See Pages 82/83.

Yours truly, Jock

UNITED IN EFFORT

THE STORY OF No.53 SQUADRON

ROYAL AIR FORCE

1916-1976

by Jock Manson

An Air-Britain Publication

Copyright 1997 by Jock Manson

Published in Great Britain by

Air-Britain (Historians) Ltd
12 Lonsdale Gardens, Tunbridge Wells, Kent

Sales Dept: 5 Bradley Road, Upper Norwood
London SE19 3NT

Correspondence to:

J.J.Halley, 5 Walnut Tree Road,
Shepperton, Middlesex, TW17 ORW
and not to the Tunbridge Wells address

ISBN 0 85130 260 2

Cover painting by Trevor Lay

Printed by
Hillman Printers (Frome) Ltd
Frome
Somerset

"UNITED IN EFFORT"

Contents

FOREWORD

by

Air Vice Marshal J D Spottiswood CB CVO AFC MA

There can be few more pleasurable occurrences than to be invited to write the foreword to a squadron history; particularly so when one has been fortunate enough to command that squadron. I was delighted therefore when Jock Manson asked me to pen these few words in introduction to his immaculately prepared and detailed account of No.53 Squadron from its birth in Yorkshire on 15 May 1916 to its disbandment on 14 September 1976.

The squadrons of the Royal Air Force are the very heart and lifeblood of the Service. Though our history is short in comparison with the Royal Navy and the British Army, the squadrons of the Royal Air Force have made an incalculable contribution to the restoration of peace in two World Wars and to the maintenance of peace in the intervening years before and after those Wars. It is of vital importance that the contribution of our squadrons and their members to this noble purpose be accurately and fully documented; this Jock Manson has admirably achieved with his fascinating and immensely readable account of the sixty years of No.53 Squadron.

All who have been privileged to serve in the Royal Air Force have a favourite squadron. These fond memories stem from the companionship of fellow squadron members, the challenge in flying and operating the aircraft effectively and the leadership and example of particular individuals. I count myself particularly fortunate to have been a member of No.53 at a time when we were all inspired by the character and

leadership of a former CO, Lt Col Pat Hannay OBE MC. As Jock so vividly describes, Pat was CO of No.53 in the late thirties.

Though a soldier and Cameron Highlander, he had an abiding love of flying and No.53 Squadron and he never forgot a squadron birthday or anniversary. I and a whole succession of Commanding Officers benefitted from his wise counsel and guidance. I shall never forget his speeches at Guest Nights when he spoke so movingly of his pride in his country, the squadron and the Royal Air Force. He was truly the unforgettable character of No.53. It was Pat Hannay who was responsible in 1939 for the design of the Squadron Badge based as it is upon that of the Cameron Highlanders. The Army connection and the Scottish connection pervades the history of the squadron. It was entirely fitting therefore that on disbandment, the Squadron Standard was laid up in St Giles Cathedral in Edinburgh.

I would like to pay a tribute to Jock Manson for the history of No.53 Squadron; a labour of love which he has so painstakingly carried out over a number of years. We are all most grateful. I would also like to pay my tribute and that of the Royal Air Force to all those splendid young men throughout the history of No.53 Squadron who lost their lives, were missing in action or were wounded in the service of their country.

"UNITED IN EFFORT"

CHAPTER 1

BORN IN YORKSHIRE

B.E.2b 2781 was issued to No.53 Squadron at Catterick

The garrison town of Catterick in Yorkshire saw the birth of No.53 (Home Defence) Squadron on 15 May 1916. The unit came under the 19th Wing of the RFC which had been formed at Newcastle on 1 May. At first, No.53 consisted only of nucleus flights under the parentage of No.14 Reserve Squadron which was to ensure a supply of experienced pilots. Initial equipment was to be four B.E.2cs for operations against airships at night. They were to be armed with a Lewis gun fitted so that the pilot could fire upwards and either four bombs or a box of Ranken darts. As far as it can be determined, the first aircraft to be allotted to No.53 were B.E.2cs 2661-2663. The first two were diverted to 47 Squadron within days to make good losses, so it is rather doubtful that 2663 arrived either. B.E.12 6490 was allotted on 26 May but was soon passed on to 36 Squadron.

By 8 June, "B" and "C" Flights were up to strength and it had now been decided that No.53 was to be equipped with Armstrong Whitworth F.K.3s and Avro 504As. Capt A C Wright (restyled Capt A Claud Wright later in the war) arrived from 19 Squadron at Filton to take command on 17 June. It was also on this day that the SNCOs and Airmen were taken off the ration strength of 14 RS and transferred to 53 Squadron. The first F.K.3s, 5512 and 5526, were allotted on 20 June and the first Avro 504A, 7951, on 12 July; 7949 and 7950 followed the next day. Martinsyde S.1 Scout 5446 also appeared on 13 July, followed by 2449 and 4246 on 17 July.

No.53 was one of the earlier units to be equipped with "wireless apparatus" and was allocated the call letters "NF" on 180 metres on 5 August. This equipment consisted of a transmitter carried in the aircraft sending messages to a receiver on the ground using Morse Code. Should the ground unit wish to communicate back to the aircraft, this was done by laying out white panels (known as Ground Strips) in set patterns on the ground.

Still no particular role in Home Defence had been decided for the Squadron but it was held in reserve for emergencies either at home or abroad. On 31 August, it was finally decided that No.53 was to be an artillery squadron equipped with R.E.8s. F.K.3s had remained in short supply and the position with the new R.E.8s was no better. In the end, it was decided that No.53 should have B.E.2s as a stop-gap and so the first two, B.E.2bs 2771 and 2781, appeared on 11 September. On 28 September, the radio call letters were changed to "RG". By the end of October, re-equipment with B.E.2s had been completed.

Major C S Wynne-Eyton took command on 14 October and, on the 23rd, it was announced that No.53 would be required for service with the Expeditionary Force in France but no date for the move was given. The Squadron suffered its first casualties on 3 December when B.E.2d 5837 spun-in off a steep turn at 300 feet over Catterick. Capt H N Steward and 2Lt M Thornely were killed.

On 7 December, No.53 was ordered to move south to Southern Aircraft Depot, Farnborough to prepare for its move to France. It was to be re-equipped with 18 new B.E.2e/gs. The move took place on the 11th and the new machines quickly began to appear from the depots at Hurst Park, Filton, Lincoln, and Ascot. It was also decided to supply some 25 B.E.2e/gs "to allow for wastage".

The B.E.2e/g was the result of a marriage between the wings of a B.E.2e and the fuselage of a B.E.2d. It retained the dual controls of the latter and was always referred to in returns and documents as a "Betug", to avoid confusion with any other type of B.E.2. The aircraft was a two-seat biplane with a wing-span of 40 feet 9 inches on the upper wing and it was designed primarily for reconnaissance and photography duties. In addition, two 112-lb bombs could be dropped. The engine was an air-cooled V-8 R.A.F 1a of 90-hp and the armament consisted of a single 0.303-in Lewis machine gun. This was carried by the observer who occupied the front seat, so he had to be particularly careful when firing the Lewis gun since he was surrounded by vital aircraft structure! The top speed at sea-level was only 90 mph and it took the better part of 25 minutes to lumber up to 6,500 feet. It is therefore hardly surprising that the Germans considered the B.E.2 to be an easy target.

An Armstrong Whitworth F.K.3 in used by No.53 Squadron at Catterick in July 1916 (R. Vann collection)

CHAPTER 2

TO FRANCE WITH

THE B.E.2

B.E.2e/g 7257 at Bailleul,
April 1917 (R. Vann collection)

On 26 December, No.53 was on the move to St Omer. The ground crew went via Bristol, Le Havre and Rouen, arriving on 1 January 1917. Then it was on to their new base at Bailleul/Town Ground where the first machine, 7250, landed at 2.15pm on 4 January. The move went smoothly when judged by 1917 standards; 6316 was wrecked near Calais on the way to St Omer and 6313, flown by 2Lt Pascoe made a forced landing in a ploughed field two miles east of Hazebrouck when the engine failed en route to Bailleul. Out of the original allocation, the author has no evidence of the following B.E.2e/gs going to France with No.53; 6314, 7229-31, 7237 and 7246.

No.53 came under the command of 2nd Corps Wing, 2nd Brigade RFC and was attached to the IXth Army Corps which was then in the trenches in the Messines sector. The squadron settled into Bailleul alongside 42 Squadron which was also equipped with B.E.2s. The first 53 Squadron casualty in France came on 6 January when Lt H Blofeld hit a tree and then a house on take-off in 7256. His observer, Lt D W L Young, was killed and the wreckage ended up on the roof of IX Corps HQ. Lt S E Goodwin was injured and 6317 wrecked near Wormhoudt on the 22nd. On the 24th, Lts T F Preston (1st Norfolk Yeomanry) and C M Buck (31st Lancers) in 6308 were shot down and killed in German lines near Warneton. It is thought that they were downed by Vzfw Ulmer of Jasta 8.

On 25 January, Capt F W H Simpson was taking photographs of the line near Deulmont in 6311 when he was attacked by a Fokker biplane whilst also under intense fire from the ground. He made good his escape by spinning down to the ground but his observer, 2Lt J R Houghton, was wounded. Photography was a vital task but it was also a particularly dangerous exercise in that it called for a very steady course to be flown and the aircraft was vulnerable to attack from all directions.

Artillery observation was not without an element of danger either. Basically, the aircraft "spotted" where the artillery shells were landing and then sent corrections to the guns via the wireless operator attached to the artillery unit. On 16 February, Capt F W H Simpson (RA) and Sgt Trumpeter C J Edlington (2nd KEH) in 6313 were on such an operation when they were seen to come down from 9,000 feet in the vicinity of Armentières and were killed. Later on in the day, Lt D McC Kerr and Lt F C Elstob in 6315 attacked a Halberstadt over Wytschaete without causing any apparent damage.

A variation of artillery observation had also been developed known as the "zone call procedure". Under this system, certain batteries within a given zone were placed on readiness to attack targets of opportunity which might be spotted by the aircraft. It was to prove to be an excellent system and many hitherto-unseen targets were successfully attacked.

2Lts T H Butler (3rd Border Regt) and V G Southern MC (3rd Yorks & Lancs) were injured on 26 February when 7250 was wrecked on the approach to Bailleul. Lt R W Scoles (GL) was seriously injured and 2Lt B A Morgan (RFA) died on 4 March in a similar accident when 6311 hit the side of a house on final approach. This was 2Lt Morgan's first flight with No.53. A welcome respite lasting for two weeks then came, during which the weather was too bad for flying.

2Lt A Pascoe wrecked A2779 on 17 March when he hit a pole on the edge of the aerodrome on his return. Cpl T W Willis (AG) was injured. B.E.2e/f A3152 ("From the British West Indies") came to grief on the 23rd when Major S A Hargraft (90th Canadian Infantry) ended up in a pond just off the aerodrome after the engine failed! The B.E.2e/f ("Betuf") was a B.E.2c fuselage fitted with B.E.2e wings. March ended with Lt J Butler MC (1st Royal Irish Fusiliers) and 2Lt H C Benstead (North Staffs Regt) in 7257 being attacked by a Halberstadt over Houthem on the 28th whilst taking photographs. The enemy machine made off when a Nieuport Scout came along.

No.53 went bombing for the first time on the night of 6 April when Lt L S Bowman dropped two 112-lb Hales bombs on a shed near Warneton Dump. Three other aircraft attacked an ammunition dump at Vyfwegen. The following night, Lt F Adams in 7251 dropped one bomb on Menin station and another on Wervicq aerodrome. The latter replied by firing back with "flaming onions".

B.E.2c 2092 arrived from No.1 AD on 12 April. This machine was an "armoured B.E.2c" and it is believed that it was intended to be used as an escort to aircraft taking photographs. Whether or not it deterred the enemy to any great extent is open to debate and it probably lapsed into the role of being the "squadron hack". In any event, this B.E.2 outlasted all of the others and was finally returned to No.1 AD on 14 October on Brigade instructions.

2Lt N J Wenger took off at 4.25 am on 13 April armed with two Hales bombs. He found a column of enemy motor lorries which he attacked successfully, claiming two "destroyed" and one "probable". Strong west winds had blown him off course and he found himself over Tournai. He was attacked by a German aircraft east of Seclin but he put the nose down and managed to escape. He was then caught in the beams of three searchlights and subjected to heavy ack-ack fire while crossing the lines but managed to land safely near Bruay at 7.30 am.

It should be noted that the westerly wind, which normally blows in this part of the world, was of distinct advantage to the enemy. Should German flyers be caught behind the British lines, they had the great benefit of a tail wind as they headed for home. On the other hand, the British flyers often had to battle against strong headwinds in order to get back over the lines and the B.E.2 was not very swift to start with!

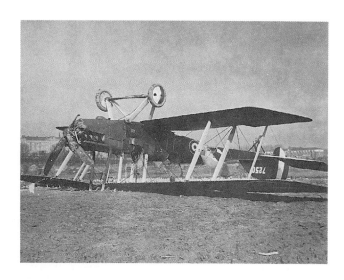

Right: 7250 crashed at Bailleul on 26 February 1917 and was taken to No.1 Aircraft Depot for repair (JMB/SL collection)

Below: The hangars of Bailleul/Town Ground airfield are on the upper part of this photograph. The airfield was occupied at this time by Nos.53 and 42 Squadrons. (The late Capt C.C.L. Dowdall MC)

9

CHAPTER 3

THE R.E.8 FINALLY

ARRIVES

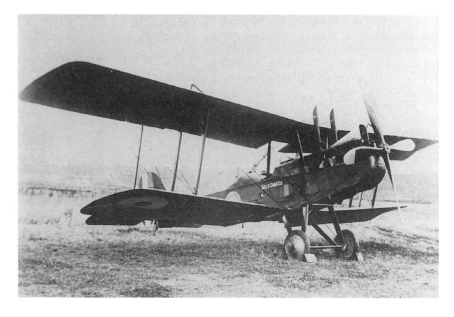

R.E.8 D6801 was a presentation aircraft titled 'Gold Coast No.5' received by No.53 Squadron on 4 September 1918.
(Norman Parker via Colin Waugh)

April of 1917 was a particularly bad month for the RFC and was to become known as "Bloody April". Rather curiously, No.53 suffered no casualties during the period. The first six R.E.8s arrived from No.1 AD on 23 April and re-equipment with the new machines had been completed by 26 April. The R.E.8 was designed to be the replacement for the B.E.2 but the improvements were not great. In fact, the wings were almost identical to those of the B.E.2e but the new centre-section increased the wing span of the upper wing to 42 feet 7 inches. The engine was an air-cooled V-12 R.A.F.4a of 140-hp which allowed 103 mph to be achieved at sea level and 6,500 feet could now be reached in just 21 minutes. The observer had been moved to the rear cockpit and this allowed him to have a much-improved field of fire for the Lewis gun. A 0.303-in Vickers machine gun was fixed to the port side of the fuselage and it was fired by the pilot through the propeller arc by means of a mechanical interrupter gear.

The first R.E.8 casualty came on 4 May when A4207, flown by Lt W Turnbull, was hit by ack-ack. His observer, Lt J R Geddes (Canadian Local Forces), was wounded in the head. Next day, 2Lt Fulljames stalled on take-off and wrecked A3237. On 12 May, 2Lts F Adams (GL) and O R Kelly (20th Northumberland Fusiliers) were taking photographs in A3243 when they were shot down by Lt Max Ritter von Müller of Jasta 28 near Hollebeke. Their machine broke up and the crew fell to their deaths since parachutes were not carried. The new R.E.8s were proving to be a bit of a handful close to the ground. Landing accidents claimed A4592 on 13 May and A4591 on 18 May. A4269 was wrecked on take-off, also on 18 May. A4239 was very badly damaged by ack-ack over the lines on 31 May but Sgt Haydon managed to land safely on the aerodrome.

June started with Lt Harvey and 2Lt Paton in A3690 having their controls shot away by AA fire whilst on artillery observation and they ended up tangled in the wire at the British front. Danger was in no way confined to No.53's aircrew. Also on the 1st, 1/AM L E Tucker, a wireless operator attached to 53 Squadron at the front, was caught in a German gas attack. Another, 2/AM J S Baley, was gassed next day.

The Battle of Messines was about to start and during the weeks leading up to the battle, No.53 had been practising flying "contact patrols" under the eagle eye of Capt J O Archer, "B" Flt Cdr. This highly dangerous activity involved flying up and down the front line at low level, gathering intelligence as to the disposition of enemy and friendly forces. Special contact patrol maps were prepared to a scale of 1/10,000 and when they had been completed, the observer dropped them at the Scherpenberg dropping zone from whence they were conveyed by runners to IX Corps HQ.

For weeks before the battle started, the Sappers had been busy tunnelling under the German lines and had placed 19 huge land mines in their excavations. At 3.10 am on 7 June, these enormous mines were exploded. This spectacular event was then followed by a heavy artillery barrage. By the standards of siege warfare, this battle was a great success and the infantry managed to advance some 2½ miles.

Lt L S Bowman (4th Royal Lancs) was injured while flying on a contact patrol at 3.30 that morning when the engine of A3464 failed over the line. Lt N J Wenger (1st Staffs Yeomanry) and 2Lt E B Hamel (11th South Staffs) were also injured when A4308 was hit in the right wing by a British shell and they spun-in at 7.15 am.

Although a great deal of fighter cover had been arranged for the operation, it was not enough to prevent 2Lts F P Brown (GL) and H E Wells (RFA) in A3240 being shot down by a German machine over the Oosttaverne line. The R.E.8 came down vertically into a shell hole and both were badly wounded. It is interesting to note that No.53 were responsible for a 3,000-yard section of the front and, within this rather limited area, were operating no less than four R.E.8s on artillery observation alone.

On 8 June, 2Lts T C S MacGregor (HLI) and R W Spooner (RFA) were flying a contact patrol in A3684 along the Oosttaverne line when they took a direct hit from AA fire and were both killed. An accident on take-off killed 2Lt C L Green (11th Essex Regt) in A4292 on 9 June. His observer, 2Lt M D R Paton (22nd City of London Regt) died of his injuries three days later. On the same day, 2Lts J A Loutit (1st Cambridgeshire Regt) and V J Holland (RFA) in A3463 spotted five Albatros Scouts and a two-seater overhead Houthem at 6,000 feet. Three scouts made an attack from above and behind and the first burst of fire hit 2Lt Loutit in the leg. One Albatros then dived straight down from above and 2Lt Holland opened fire at 100 yds with one drum of ammunition. The Albatros was seen to make a half-loop and to fall "out of control". The rest broke off the attack but not before 2Lt Holland had also been wounded.

R.E.8 B6598 at Villeselve, early 1918 (Colin Waugh)

R.E.8 C5026 arrived at Bailleul on 16 October 1917 (Vann)

By now, a network of Central Wireless Stations had been set up. They fulfilled a variety of purposes such as enabling an aircraft to make contact with a battery which was not responding in the usual way. The aircraft simply made contact with the appropriate CWS which then contacted the guns by field telephone and relayed the information. Artillery units were often reluctant to lay out Ground Strips when hostile aircraft were in the vicinity as this practice rather advertised their presence. They could now signal back to their aircraft by having Ground Strips laid out at their nearest CWS. It is interesting to note that 42 Squadron started to make experiments with airborne wireless receivers during June. A contemporary account states that "the possibilities of wireless communication from the ground would seem to be very great". This was certainly to prove to be the case!

2Lt W Turnbull and 2Lt W B Protheroe were taking photographs in the Warneton area on 12 June in A4207 when they were shot down and killed by hostile aircraft. They fell in flames and crashed at Oosttaverne, at which point the enemy artillery opened fire on the wreckage. On 18 June, Lt M E Newton (17th Bat London Regt) and 2Lt H M Jackson (Royal Irish Rifles) were shot down and killed in A4617 ("Zanzibar No.1"), followed by Lt L S Bowman (4th Royal Lancs) and 2Lt J E Power-Clutterbuck (RFA) in A3847 on 25 June.

2Lt R E G Fulljames and 2Lt W E Watt in A4236 were set upon by "five enemy machines with red fuselages" over Wytschaete on 29 June. They escaped by spinning down almost to the ground and then recovering from the spin at the last possible moment. Even at this stage of the war, spinning was still not a fully-understood manoeuvre and Fulljames had only recently completed the "spinning course" at Gosport. Despite his Lewis gun jamming several times, 2Lt Watt managed to get off 300 rounds and hit one of the enemy machines which was then seen to break off the attack. Later, "S Group" of the artillery and their wireless officer were able to confirm the destruction of this aircraft. 2Lt Watt was wounded in the action and the R.E.8 badly damaged.

Sgt H A Whatley (2056) and 2Lt F G B Pascoe (7th Royal Irish Fusiliers) were shot down and killed in A3538 on 2 July. They fell in flames behind Comines and Manfred von Richthofen claimed them as his 57th victory. At about the same time, Capt W P Horsley MC (GL) and 2Lt A G Knight (GL) were escorting an R.E.8 taking photographs when they were shot down in A3249 near Ten-Brielen. Capt Horsley died and 2Lt Knight was badly wounded. His brother, 2Lt W E Watt, was also serving on 53 Squadron at this time.

Enemy aircraft brought down A4621 ("Ceylon") on 12 July. Sgt R Kay was wounded and Lt B W Binkley (15th

Canadian Reserve Bat) was killed. 2Lts P J Rodocanachi (GL) and N L Watt (1st King Edward's Horse) were on artillery duty in A4303 on 27 July near Wytschaete when they were also shot down by enemy aircraft. 2Lt Rodocanachi was killed and 2Lt Watt was taken to the aid post at Torreken Farm where he died of his wounds. His brother, 2Lt W E Watt, was also serving on 53 Squadron at the time.

The Third Battle of Ypres started on 31 July. The German front line was rapidly overrun at first but it started to rain and the whole of August was wet. The troops became bogged down and it was not until 6 November that they succeeded in capturing one of the primary objectives, the village of Passchendaele. By the end of this dreadful battle, British casualties numbered some 240,000 and the Germans, some 400,000.

On 10 August, Lt G I L Murray (Australian Flying Corps) and Lt S H Short (Canadian Field Artillery) were shot down and wounded in A3260 near St Etoi. 2Lts J E Goodman (GL) and F E Kebblewhite (8th Sherwood Foresters) in A3838 were brought down by enemy aircraft and killed on 14 August whilst on "flash reconnaissance". This activity involved seeking out hitherto unknown enemy artillery positions which betrayed their presence by the flash of the gun being fired.

Bailleul aerodrome was attacked by German aircraft at 9.45 pm on 17 August. R.E.8 A4295 was damaged by a bomb while standing in a hangar. Lt F H Holmes and 2Lt J B Pierce in A3605 were engaged on artillery duties with the 161st Siege Battery on 20 August when they saw five enemy machines approaching. One of them, an Albatros D-III, attacked. Pierce opened fire at 200 yards. The Albatros went down at a steep angle and appeared to hit the ground near Comines. The artillery later confirmed that the Albatros had indeed crashed.

On 22 August, 2Lt D McC Kerr and 2Lt W A Knight in B3402 attacked a Rumpler two-seater over Hollebeke which then appeared to go down near Houthem. Aerial combat continued on 3 September when Lt Holmes and 2Lt Pierce in A3605 ("Punjab No.7 Faridkot") encountered four Albatros D-IIIs at 10,000 feet whilst taking photographs over Ten-Brielen. One Albatros made an attack but the observer fired off one drum of ammunition at it. The Albatros appeared to go down out of control and this was later confirmed by Lt Reeves of 1 Squadron, based at Bailleul/Asylum Ground with Nieuports.

On 14 September, 2Lt H W Westaway (GL) and 2Lt L Hodkinson (15th Royal Welsh Fusiliers) were on artillery co-operation duties in A3238 when they were shot down by ack-ack fire from Flakzug 162 commanded by Lt Eckhardt. 2Lt

Reconnaissance photographs of the area around Wytschaete village taken by R.E.8s of No.53 Squadron. The upper photograph was taken on 24 May 1917, the lower on 12 June. The remains of the houses of the village seen in the upper photograph have virtually vanished three weeks later, replaced by interlocking shell craters.
(The Late Capt C.C.L. Dowdall MC)

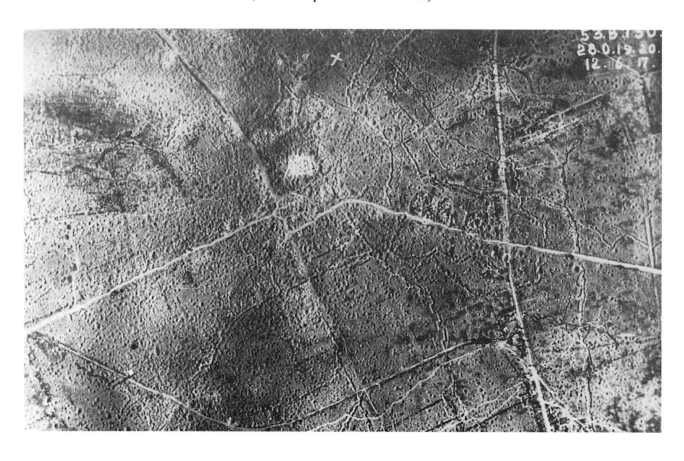

Captain H.L. Tracey, formerly of the Canadian Infantry, served with No.53 from September 1917 until March 1918.
(Colin Waugh)

Left to right: Capt J.O. Archer (OC 'B' Flt), Major C.S. Wynne-Eyton (CO) and Capt J.B. Home-Hay (OC 'C' Flt) at Bailleul (The Late Capt C.C.L. Dowdall MC)

Westaway was slightly wounded but 2Lt Hodkinson was killed. Capt J B Home-Hay MC and Cpl W Metson were on artillery duties in A3619 on 16 September over Hollebeke when they were attacked by five Albatros Scouts. They escaped by spinning down and Cpl Metson managed to fire a drum of ammunition at two of them at a range of 50 yards. Lt Potts of 56 Squadron was on the scene in an S.E.5a and he later reported seeing one Albatros "crash" and one "out of control". Capt Home-Hay (7th Argyll & Sutherlands) was a Flight Commander and had been with No.53 since July, 1916.

On 20 September, the assault on Gheluvelt Ridge began. The next day, Capt R N F Mills (ASC) and Lt W A Browne (8th Royal Iniskilling Fusiliers) were up in A3617 ("Punjab No.23 Karnal") at 6.35 am on artillery observation near Warneton when they were shot down by an Albatros flown by Lt Erwin Böhme of Jasta Boelcke. Their deaths were later confirmed. An Albatros Scout attacked 2Lt Watts and 2Lt Ripley in A3605 on 23 September over Kruiseecke and one drum was fired at a range of 100 yards. Tracer was seen to enter the enemy machine which then dived vertically out of control and was lost to sight due to cloud cover but its demise was confirmed later. Gheluvelt Ridge finally fell to General Plumer's IInd Army on 26 September.

At 4.15 pm on 1 October, Lt A R Reeder and Cpl G Holmes in B3402 were attacked by a "single-seater with

yellowish wings" over Zillebeke Lake. Cpl Holmes fired one drum from a range of 100 feet and saw the enemy machine fall out of control. It was later confirmed that the artillery had seen the R.E.8 shooting down this machine which broke up in the air. Next day, 2Lt S A Gilray was on his very first operational flight on 53 Squadron with Lt H W Smith in A4376 at 6.30 pm over Ypres. It was getting dark and the observer was trying to locate a "flash" when two Albatros Scouts suddenly loomed up in front of their R.E.8. Lt Smith was immediately shot in the ankle but he managed to open fire at very close range. One Albatros caught fire and was last seen falling enveloped in flames. The other Albatros then made off for home on seeing the fate of his companion.

On 8 October, 2Lt H W Laird (GL) was killed and 2Lt J T Long (GL) was badly injured when R.E.8 A3261 was caught by a gust of wind on take-off, stalled and nose-dived into the ground. 2Lt Long died two days later. It was around this time that No.53 first became involved in "retaliation and offensive patrols". These involved machine-gunning and bombing the enemy trenches from low-level. A typical sortie was flown by Capt W A L Poundall MC (South Lancs) and 2Lt H F Lambert (GL) in A4236 on 27 October. Four 20-lb bombs were dropped in the region of Houthem and then 200 rounds from the forward-firing Vickers gun and four drums from the Lewis gun were fired into the trenches. However, luck was running out for Capt Poundall. On 31 October, he

Hangars at Bailleul, shared with No.42 Squadron, one of whose B.E.2es can be seen on the left.
(The Late Capt C.C.L. Dowdall MC)

set off at 11 am with 2Lt E R Ripley (GL) in A4214 for artillery co-operation with the 188th Siege Battery. They were posted missing and later confirmed dead.

No.53 entered the propaganda war on 7 November when Lt Hutchings and 2Lt Pierce in B5037 dropped 500 copies of "literature" around hutments at Gheluwe. At the time, the Germans took an extremely dim view of leaflet dropping. Should any crew member fall into their hands whilst engaged in this activity, they were liable to be court martialled and even sentenced to death! Next day, 2Lt L W Middleton (GL) and 2Lt F J McCullough (RGA[SR]) took a direct hit from a shell in A4664. The wreckage fell in "no man's land" and they were later confirmed dead. 2Lts Napier and Cook in A4632 ("Punjab No.47 Ravi") later reported seeing what looked like the fuselage of an R.E.8 falling in flames at 10.30

am; such were the horrors of this war.

Major C S Wynne-Eyton, who was now proudly wearing the DSO, was posted back to England on 20 November. Major G Henderson (38th Central India Horse) took over as CO. Throughout November, many encounters with enemy aircraft were reported but little damage was sustained. 2Lts Jarrett and Arthur in B6464 met five Gothas over Dickebusch on 10 December which they attacked to little apparent effect. 2Lt F A Lewis and Cpl G Holmes in C5026 were set upon by a formation of about ten Albatros D-Vs over Gheluvelt on 18 December but landed safely. Lt W R Bucknall (Black Watch) became No.53's last casualty of 1917 when B6463 caught fire at 6,000 feet on 28 December. Sadly, his legs were badly burned but Cpl W Metson (7th Corps Cyclists Battalion) was unhurt.

Officers of 'C' Flight at Bailleul in 1917. (The Late Capt C.C.L. Dowdall MC)

CHAPTER 4

FAREWELL TO

BAILLEUL

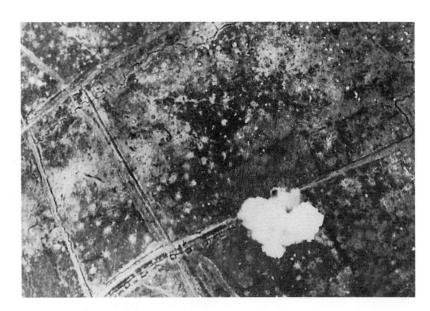

'Archie' exploding beneath an R.E.8
of No.53 Squadron (Dowdall)

After over a year at Bailleul, No.53 moved to Abeele on 1 February 1918 and became attached to XXII Corps. On 5 February, 2Lt F A Lewis (GL) and Lt T McK Hughes (KRRC) were shot down and killed by ground fire in B6466. Lt Hughes was No.53's Intelligence Officer. The squadron moved again on 21 February, this time southwards to Villeselve near Noyon. The move did not go entirely smoothly however; B2251 was wrecked when Lt G J Hutcheson and 1/AM Dunn took off cross-wind from Abeele and crashed. Capt H L Tracy and Lt G W G Tucker in A4236 swerved to avoid B2251 and turned right over! No.53 now came under the command of 5th Brigade, 15th Corps Wing rejoining the IXth Army Corps who were planning to take over from the French in the Soissons sector. On 18 March, 2Lts Hutcheson and Cook set off in A3694 for a liaison visit with the French at Saponay. On their return, they misjudged the landing and overran into a ditch on the edge of the aerodrome.

Before the take-over could take place, the Germans mounted a massive offensive at dawn on 21 March. This was to prove to be No.53's darkest time in this war. Bombing and recce sorties were immediately called for but it was very foggy and it was some time before flying could start. No.53 was to suffer no losses this day; indeed 2Lt C A Bainbridge and 2Lt G H Parker in B5061 tangled with an Albatros D-IV with "yellow fuselage and green planes" and saw it make a very bad landing and possibly crash. Unfortunately, it was to be a different story next day.

2Lt T E H Birley (GL) and Lt E Dennis (Sherwood Foresters) were on a bombing expedition in A4400 when they were attacked by two enemy aircraft. The controls and engine were put out of action. 2Lt Birley was wounded in the back and had to land near Vendeine. Lt Dennis died some five minutes after landing and 2Lt Birley became a POW when he was captured near St Quentin. 2Lts B G Poole (GL) and G F Moseley (GL) in A4438 went missing and were at first thought to be POWs. However, some weeks later, 2Lt Moseley was found to be in a Rouen hospital and he was able to report that they had been shot down by German airmen just inside the British lines. Sadly, 2Lt Poole had been killed.

With the German forces advancing rapidly, co-operation with the artillery had become all but impossible since the guns were now falling back in some disarray. Offensive patrols were flown instead and bombs were dropped on the German troops. Many attacks were made on No.53's R.E.8s by

enemy aircraft which were very active. Lts H M Gibbs and A DeM Severne in C5037 dropped four bombs and were then attacked by an Albatros at 2,500 feet. The observer fired back with 196 rounds at close range and drove him off. Capt C W Baldwin and 2Lt Cook in A3931 dropped their bombs and were then set upon by six enemy aircraft when just one mile from the aerodrome. 2Lt Cook hit one of them with tracer and saw the fuselage catch alight for ten seconds before going out again.

Lts W M Emery and K Hall in A3619 dropped four bombs and fired 100 rounds from the Lewis gun at a German horse transport column. At 1,500 feet over Frières, they were attacked by five Albatros Scouts and driven down to 500 feet. The attack was abandoned when the observer opened up with the Lewis gun. No.53 was now ordered to pull back to Allonville and 2Lt G B Knight (GL), on his first flight with the squadron, was tasked with flying B841 to the new aerodrome. Just after take-off, he spun-in and the machine caught fire and was destroyed. He suffered head wounds and died of his injuries on 7 April. His mechanic, 1/AM A J Coleman, was injured. Finally, R.E.8s A3694 and A3721 had to be left behind at Villeselve and were burned.

There were no casualties on 23 March but 2Lt J J Quinn (GL) and Lt E L O'Leary (Canadian FA) in B6598 were attacked by six "new single-seat Rumplers with V struts" (sic). Fire was returned and one machine entered a spin and was later seen on the ground. The centre-section of the R.E.8 was almost shot through and the aileron cable had only one strand remaining. A forced landing was made at Montdidier. No.53 was told to pull back once again, this time to Fienvillers. R.E.8 B2279 had to be left behind at Allonville. 2Lt Quinn, having effected some temporary repairs, tried to catch up with the squadron but had to land at Vert Galant due to fog.

The task on 24 March was to bomb the bridges at Péronne. Lt A A Miles (GL) and 2Lt C W Cook (GL) were struck by heavy machine gun fire from the ground. Lt Miles was hit first so the observer took over but he was also struck by a bullet above the right eye. Both of them were now unconscious! 2Lt Cook came-to just a few feet above the ground but was too late to prevent a crash. Both survived but were captured and became POWs. This R.E.8 is thought to have been B6564.

2Lt G J Hutcheson and Lt F J Pullen in A3931 saw Lt Miles crash and followed Lt Napier down to investigate. At

Officers of No.53 Squadron in front of a portable hangar. Those identified are:
Centre row: Unknown, 2Lt Fulljames, 2Lt C.C.L. Dowdall, Lt. 'Toc' Hughes, Capt Jo Archer, Major C.S. Wynne-Eyton, Capt
J.B. Home-Hay, two unknown, Lt. D.P. Farley, unknown;
Third from right seated is 2Lt H.L. Tracy (The Late Capt C.C.L. Dowdall MC)

1,500 feet, Lt Pullen (Welsh Regt) was hit in the leg by machine gun fire. Worse was yet to come as Capt R H Martin (Western Ontario Regt) and 2Lt G H Parker (GL) were reported missing in B5061 and then confirmed dead. 2Lt Quinn and Lt O'Leary finally arrived from Vert Galant in a very badly damaged B6598 at lunchtime. Both were awarded the MC in May. Meanwhile, 2Lt C W Turner and 2Lt R A Carter in B2282 had landed at Vert Galant owing to the pilot feeling unwell. After he had recovered, they took off but crashed on the aerodrome when the engine choked.

R.E.8 A4400 at Abeele in February 1918; it was shot down on 22 March 1918. (Colin Waugh)

At this point it was decided to pull 53 Squadron back from the front to Boisdinghem (2nd Corps Wing, 2nd Brigade) to rest and to re-equip. The move took place on 25 March in foul weather and most aircraft had to force-land on the way in conditions of gales, low cloud and mist. Nevertheless, the only casualty was D4966 which crashed at Hesdin whilst making a forced-landing. It was being flown by 2Lt Turner (again) and 2/AM C Aston, both of whom were uninjured. R.E.8 B6598 was left behind at Fienvillers.

This crashed R.E.8 shows No.53's crescent marking and individual aircraft letter.
(J.M. Bruce/S. Leslie collection)

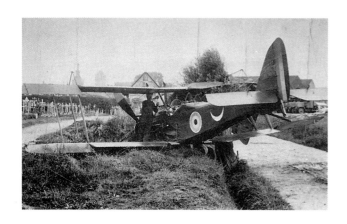

CHAPTER 5

THE ROYAL AIR

FORCE IS BORN

An aerial view of a German gas attack at Ypres. (Dowdall)

The Royal Air Force came into being on 1 April. It was a fine clear day and the German advance was slowing down. Having made good its losses, 53 Squadron moved again on 6 April to Abeele. They were now part of IXth Corps, which was taking over part of the line in the Ypres-Armentières sector. On 9 April, Field Marshal von Hindenburg switched his main assault towards Ypres and this was to cause No.53 further heavy casualties. Aircraft were sent to bomb the advancing German infantry on 10 April and all returned safely. 2Lt J Craig and Lt K Hall in B8890 were brought down in flames near Béthune on 11 April whilst on a "counter attack patrol" (CAP). 2Lt Craig died of his injuries and Lt Hall (RGA[T]) was badly wounded. These patrols were started around August 1917 and were specifically tasked with looking for evidence of the enemy preparing to mount counter-attacks. Lt R S Barlow and 2Lt F E Pashby were shot down in E18 by heavy machine gun fire but survived injury. 2Lt R D Best (ASC) and Capt C G White MC (RFA) in B4021 were similarly brought down and 2Lt Best was wounded. Lt E H N Stroud was forced to land near Bailleul in A4452 and 2Lt W R McCoo, his observer, was hit. Finally, 2Lt A C Jones and 2Lt C E Lovick in E16 made a forced landing when their engine stopped at 400 feet. They effected temporary repairs but crashed on take-off at 7.45 pm. CAPs were proving to be dangerous.

2Lt G J Hutcheson and 2Lt F E Pashby (Royal Berks Regt) were on a recce flight at 7 pm on 12 April in A3931 when three Albatros Scouts suddenly came out of a cloud and attacked them. Fire was returned by 2Lt Pashby who suddenly shouted and fell over the front of the observer's seat, wounded. 2Lt Hutcheson managed to shake off his attackers and saw Abeele not far away where he landed and sought help from 10 Squadron. Sadly, 2Lt Pashby died next day. No.53 was now ordered to retire to St Marie Cappel with immediate effect due to enemy pressure. On arrival there, further orders were issued to proceed to Clairmarais South. 2Lt F Green (DCLI) and Lt A De M Severne (RFA) set off for the new aerodrome at 7.35 pm in A4376. Although it was now quite dark, the authorities at Clairmarais were most reluctant to light flares due to the presence of enemy aircraft. A4376 was wrecked on landing and both crew were injured.

2Lts K A Ranney and C E Lovick were observing the enemy massing for an attack from Wytschaete to Kemmel on 16 April when ground fire hit their R.E.8. 2Lt Lovick (RFA[SR]) was wounded. B7718 was very badly damaged when a snow storm forced 2Lts A N Pitchford and J Harrison down north of Steenvoorde on 19 April. Lt E H N Stroud (GL) and Capt C G White MC (RFA[T]) set off in C5037 ("Punjab No.7 Faridkot") on a CAP of the Kemmel area on 21 April. They went missing and it was later learned that they had been killed. A3931 was wrecked this day whilst parked on the aerodrome when it was struck by a 1 Squadron S.E.5a taking off.

Later in the day, 2Lt J J Quinn and Lt A Lomax in D4690 spotted a "golden rain" rocket coming up from the front. No action followed but then a two-seat Albatros marked with small black crosses inside black circles flew over them but was chased away. Lt W M Emery and 2Lt W W Porter were on artillery duty over Mont Rouge in B7827 when two Albatros Scouts (marked with black tails and with two blue rings around camouflaged fuselages) attacked. They were driven down from 4,000 feet to 20 feet and pursued at ground level to the west of Reninghelst. The forward-firing Vickers gun had failed and the enemy aircraft fired continuously, closing to 10 yards behind them, but were driven off eventually by gun fire. 2Lt C A Bainbridge and 2Lt L F Thurlow in C2259 saw this attack but were unable to assist as they were already under attack from another three enemy aircraft! It was on this day that Manfred von Richthofen died.

Several "flash patrols" were flown on 22 April. Lt S H Evans and Lt W A B Buscarlet in C5083 managed to steer clear of two two-seaters at 11.20 over Steenwerck and then saw large formations of scouts above at 10,000 feet over Ploegsteert. Shortly after, they spotted two Bristol Fighters down in a field. They were lettered "K" and "R" and one of them had crashed. Capt J Hutchings and 2Lt L F Thurlow in B5037 were attacked by an enemy aircraft but managed to drive it off.

Lt G J Hutcheson and Lt R A Carter left on a recce at 8 am on 25 April in C2244 and they had just passed over Mont de Cats when they were set upon by nine Albatros Scouts. Lt Carter managed to hit one of them on the first pass but the third machine to attack wounded Lt Hutcheson and they were forced down to the ground and crashed. Before they were able to get out of the wreckage, an Albatros dived and fired at them so Lt Carter manned the Lewis gun and fired back with the remainder of his ammunition until the Albatros gave up

Major C.S. Wynne-Eyton, Commanding Officer of No.53 Squadron in his office. (The late Capt C.C.L. Dowdall MC)

and flew off. Lt Hutcheson died of his injuries on 27 May. Lt Carter was later wounded by ground fire on 30 April near Ypres in D4690.

At 9.50 am, Lt G W T Glasson and 2Lt W W Porter in B7827 were on a CAP when a formation of eight or nine Albatros and Pfalz Scouts was seen above. Two Albatros D-Vs dived down on them and started firing from above and behind. Although the R.E.8 landed safely, all four wings, the tail, oil tank, fuselage, centre section and a wheel had been damaged. The rudder control wire was severed, except for one strand but B7827 was rebuilt as F5889 and returned to No.53 on 24 July. Capt H M Gibbs and Lt A Lomax went missing in B6615 whilst on a CAP but turned up later suffering from wounds. Lt Lomax was awarded the MC on 5 May.

On 29 April, Lts Evans and Buscarlet were on CAP at 6.40 am in A3629 when they were chased from the line by fifteen enemy machines. Five of them attacked a balloon over Steenvoorde and brought it down. Another five chased the R.E.8 to Poperinghe before they turned away. Luck was running out for A3629 however for Lt H W Auerbach and 2Lt A Todd were attacked by three enemy aircraft near Locre while on CAP in it at 11.30 am. The engine failed when south of Abeele and they crash-landed. Luckily, they were unhurt but the R.E.8 was wrecked. At 2.15 pm, Lt A N Pitchford and 2Lt L F Thurlow in C2315 were on a CAP when their engine cut out over Cassel. They just managed to get to St. Marie Cappel aerodrome but had to land downwind and the R.E.8 turned over on its nose. It was rebuilt as F5891. The German advance had now ground to a halt. Though it had been a great success in terms of territory gained, some 350,000 Germans had lost their lives in the battle and British casualties stood at around 260,000.

Lt H T Rushton and 2Lt J B Sanders in C2311 were over Kemmel on 3 May taking photographs at 7,000 feet when they were attacked by six enemy aircraft. Although both were wounded, they managed to land at Abeele. One hour later, two Pfalz single-seaters forced Lt Evans and 2Lt Todd in C5083 ("Punjab No.9 Kalsia") down into a field near Abeele where they crashed but were unhurt. The aircraft was rebuilt as F5899. On 4 May, Lts S F Pickup and C E Lovick were on CAP near Kemmel in A4452 ("Mauritius No.6") when they were hit by heavy machine gun and rifle fire. They escaped injury but the R.E.8 was very badly damaged and was rebuilt as F5894.

On 7 May, Lts K A Ranney and C E Lovick in C2293 had an eventful flash patrol. At 3.50 pm, they were attacked by seven "triplanes" over Kemmel but escaped unscathed. At 4.5 pm, five Albatros Scouts set upon them. Lt Lovick fired a drum from the Lewis gun into the leading machine which became enveloped in smoke and nose-dived to the ground behind Kemmel. The R.E.8 was hit several times and when they went back at 4.15 pm to see if they could find where the Albatros had gone down, they were driven off by the remaining four Scouts. Lt G W T Glasson was later wounded by machine gun fire near Dranoutre. Lt J W Foreman was injured at Clairmarais whilst practising landings in C2259 on 9 May. C2259 was rebuilt as F5873 and returned on 30 June. IX Corps was relieved at the front by II French Cavalry Corps on 19 May and No.53 continued to work in the French area.

Lts G Davis and B E Scott were taking photographs at 7,500 feet near Dickebusch Lake in C2308 on 15 May when three enemy aircraft dived on them out of a cloud. Lt Scott returned the fire of the leader who was on their tail. He banked vertically, showing black markings, and disappeared into a cloud. The remainder dropped back as they crossed the line and were then seen to dive into cloud pursued by a friendly scout.

2Lt T E Read was wounded on 4 June in a bizarre incident. He was standing behind a tree waving a handkerchief for 2Lt Raby to aim his gun at but left his hand and wrist exposed! Around this time, No.53 was issued with Nieuport 27 Scout B6819. Presumably this machine was intended for use as an escort. "A" Flight was detached to No.4 Squadron at nearby St Omer on 9 June. Lt W H Williams and 2Lt L F Raby were injured in C2291 on 13 June when their engine failed and they struck telephone wires whilst trying to land in a field. Lt B Pepper and 2Lt J W Perks in C2310 were looking for targets to bomb between Ypres and Bailleul on 15 June when two Albatros and one Fokker biplane attacked them near Locre. Some shots were seen to hit the Fokker and the R.E.8 was badly damaged. Ten minutes later, Lt H H Blackwell and Lt D C Burke in D4811 were flying over Ridge Wood when they were attacked by three Fokker biplanes which had been following along behind seven Bristol Fighters. Right at the beginning, the petrol tank was pierced in three places so that the remainder of the fight took place without an engine! There were no injuries but D4811 was badly damaged in the ensuing forced landing.

Lts G C Brown and H Dyson were flying C2364 on artillery duties (while attached to 4 Squadron) at 4.30 pm on 16 June when another R.E.8 was seen to be hit by one of our own shells over Merris. It was blown to pieces and both pilot and observer were seen to fall to the ground from 4,000 feet. Earlier in the day, Lt J N Gatecliff made a bad landing in C2405 at St Omer and it was struck off charge on 19 June.

R.E.8 A3619 ("Johore No.10") was written off on 23 June when Lt Dobell made a bad landing after dark. Although landing accidents were common, this one involved No.53's "high-time" R.E.8. A3619 had achieved some 369 hrs 25 mins when SOC, a remarkable achievement for the day. "A" Flight at St Omer sent 2Lts K D Handel and H Dyson on a recce of the XVth Corps front in D4966 at 4 am on 25 June. It became very misty and they got lost making a forced landing at 6.45 am. Both received injuries and 2Lt Handel died soon afterwards. 2Lts J N Gatecliff and J Harrison were killed on 29 June whilst on artillery duties at the XVth Corps front when D4834 crashed and burst into flames.

Nieuport B6819 had been damaged in a forced landing on 19 June and was sent to No 1 ASD for repair. It did not return until 31 August. From 1 July, an S.E.5a was borrowed and this machine proved most useful for escorting R.E.8s taking photographs. Lts D C Dunlop and B E Scott MC in C4574 were on CAP on 5 July when their petrol tank was pierced by a bullet. Although they were only at 1,500 feet and under heavy anti-aircraft and machine gun fire at the time, Lt Scott climbed out on to the wing to survey the damage. He plugged the hole with his swagger-stick and his leather helmet. They then completed the recce and even dropped a message at HQ on the way home! Lt Scott was later awarded the DFC. On 10 July, 2Lts H F Redmond and W Cowden in B4090 were seen to come down in a nose-dive from 500 feet whilst on a flash patrol. All of the fuselage was destroyed save for the last five feet from the tail. 2Lt Cowden was badly injured and 2Lt Redmond died next day. No.53 was now attached to the Xth Corps which had taken over in the Dranoutre sector. 2Lt A F Stokes and Lt H Walpole (Notts & Derby Regt) were injured in C2503 on 17 July; they crashed approaching the aerodrome and the aircraft caught fire.

The French Xth Army (reinforced by two British divisions) made a counter-attack on 18 July towards Soissons and this event was to prove to be the beginning of the end for the German forces. Soon, the French VIth and IXth Armies had joined the fray (reinforced by three American divisions) and the German forces started to pull back.

On 31 July, Lt K A Ranney and 2Lt H S Smith (London Regt) set off at 10.30 pm in C2308 to make an "experimental night flight" in the area of St. Sylvestre Cappel. Several enemy aircraft were known to be in the area so they fired off several "greens" to advertise their presence but were nevertheless shot down by machine gun fire from our own troops. Both were killed and the aircraft was completely destroyed by fire.

The British IVth Army joined in the battle on 8 August when they began an assault towards Amiens. On 10 August, Lt S W Cowper-Coles and 2Lt G L Pargeter (Royal Fusiliers) had their petrol tank holed by shrapnel. The pilot was saturated in petrol and the observer climbed out onto the lower wing and managed to plug the hole with his glove. He remained on the wing until just before landing! At 5.30 pm, Lt D C Dunlop and 2Lt T G Evans were taking off in F5889 (B7827 rebuilt) when a wheel sheared off. The aircraft was badly damaged in the ensuing landing and rebuilt yet again as F6385. Lt G L Dobell and 2Lt A W Baker were killed when C2265 came down out of control and burst into flames on 11 August. They had probably been hit by enemy fire. E48 ("Jamaica No. 2"), flown by Lt St Jean and 2Lt Cooper (West Yorks), was wrecked in a forced landing while on a shoot with the 352nd Siege Battery on 19 August. E48 was rebuilt as F6391.

No.53 went supply-dropping for the first time on 22 August when nine coils of barbed wire and four boxes of equipment were dropped on the Xth Corps front by parachute. On 24 August, Lts Cowper-Coles and Sanders in C2244 were on a trench recce near Bailleul when they saw a D.F.W. two-seater carrying streamers from its struts at 1,400 feet. They dived on it and opened fire but when they levelled off, were unable to catch up with it! 2Lts Leach and Sanders in F5897 met with an enemy formation of nine or ten aircraft near Neuve Eglise whilst spotting for the guns on 27 August. A Fokker triplane attacked, followed by two other aircraft. Luckily, some Sopwith Dolphins appeared, so they were able to escape but not before their wireless batteries had been shot away, the transmitter damaged and the aircraft hit in several places.

Lt Cowper-Coles and 2Lt Pargeter were on a contact patrol on 1 September in C2244 when their petrol tank was holed yet again by AA fire. 2Lt Pargeter repeated his wing-walking act and managed to plug the leak until they reached the aerodrome. He was later awarded the DFC. Next day, 2Lts A J MacQueen and D A Watson were brought down in D4903 by AA fire but were unhurt. On 3 September, Lts D C Dunlop and B E Scott MC DFC (Canadian FA) came under machine gun fire whilst flying in C2377 on a flash patrol. Lt Dunlop managed to land at Clairmarais where he found that Lt Scott was severely wounded. Lt J B Pierce and 2Lt M W Wakeman in C2364 were spotting a hostile machine gun post near Ploegsteert Wood next day when a D.F.W. dived on them. Fire was returned and the D.F.W. made off after a few minutes. Since its rear gun had not been used, it was assumed that either the gun had jammed or that the observer had been put out of action. The R.E.8 was badly damaged in the encounter.

On 11 September, No.53 moved to Abeele East. Major Henderson was awarded the Croix de Guerre on 21

September. Next day, 2Lts J P Sharp and S A Bird in C2506 were both wounded by machine gun fire at the Xth Corps front. The aircraft was badly damaged in a forced landing on Proven aerodrome. Twenty five minutes later, Lts Aitken and Vickerton were on artillery duties in C2549 near Ploegsteert Wood at 8,000 feet when five Pfalz Scouts dived out of the sun and opened fire on them. They span down to 4,000 feet followed by just one Pfalz. As soon as they returned fire, it broke off the attack and flew off.

At the end of September, the Allies renewed their offensive and the Germans were on the retreat again. It was slowly beginning to dawn on them that they were going to lose this war and the first tentative steps were taken towards seeking an armistice during the first week of October.

On 1 October, Lt G C Brown and 2Lt L F Raby were brought down in C2549 by machine gun fire but escaped unhurt. Tragedy struck the next day when Lt J B Pierce and 2Lt M W Wakeman went missing in C2742 on a CAP. Lt Pierce was confirmed as being killed and 2Lt Wakeman died of his injuries on 19 October. 2Lts B R Ronald and H Walpole were attacked by an enemy aircraft whilst flying C2534 on the 3rd. The petrol and oil tanks were shot through and a forced landing was made at the front.

A close relationship between 53 Squadron and "M" Flight began on the 6th when Lts D C Dunlop and J A Lewis became the first of many to be posted between the two units. "M" Flight was one of five long-range reconnaissance units ("L"-"P") which had been set up in the autumn of 1918 equipped with Bristol Fighters. Although it is not strictly part of No.53's history, it is interesting to note that Lts Dunlop and Lewis were responsible for "M" Flight's first combat success when they shot down a Fokker biplane on 14 October over Roncq.

Lts A H A Alban and G W L Day were taking off in D4943 on 8 October when they hit a notice board on the edge of the aerodrome which broke the propeller. The engine rapidly over-revved and a crash became inevitable! The crew made off at speed while the R.E.8 was totally destroyed by fire. Next day, Lt G C Brown and 2Lt L F Raby in D6804 were shot down by a hostile aircraft at the front. Lt Brown was severely wounded and died next day. 2Lt Raby was killed. On 17 October, Lt G W E Whitehead and 2Lt R H Griffiths (Welsh Regt) went missing in D6799 and were later confirmed to be dead.

The Germans were now well and truly on the retreat and No.53 moved further east to Menin/Coucou on 21 October. Lts A H A Alban and R A Neilsen (Canadian FA) were in C2935 on 24 October when they came under machine gun fire on a CAP. They were able to land unhurt at Coucou but the R.E.8 was badly damaged. Lts H H Blackwell and P G Hutson in C2558 were taking photographs on the 30th when they were hit by AA fire. Lt Hutson (Middlesex Regt) was wounded by shrapnel. The dubious honour of being No.53's final casualty of the war fell to Lt Alban (RFA). He was shot in the hand by AA fire on 3 November.

No.53 moved to Sweveghem near Courtrai on 5 November. Lts L J StJean and P J Swan-Taylor wrecked C2563 when they landed in a shell hole on the new aerodrome. H7262 was badly damaged when the front of a hangar collapsed on top of it on 7 November. Lt C C Allinson and 2Lt J M Calneck wrecked D6723 whilst landing on unfamiliar ground to make a report at X Corps HQ on 9 November at 6.05 am. Two hours later, Lt V Foster (South Lancs) and 2Lt G W Pearce (RE[T]) came under heavy

machine gun fire in E1109. The engine was shot through and a forced landing was made at the front. This most horrid of wars ended on 11 November when the Armistice was signed. Some 671 successful artillery shoots had been carried out and 27.83 tons of bombs had been dropped by 53 Squadron since 1 October 1917. The squadron records prior to this date cannot be found.

16 November saw No.53 on the move again to Seclin near Lille and transferred to 81st Wing in the 10th Brigade. One Flight went to Avelin under 80th Wing on attachment. A further move to Reumont was made on 24 November (15th Wing, 5th Brigade). 2Lts W H Sissons and J J V Barlow in C2613 overshot on arrival at Reumont and hit the top of a shrine situated on the edge of the aerodrome! Both were injured and the R.E.8 ended up on its back. No.53 were ordered to Laneffe near Charleroi on 28 November. Lt V Foster wrecked C2743 on take-off from Reumont on 30 November en route to Laneffe.

No.53 was now part of the Reserve Army of Occupation and Laneffe was to be their home for some four months. Hangarage was limited and the airfield would appear to have been a somewhat bleak and windswept place. R.E.8 E1112 was blown over and wrecked by a strong wind on 27 December, despite being picketed down. 2Lt A Knox was on his way back from Ochey on 30 December when he had an engine failure in C2870 and forced to land. He struck a sunken road and then the machine blew over in a violent gust.

Having to keep the aircraft outside exposed to the elements was proving to be a costly business. Eight R.E.8s were struck off squadron strength on 6 January 1919 due to damage caused by water ingress. Glue joints were softening, woodwork warping and metal fittings rusting. The first eight to be struck off were C2545, C2602, C2901 ("Mauritius No.6"), D4871, D6703, F5897, F6018 and H7033. Five more were struck off on 9 January; C2593, C2930, C3474, D6801 ("Gold Coast No.5") and H7022. Morale was on the decline now that the euphoria generated by the end of the war was dying down. A contemporary note points out that it was possible to get into lots of trouble in Charleroi and several of the squadron members managed it! Most just wanted to go home and be re-united with their families.

A proposal to re-equip No.53 with Bristol Fighters was made on 10 January with an ultimate destination of Yatesbury, amended to Old Sarum on 20 January. Capt G B A Baker took over as temporary CO on 19 January. No.8 Squadron had received instructions to supply one Bristol Fighter (Arab), one pilot and one engine fitter to No.53 on 22 January. Other aircraft are believed to have followed. Capt F H Davies became temporary CO on 3 February. 2Lts J H Weatherill and T R Young struck a tree on take-off and wrecked C2908 two days later. Major G H B McCall took over as CO on 11 February. An order to pass all Bristol Fighters on to 59 Squadron was received on 13 February. These were to be replaced by a similar number of R.E.8s.

No.53 was then ordered to waste to cadre strength and its machines were to be flown home to demobilisation aerodromes by their own pilots. Some of the R.E.8s, including D6722 and D6839, are thought to have been passed to 13 Squadron at St Omer. No.53, consisting of 48 Officers and 182 O/Rs, was struck off the strength of 2nd Wing on 21 February. Capt J L Vatchell took command of the cadre, which embarked at Boulogne for Folkestone on 18 March. The final destination was Old Sarum where 53 Squadron officially disbanded on 25 October 1919.

CHAPTER 6

RE-FORMED AT

FARNBOROUGH

*Hector K9703, coded D, carried the
squadron badge in a star on the fin
(The late Lt Col A.P.C. Hannay)*

Some twenty-one years after leaving Farnborough for France, No.53 came back again when it was re-formed there on 28 June 1937 as No.53 (Army Co-operation) Squadron. The new CO was Major A P C Hannay MC (Queen's Own Cameron Highlanders). He was given the honorary rank of Squadron Leader and was the first Army officer since the end of the First World War to command an RAF squadron. F/O B G Carroll was put in charge of "A" Flt, Lt E D Joyce (RA), "B" Flt and Capt K J McIntyre (Royal Tank Corps), "C" Flt. New Hawker Hectors with 790 hp Napier-Halford Dagger III engines were collected from the Westland factory at Yeovil and by the end of July, the squadron strength had reached sixteen aircraft.

Although the Hector was a great improvement on the R.E.8, the tasks which No.53 were asked to perform had a familiar ring to them. Night recce exercises were flown from Upper Heyford from 4 September for a week. Some aircraft also went to Debden and took part in a War Office exercise on 20 September. The squadron was now part of No.22 Group. Group HQ was situated right across the road from No.53 which was rather too close for comfort. Certainly, the AOC did not have far to travel when he conducted his annual inspection on 20 October!

By 31 October, 14 officers and 148 NCOs and airmen were on the strength of 53 Squadron and "survey photography" had been added to "night recce" and "more-distant tactical recce" as squadron tasks. As a result of this, F/L M B Edwards, who was a specialist in photography, was posted in to command "A" Flt which gradually became known as the "Survey Flight". On 1 March 1938, eleven Hectors flew up to West Freugh for the annual practice camp. The squadron was there for a month and fired off 36,014 rounds of ammunition. Some 490 practice bombs were also dropped.

No.53 moved to nearby Odiham on 8 April 1938 to join No.50 (AC) Wing which was commanded by No.22 Group. Odiham had been used as an exercise landing ground since 1924 and was now in the process of becoming a proper airfield. The new offices and hangars were not yet completed, so 53 Squadron moved in with Nos.4 and 13 (AC) Squadrons to start with. Avro Tutor K4823 was taken on strength from No.13 on 24 April and used for training. Even more interesting was the arrival on 28 April of Vickers Valentia K2344 from Cardington. This aircraft was to be used for

troop-carrying and was flown by F/L Roberts and F/O Campbell-Voullaire.

Hector K9702 was written off in a landing accident on 4 May. F/O J F Hyde was slightly injured. K8150 (P/O D P Hughes) and K9695 (Capt K J McIntyre) were damaged on 11 May when they collided on take-off during a practice for the Empire Air Day display. Both were able to land without further damage or injury. On 16 May, the squadron was finally able to move into its new hangar and offices. The Empire Air Day display on 28 May gave No.53 an opportunity to fly a squadron formation in the No.50 (AC) Wing fly-past and then to give a demonstration of supply-dropping and message pick-ups. By the end of May, Valentia K2344 had carried 860 troops in 11 days of flying.

A final rehearsal and Press night for the Aldershot Tattoo took place on 2 June. Three Hectors appeared in the Tattoo which took place between the 7th and the 18th. Miles Magister L8166 was collected from the factory at Reading on 9 June. On 16 June, the driver of a road-roller who was working on the airfield, decided to go off to lunch. Unfortunately, he left his roller parked on the landing area. Major Hannay was returning in K9688 from a Staff College exercise and failed to spot the roller which was hidden from view by the long nose and lower wings of his Hector. The resulting collision was, perhaps, inevitable and the roller driver was never to be allowed through the gates of RAF Odiham again! During the month, the Valentia carried 1,380 troops in 16 days.

No.53 took part in several exercises during July including one at night in the Longmoor-Bordon area in order to see how effective a proposed black-out might be in time of war. K9712 was damaged on 22 July when a gust of wind caught the aircraft on landing and it ended up on its nose. The pilot, Capt M D Khalifa (Egyptian Air Force), was unhurt. The Valentia flew 2,920 troops in 20 days during July. It was then switched to supply-dropping tests which were completed on 11 August. The aircraft was then taken off strength having carried a total of 5,160 troops in three months.

Exercises continued throughout August including a flight of Hectors being detached to Worthy Down on the 16th to co-operate with the 1st Cavalry Brigade. The biggest event of the month took place on 26 August when seven Hectors set off on what was then termed a "Long Distance Flight". On the first day, they flew to Sealand and Abbotsinch. Then it was on to

K9712, tipped up on landing, shows clearly the details of the aircraft. Coded 'U', it has the squadron badge on the fin and is in the overall silver colour scheme used prior to the Munich crisis. (Philip Jarrett collection)

Hectors of No.53 at Farnborough, with the buildings of the Royal Aircraft Establishment behind. (Lt Col A.P.C. Hannay)

Montrose and Evanton on 27 August where it was reported that the two aircraft fitted with W/T were still able to contact Odiham from Stirling, some 400 miles away! No.53 became the first RAF squadron to visit Orkney when they landed at Kirkwall on 29 August. A great deal of interest was shown in the visit and after refuelling, the journey was continued back to Evanton and then on to Montrose. The Hectors returned to Odiham on 30 August via Driffield and Feltwell. Tutor K4823 was passed to No.1 AACU Farnborough on 27 August.

F/O A C Brown became OC "C" Flt on 5 September when Capt K J McIntyre returned to Army duties. War clouds had been building up in Europe and it was beginning to look as if a war with Germany was becoming likely. Hitler was threatening to annex Sudetenland and to occupy Czechoslovakia. On 26 September, No.53 were brought to a state of precautionary mobilisation, which meant that they were to prepare to evacuate Odiham and proceed to Digby to adopt the secondary role of a two-seat fighter squadron! This caused a deal of consternation since 53 Squadron had absolutely no experience of this sort of activity.

Apart from anything, all of the air gunners on the squadron were volunteers from the ground trades who were paid one shilling a day and entitled to wear the "Flying Bullet" badge on the left sleeve. As it happened, there were not enough of them around to give each pilot a gunner, so

The A.O.C.'s Inspection at Farnborough on 20 October 1937

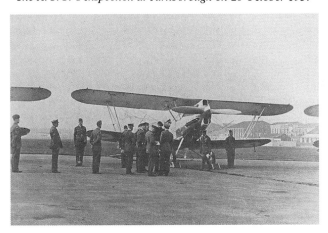

At Kirkwall Airport on 29 August 1938. (Gp Capt J.B. Wray)

No.53's 'Flying Bullets'. Left to right: AC Newton, AC Rogers, AC Templing, Cpl Woods, AC Wallace, Sgt Pritchard and AC Ferre at Kirkwall on 29 August 1938. (Gp Capt J.B. Wray CBE, DFC)

other volunteers were immediately sought. Very few of those who came forward had ever fired a Lewis gun and had little or no flying experience. Since the sight for the forward firing Vickers gun was pretty rudimentary, orders were received to mark a series of vertical lines on the forward windscreen at set distances. The theory was that when the Hector was flown up behind an He 111, for example, and its wing tips and the outside vertical lines on the windscreen coincided, then the

Hectors with flares running up before leaving to take part in the Aldershot Tattoo. (Philip Jarrett collection)

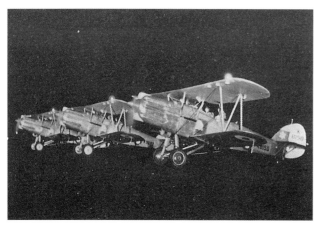

distance was 150 yards and it was therefore time to open fire! P/Os John Wray and Jasper Read were issued with a Local Purchase Order and instructed to proceed to the chemist in Odiham village in order to buy lipsticks for marking these.

Wishful thinking continued with the instruction that bombers were to be attacked from behind and then to be overtaken (!) from underneath so that the gunner could bring the Lewis gun to bear. The Hectors lost their beautiful silver finishes and were roughly camouflaged to a pattern provided. Mercifully, the squadron never had to go to war as No.53 (F) Squadron. The Prime Minister, Mr Neville Chamberlain, came back from his meeting with Hitler in Munich and made his famous "Peace in Our Time" speech. The crisis was deemed to be over and No.53 (AC) Squadron came into being again on 5 October. The annual AOC's inspection went ahead as planned when AVM B E Sutton DSO OBE MC visited on 14 October in his capacity as AOC No.22 Group.

On 28 October, F/L W B Murray was posted in from the School of Photography at Farnborough to take over the Survey Flight from S/L M B Edwards who had been promoted. Bill Murray was a keen glider pilot and had recently broken the two-seater endurance record when he and John Sproule had stayed airborne in a Slingsby Falcon for over 22 hours at Dunstable Downs. On 17 November, King Carol and Prince Michael of Rumania paid a visit to Odiham and 53 Squadron.

24

CHAPTER 7

FIRST TO FLY THE

BLENHEIM IV

A trio of Blenheim IVs of 'C' Flight
before squadron codes have been applied

News was received on 24 November that the Hectors were to be replaced with Bristol Blenheims. It was becoming increasingly obvious that the Hector was incapable of operating far behind enemy lines and that the Survey Flight, at the very least, needed more modern equipment. It had therefore been decided that No.53 should be the first squadron to be equipped with the new Mk.IV version of the Blenheim. Crews were sent to Bicester and Harwell on the 28th for training on the new type. In addition, F/L Robinson of 107 Squadron brought Blenheim Mk.I L1310 to Odiham from Harwell in order to instruct the pilots remaining at base.

The first of the new aircraft, L4836, arrived from Filton on 19 January 1939. From the pilot's point of view, the Blenheim IV represented a huge advance in speed and technology on the Hector. It was faster than many of the fighters still being flown by the RAF and was powered by two Bristol Mercury VIII engines driving variable-pitch propellers. Later Mk.IVs were fitted with Mercury XVs. The crew was no longer accommodated in an open cockpit and the aircraft was equipped with retractable undercarriage and wing flaps.

Hector flying continued in the meantime and an interesting incident took place on 24 January during a session of local night flying practice. This was the first time that camouflaged Hectors had been used for this purpose and the new paint scheme was so effective that P/O P F G Jameson in K9695 failed to see K9687 flown by F/O W S G Maydwell (Somerset Light Infantry) and taxied into the back of it! F/L

Brown set off for Harwell in K9712 on 17 February to collect some Blenheim spares. Unfortunately he hit some rising ground on landing there and the Hector was written off when the undercarriage collapsed.

Tragedy struck on 30 January when P/O Peter Jameson was killed in Blenheim L4836 when it crashed half a mile from Odiham after an engine failed. As history was to prove, he was to be the first of many to die in a 53 Squadron Blenheim. The re-equipment with new Blenheims was completed on 21 March and, by the end of the month, squadron strength was 17 Blenheims, 10 Hectors and one Magister. On 1 April, F/L Murray was promoted to S/L and so took command of No.53 on 21 April. Major Pat Hannay MC went back to his Army duties and he was sadly missed by all. He had been a well-respected and just CO and in years to come was never to lose touch with "his squadron".

No.53 went north to Leuchars on 26 June for the annual practice camp. Apart from one over-enthusiastic Blenheim pilot who put six bullets through the Fairey Gordon target tug with his forward-firing wing gun, all went well. Luckily, there were no injuries but the author has it on good authority that the Gordon never flew again. By the end of June, only one Hector remained.

Crews were now able to concentrate on the Blenheim. Although these early Mk.IVs were a great advance on the Hectors, not a lot of thought had gone into equipping them. No intercom system was fitted so it was pretty well impossible to communicate with the gunner, who was isolated

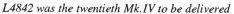

L4842 was the twentieth Mk.IV to be delivered

Engine repairs on L9043

No.53's Blenheim IVs lined up on the occasion of a Press visit to Odiham early in 1939. All but one have the revised roundels

in his turret behind the wing spar. No.53 got round this problem by rigging up a continuous pulley made of strong twine which ran from alongside the pilot's left ear back over the spar to the gunner. Communication was now made possible by attaching written notes to the pulley with clothes pegs! Thoughtfully, some kind person had fitted the Morse key into the right-hand arm rest of the pilot's seat. This, combined with a multitude of new knobs and levers, ensured that the pilot would never get bored. The notion that the gunner might be able to cope with a radio had yet to dawn.

Until 1936, pilots were responsible for navigating aircraft in the RAF. As aircraft became more and more complicated and flew longer distances, it became obvious that pilots had less and less time to devote to the essential task of navigation. As a result, the Observer brevet was re-introduced on 21 October, 1937 and schools were set up to teach suitable candidates the rudiments of navigation. In the interim, No.53 had found several volunteers from the ground trades who were largely self-taught and who had learned their skills whilst serving in such places as the Middle East and India. One of the best of these was Sgt W J Cronin who was also the Sergeant Fitter in "A" Flight.

War clouds were looming over Europe again and the order that No.53 and the other squadrons which made up the

Field Force were to prepare for mobilisation was received on 23 August. At 1700 hours on 1 September, general mobilisation was ordered as a result of the invasion of Poland by Germany. Instructions were received to change the squadron code letters, which were painted on the sides of the aircraft, from "TE" to "PZ". A state of war with Germany was declared on 3 September and the mobilisation of 53 Squadron was completed on 6 September. Since No.53 was a mobile squadron with its own photographic and W/T units, some 300 personnel were on strength. The ground party left Odiham on 14 September for France via Southampton and Cherbourg in a convoy of 48 vehicles and 5 trailers.

The air party, consisting of 12 Blenheims, left Odiham on 18 September led by S/L Murray. Since it was necessary to carry some ground crew, only the CO and the Flight Commanders had observers on board. The course for Newhaven was set and then to Le Tréport where the CO was to fire the colours of the day before proceeding to Reims/Champagne. The visibility was very bad over France and it became obvious that the squadron was lost when the CO started to orbit a big town with a large church in the centre. "A" Flt, under the command of F/L Clements (RCAF), became detached from the rest and while they circled in the gloom, he flew very low and very slow over a

Above: The spartan surroundings at Poix, with the squadron's Tiger Moth in the foreground

Below: Poix's watch area with Magister L8166 and a visiting French Curtiss Hawk 75A

Although not confirmed, this could be either L4862 or P6916 involved in a ground accident at Metz, the codes appearing to be PZ-E. On 2 May 1940, a small party of ground staff was sent to Metz to maintain detached Blenheims. The Potez 25 that has rammed the tail carries the chequered lozenge that warned passing aircraft that it was engaged in instrument flying training

railway station and read off its name. The station staff ran out on to the platform and manned what appeared to be an old Gatling gun but fortunately missed! Sgt Cronin then set course for Reims where "A" Flt were the first to arrive. F/L Bill Clements was attached to No.53 from the RCAF and had made up his own identity tag numbered "RCAF 1" since he figured that he was the first of his colleagues to go to war. The remainder of No.53 arrived in ones and twos, the last to arrive being the CO who had landed in a field to ask a passing cyclist for directions!

Sealed orders were then received ordering No.53 to proceed to Plivot, near Epernay, the centre of the champagne industry. It was a small grass airfield which had once been an emergency landing ground for Imperial Airways. The squadron accommodation at Plivot was of the tented variety, the officers were billeted in houses and the others in haylofts and barns in the village about a mile away. Contact was quickly made with a young man called Pol Roget who organised a visit to his champagne factory and arranged supplies at an extremely favourable rate.

No.53 was now part of the Air Component of the Field Force and under the immediate command of AVM C H B Blount OBE MC who was, in turn, under the command of the C-in-C, British Expeditionary Force, General The Viscount Gort VC KCB CBE DSO MVO MC. Due to the late arrival of Nos.18 and 57, both of which were planned to be bomber squadrons within the Advanced Air Striking Force, No.53 was attached to the AASF for a few weeks. Some training started immediately and the squadron was told on 23 September to prepare for long range recce flights over Germany in the area of Brunswick-Rheine-Düsseldorf. A photo-survey of northern France was also undertaken as a matter of priority.

On 29 September, newly-promoted S/L Clements and P/O Read positioned their Blenheims to Metz to prepare for recce flights over Germany. S/L Clements took off in L4842 just before midnight to cover the area Bremen-Osnabrück-Münster followed by P/O Read in L4840 on his way to Hanover-Minden-Hamm. At first it was clear, but the weather rapidly got worse and very little useful information was obtained although both of the areas were covered. S/L Clements even tried coming down to 1,000 feet but to no avail. Both aircraft had been ordered to return to Villeneuve but no bearings could be obtained from this station. P/O Read finally found an aerodrome with lights on and landed to discover that Villeneuve was some 30 miles away. He took off again and landed there at 0350. Unfortunately, when clearing the flarepath, he mistakenly raised the undercarriage instead of the flaps. The Blenheim cockpit was an ergonomically unfriendly place and the knobs for operating the flaps and the undercarriage were right beside one another! In fact, it took a long time to get them separated, for the author well remembers almost doing the same thing in a Vampire over twenty years later!

S/L Clements was also unable to find Villeneuve. By 0515, he was getting very short of fuel, so he set up a forced-landing pattern over a large dark area. At 800 feet, both of the engines stopped so he lowered the flaps and the undercarriage and switched on the landing light. To his astonishment, he found himself smack in the centre of a very large stubble field near Essertaux! A quick look round after landing revealed absolutely no damage whereupon he produced a large flask of whisky which he and his crew promptly demolished. At the time he set off on this flight, his total night flying experience on the Blenheim was four hours; the most experienced was F/O Wray with ten! It was

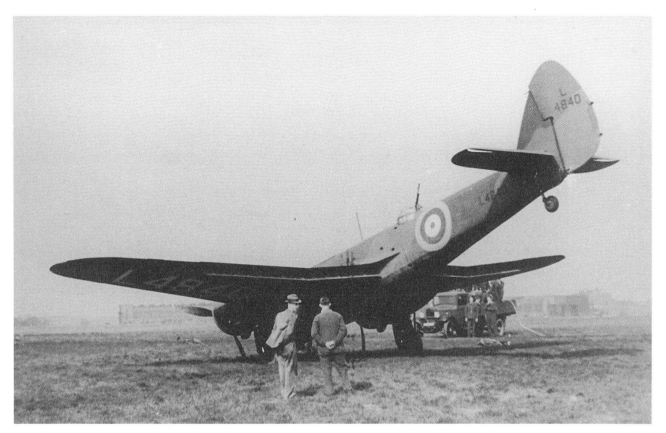

Blenheim L4240 tips up on soft ground at Odiham, with a rescue team preparing to get the tail back down.
(Gp Capt W.S.G. Maydwell DSO, DFC)

discovered that the reason no bearings had been forthcoming from the D/F station at Villeneuve was that the operator had thought the Blenheims to be German aircraft trying to home in on them.

F/L Joyce, F/O Wray and P/O Rochfort positioned to Metz for recce flights on 1 October. They were sitting in the sun watching the antics of six new French Curtiss Hawks patrolling up and down overhead the airfield which was close to the border with Germany. A French biplane took off and started practising circuits and bumps. Suddenly, a Bf 109 appeared and promptly shot it down. The Curtiss Hawks just continued to patrol up and down. Then the fog rolled in and the sorties for that night were cancelled. The recce flights were made the following night and Villeneuve was reached without difficulty. Once again, little intelligence of any value was gained and so AVM Blount decided, on 3 October, that future recce sorties would have to be flown in daylight.

It is interesting to note that the use of powerful parachute flares at night by No.53 was forbidden at this stage of the war on the grounds that they might cause damage to life and property in Germany! It was felt that this might provoke the enemy into taking retaliatory action. The first daylight recce flights were flown on 6 October by P/Os Rochfort and Bone. They were briefed to land back in England at Mildenhall and then return to Plivot after de-briefing. It was felt that it would be unwise to try to fly back to base, since the Germans would have been alerted to their presence on the outbound journey and would be quite likely to shoot them down on the way back. In any event, the weather continued to be unhelpful so little of value was learned.

An advance party of No.53 set off for Poix-de-Picardie, south-west of Amiens, on 7 October. Once again, the squadron came under the direct command of No.50 Wing of the Air Component. P/O A J Mackay and three airmen arrived there with a Tiger Moth which was to be used for communication purposes. F/L Brown and F/O Panton made recce flights over Germany on 8 October and both encountered heavy AA fire. F/O Panton in L4847/D was photographing the railway line near Bremen when he saw nine Bf 109s taking off from Stuhr aerodrome with him as the apparent target. He put the nose down and flew out to sea at 10 feet to make good his escape. Both landed safely at Mildenhall. The move to Poix was completed on 12 October. The squadron was to share the airfield with 59 Squadron which was also equipped with Blenheim Mk.IVs.

On 23 October, Vitry-en-Artois was nominated as the advanced landing ground to be used by the two squadrons and F/L Joyce and 26 airmen were sent there to set up a detachment. The squadron had now started a survey of north-east France and the Belgian border. F/O J B Wray became No.53's first casualty in France when he was badly concussed in goal during a football match against 2 Squadron. He was sent back to England on medical leave and later in the war, went on to command 137 Squadron equipped with Westland Whirlwinds. He retired as Gp Capt Wray CBE DFC. The No.53 Squadron Badge, which had been designed by Major Hannay, was approved on 26 November. HM King George VI inspected units of the Air Component at Douai on 5 December. Two Blenheims and crews from No.53 were in attendance. On the last day of 1939, Poix was inspected by the Under Secretary of State for Air, Capt H Balfour MC MP and the ACAS, AVM Sholto Douglas MC DFC.

On 1 January 1940, S/L Clements was posted to No.52 Wing HQ and F/L B B StG Daly (Lancashire Fusiliers) took over "A" Flight. The weather became bitterly cold and it proved to be impossible to start the aircraft engines on several

29

Blenheim L4843, coded TE-J, fitted with Light Series bomb carriers under the fuselage and the turret unretracted.
(Gp Capt W.S.G. Maydwell DSO, DFC)

occasions. The surface of the airfield froze hard and a new enemy appeared in the shape of frozen molehills! They were to damage several Blenheim stern frames and, since there was only one small hangar at Poix, the groundcrew were forced to erect a tent over the tail of the aircraft in order to carry out repairs in a very hostile environment. In fact, it turned out to be one of the coldest winters in living memory. Engine starting problems were never to be solved and on one notable occasion, only two engines had been started on the entire squadron after a four-hour struggle. Unfortunately, they were on different aircraft!

A new command structure came into being on 15 January. BAFF (British Air Forces in France) was formed to directly command the Air Component and the Advanced Air Striking Force (AASF), which had hitherto been controlled by Bomber Command. The new Commander was Air Marshal Sir Arthur Barratt CB CMG MC.

The aircraft establishment was increased to 18 Blenheims on 24 January and the command of No.53 Squadron became a Wing Commander post. AC1 T J Hotten, a wireless mechanic, became the first casualty of 1940 when he was found dead in a tent filled with spares on 12 February. He had been on guard duty on a very cold night and had been overcome by fumes from a paraffin heater.

The weather improved at the end of February and operations were able to be started again on 1 March. P/O Bone landed at Poix at night on 4 March in L9190 and fell into the trap of retracting the undercarriage instead of the flaps. No.53's first medals of the war were awarded on 8 March; F/O A D Panton got the DFC and Sgt W J Cronin and AC1 H A Ferre, the DFM. An important visit took place on 20 March when No.53 were inspected by the C-in-C BEF, General Gort, the CGS, Lt Gen Pownall and the AOC, AVM

Blount. Survey flights continued whenever the weather was suitable, and some night recce flights over north east France also took place.

No.59 had taken over the task of flying recce flights over Germany, but No.53 started again on 2 May. P/O J L G Butterworth, Sgt M G A Pearce and AC2 R A Wood took off from Metz at 2020 on 3 May in L9329 to carry out a recce of Ruhr-Hamm-Minden-Osnabrück-Münster but failed to return. They had been shot down south of Baden-Baden near Hornisgrinde and all were killed. P/O Wilson took off from Poix in L9331 at 2030 on 8 May to carry out a recce of reported movements near the German/Dutch border. He returned at 0130 on 9 May to find Poix shrouded in fog. He crashed half a mile from the airfield. Luckily, no one was badly injured. S/L Murray took off from Metz in R3634 at 2130 for a recce over Germany. He also found extensive fog over France on his return and since no airfield could be found, it was decided to abandon the aircraft. The observer, Sgt D G B Falconer, bailed out first but was killed on exiting the aircraft. S/L Murray then decided to try to make a wheels-up landing using parachute flares and this he managed to do in a field near Rosières at 0245 without further injury.

10 May 1940 was to become known as Blitzkrieg Day. At first light, the Germans invaded the Low Countries and advanced faster than anyone had thought possible. P/O Massey left Poix at 0855 in L9332 to make a recce of the German advance into Belgium. He was followed at 0925 by F/O Bartlett in L4848. Both landed safely at the ALG at Vitry, although L9332 had been struck by machine gun fire. One Blenheim set off for Metz with a spare crew on board to collect another 53 Squadron aircraft which had been left there for repairs. One of the observers, Donald McLeod, recalls arriving there and seeing a lot of brown patches on the

airfield. They managed to miss all of them on landing which was fortunate as they turned out to be bomb craters! They then discovered that the large airship hangar at Metz had been demolished and was now sitting on top of the aircraft which they had come to collect. Both crews got back into their Blenheim but struck a bomb crater on take off and wrecked that one also! They made their way back to Poix by train via Paris. These two aircraft are believed to have been L4862 and P6916. The final event of the day came when a staff car, driven by S/L Murray, was involved in an accident near Beauvais in the blackout. The CO suffered shock and P/Os Jasper Read and Jack Butterworth (later Gp Capt) were seriously injured.

P/O McPherson and crew were airborne from Vitry in L9460 at 0420 on 11 May for a recce of the German advance into Belgium and returned safely. P/O A D Panton DFC set off on his second survey flight of the day in L9459/B at 1455. He and his crew were shot down by five Bf 109s in Belgium. All three were wounded, however P/O Panton and Sgt J Christie (obs) were able to evade capture and escaped back to England. The gunner, AC2 R W Bence, was captured in hospital and was sadly to lose a leg. He was taken to Stalag XII but was repatriated later in the war.

All aircraft returned safely on 12 May but Poix was visited by the Luftwaffe after dark. The flare path was quickly put out and 40 incendiary bombs were dropped on the dummy flare path some two miles to the west. L9332 was badly damaged by ground fire over Belgium on 13 May but F/L Brown managed to get back to Vitry on one engine. His gunner, AC2 W J Cavett was wounded in the leg. P/O Collins and his crew were ordered to proceed to HQ BAFF and to come under their direct control. In fact, this developed into a No.53/No.59 Squadron detachment and consisted of up to six Blenheims. Orders to bomb-up all available aircraft came at 1700 on 14 May but all were stood down again shortly afterwards.

P/O P K Bone and crew took off at 0745 on 15 May in L9399 to take photographs in Belgium but failed to return. They were shot down over Tournai by a British Hurricane at 0900 and Bone, Sgt W J Cronin DFM and LAC J Bromley were all killed. F/L Daly and crew in L4847 were also set upon by a Hurricane but managed to escape although their aircraft was damaged. P/O McKinnon in L9460 was attacked by two Bf 109s and P/O Villiers-Tuthill in L4841 tangled with two Bf 110s but both were able to return with damaged aircraft.

P/O M G L Lovell, Sgt D McLeod and AC Kenneth set off at 0505 on 16 May for a recce of the Maastricht bridges in L4860/W. They were shot down by Bf 109s and crash-landed at Wadelincourt, near Peruwelz in Belgium. All three were wounded but managed to escape back to England with the help of the local populace. At briefing, P/O R I C McPherson was told that he could make his recce at high level and be shot down by Bf 109s or at low level and be shot down by ground fire! He set off in L4843 at 0905 and was flying at low level when he was shot down near Charleville-Mézières. Although the crew got out of the wreckage without injury, they were caught immediately by German troops and P/O McPherson collected a bullet wound in the process. He, Sgt A T Morland and AC2 S Robinson spent the rest of the war as Hitler's guests.

At 1430, F/L Daly took off in L4852 on a photography sortie. For the second day in succession, he was attacked by a British Hurricane. He tried to land at the Hurricane's base at Glisy but was attacked again on final approach, despite firing the colours of the day. He was forced to overshoot but finally did manage to land wheels-up on the airfield but not before the Blenheim had caught fire. On being quizzed about why he had ignored the firing of the colours of the day, the Hurricane pilot stated that he thought they were firing a cannon at him! F/L B B StG Daly, Sgt W R B Currie and AC2 P J Blandford were badly burned and returned to England for medical treatment. At 2330 on this dreadful day, S/L E C T "Sphinx" Edwards arrived to take over command of No.53. He had been a well-known King's Cup air race pilot before the war.

On 17 May, orders were received that all survey flying was to be abandoned for now, "due to the failure of fighter aircraft to recognise friendly aircraft after the firing of recognition signals". At 0830, the Luftwaffe attacked the ALG at Vitry but no damage was done as the bombs fell off the airfield. The Germans were still advancing quickly and many RAF units were having to pull back. At 1050, No.53 was ordered to bomb German troops coming down the Le Cateau-Cambrai road. Five Blenheims took off at 1245 and all returned safely at 1350. Blenheims L4842 and L4848 were lost this day but are believed to have been "borrowed" by another Squadron.

P/O Truscott took off in L9330 at 0530 on 18 May and spotted large columns of German infantry advancing to the south west. His aircraft collected several bullet holes, but he returned safely. P/O Bailey left 15 minutes later and went over Belgium as far as Brussels. They became uncertain of their position on the way back and landed at Soissons. Shortly after switching off the engines, the aircraft, believed to be R3700, was destroyed in an air raid. P/O L J Huggett, Sgt A C Gothard and AC1 W A Christie set off on a recce in L4841 but failed to return. They were brought down near Frévent and all were killed.

P/O P G Royle, Sgt E F Woods and AC2 A H Malkin went missing in L4861. They had been forced down into a field at Fontaine-au-Pire, south-east of Cambrai, by enemy fighters. Sgt Woods was badly wounded so P/O Royle and AC2 Malkin carried him to the village where he was taken care of by the priest. The gunner set off towards Cambrai in company with the village schoolmistress to try to find an ambulance. P/O Royle then returned to the Blenheim and destroyed it by fire. On his return to the village, he passed out as a result of his injuries. German troops poured into the village at 1600 and the priest informed them of the presence of the two RAF men. P/O Royle spent nearly two years in Stalag Luft I, Barth and organised the digging of several unsuccessful escape tunnels before ending up in Stalag Luft III, Sagan. He took part in the notorious "Great Escape" on the night of 24/25 March, 1944 when 76 officers escaped through a tunnel. P/O Royle was the 55th to escape and emerged at 0230 but was re-captured 24 hours later. He was lucky to survive, for Hitler ordered the massacre of fifty of his colleagues. Sgt Woods was taken to a hospital at Avesnes-les-Aubert where he recovered from his wounds and also became a POW. AC2 Malkin was able to escape back to England and turned up in an Evesham hospital on 29 May.

P/O Coleson landed at Vitry after a reconnaissance flight at 1810 and within minutes some Bf 110s appeared and dropped bombs on the airfield wrecking his Blenheim, six Hurricanes and the Tiger Moth. Orders were received to abandon Poix and to fall back to Crécy at 1930. All equipment that could not be moved was to be destroyed. Due to a lack of spares, several Blenheims with relatively minor defects had to be left behind.

The aircraft started to arrive at Crécy at 0500 on 19 May. A wood on the south side of the airfield offered some concealment and No.53 settled in to it as well as was

Belgian schoolgirls posing on the wreckage of L4840, shot down at Wadelincourt by a Bf 109E on 16 May 1940.
(Delforge-Basècles)

possible. However, it had already been decided to move the Air Component HQ to Hawkinge and to mount recce flights from bases in southern England. No.53's aircraft were to fly to Lympne, the ground personnel were to proceed to Boulogne and valuable equipment to Cherbourg. All aircraft had left by 1930 except for P/O Steuart-Richardson who had come back to Crécy in L4847 from a recce to find an empty airfield. His aircraft had been damaged by ground fire and, after temporary repairs, he left for Lympne at 0600 on 20 May.

At 1530 on 20 May, F/O Rochfort in L9460 and F/O Mallon in R3735 set off to join the HQ BAFF detachment which was now at Coulommiers. The remainder of the aircraft were flown to Andover at 1700. The ground party had arrived at Tidworth Barracks and they caught up with their aircraft on 21 May. It was decided to use Hawkinge as an ALG. P/O Triptree left Hawkinge in R3596 at 0415 on 22 May for a recce of Arras-Cambrai-Péronne. The aircraft was damaged by machine gun fire and crashed on arrival back at Hawkinge. The crew were only slightly injured. F/O S G L Pepys, Sgt A J Haygreen and AC2 H Spear failed to return from a recce of the Boulogne area in R3691 on 23 May. It was later learned that they had all become POWs. Another recce was flown by P/O Truscott in L9466 which was damaged by flak. Two other aircraft landed at Rouen/Boos at the end of their tasks. This airfield was to become the new ALG in France. Back at Andover, P/O Steuart-Richardson was sent in L4850 to the small airfield at Worcester to collect spark plugs. There was no wind when he got there and, unfortunately, he ran out of airfield and went through the railings at the end, hitting a car on a side road.

F/L Brown was on recce in R3605 on 24 May near St Omer when his aircraft was struck by flak. A forced landing was made at Manston. F/O Bartlett was also struck by flak on 25 May in L9466 but managed to get back to Hawkinge. P/O G M Bailey, Sgt W J K Evans and AC1 A A Gillmore took off from Boos in L8863 on 26 May and failed to return. They had crashed near Seninghem, Pas-de-Calais and all three were killed. P/O K A Aldridge was attacked by enemy fighters in R3703 on 27 May and the damage was so bad that the crew had to abandon the aircraft over St Margarets, near Dover. He and AC1 R H Trafford were injured. P/O P F C Villiers-

Tuthill, Sgt A H Payne and AC1 D B Mearns were brought down near Faumont in R3735 and all were killed. P/O Coleson in N3551 escaped from an attack by four Bf 110s on 28 May by diving down to ground level. P/O Robinson was attacked by eleven Bf 109s on 31 May and R3733 was badly damaged. Later in the day, No.53 moved from Andover to Eastchurch.

W/C E C T Edwards took command officially on 1 June. F/L A C Brown set off from Hawkinge on 2 June in L9476 to carry out a recce of the Dunkirk area. He was engaged by flak and, in the process of taking avoiding action, struck a sand dune with the starboard wing and aileron. The aircraft became very difficult to fly and he realised that they would not get back to Hawkinge so he crash-landed on the Goodwin Sands. The crew were unhurt and were rescued by HM Drifter *Shipmates*. On 6 June, P/O Bethel took off from Boos at 0520 in R3602. He was attacked by a single Bf 109 and his wop/ag, Sgt H H Wilson, was hit in the head and seriously wounded. The aircraft was badly damaged but they managed to get it back to Boos. Sgt Wilson was then flown back to Hawkinge by F/O Mallon in L9460 but died of his injuries some two months later on 7 August.

No.53 moved from Eastchurch to Gatwick on 13 June. Squadron HQ was set up in the terminal and the rest were accommodated in the racecourse grandstand. On 14 June, F/O Panton DFC in R3662 was struck by ground fire near Elbeuf and then forced to leave the area by Bf 110s. P/Os Collins and Triptree returned with their crews from detachment to HQ BAFF. The last Blenheim to return from France was flown by F/O J D Rochfort who arrived at Gatwick on 15 June. He and his crew had left Andover on 20 May and they had been "living rough" while HQ BAFF had retreated across France. They had inherited a Corporal with ginger hair who was a genius at scrounging food and accommodation. The last remnants of the RAF left in France had finally come under the command of Air Commodore J Cole-Hamilton. He and the Corporal returned with them in the well of the Blenheim. His wop/ag, Robbie Roberts DFM tells how they were confronted by an angry official wearing a top-hat on arrival at Gatwick who then proceeded to tell the crew that they had landed right in the middle of a race and had frightened the horses. F/O Rochfort laid him out cold

Sir Kingsley Wood, Sec of State for Air, visits Odiham. From left, Sir A. Campbell, W/C L.O. Brown, Major A.P.C. Hannay and ACM Sir C. Newlands, Chief of Air Staff. (Lt Col A.P.C. Hannay)

with just one punch!

The joint No.53/No.59 detachment had been sent out daily to find out where the front line actually was. This they did by flying in several directions until they were fired at! Despite this dubious practice, No.53's casualties were remarkably light. On 6 June, F/O Rochfort and Sgt Clayton had been slightly wounded by flak shrapnel and their aircraft, TR-X, badly damaged. Other aircraft used included, TR-C, TR-E, TR-Y, R3631, R3632, R3694 and R3699.

Two sorties were flown over France on 16 June and news came that No.53 and No.18 were to be given priority for re-equipment. On 18 June, orders were received to send

three aircraft to Nantes and three to Jersey at first light. Eight sorties were carried out without loss. F/L I H Bartlett came back from Jersey with an added bonus having "found" F/O Dick Maydwell who had been missing for weeks. He had been in England with his crew on leave when the Germans invaded on 10 May. On his way back to join No.53, he had been commandeered to run a refuelling and rearming unit near Rouen which looked after the Hurricane squadrons that came over from England every day. They had fallen back through Dreux, Dinard and then through St Malo to Jersey. On return to Gatwick, he was promoted to F/L and given command of "A" Flt.

L4837 on the tarmac at Odiham. (Ken Smalley)

P/O R. V. Muspratt, Sgt D. Smart and Sgt R. Cole at Detling

CHAPTER 8

INTO COASTAL

COMMAND

*A Blenheim IV running up at dispersal
at Thorney Island, January 1941.
(S/Ldr R. Walton MC AFC)*

News was received on 29 June that 53 Squadron was to be transferred to Coastal Command and was to proceed to Detling on 1 July. This was to signal big changes for the squadron. The main ground party and the air party, consisting of 20 Blenheims, moved to Detling on 3 July. No.53 HQ was established in Owen's Garage on the south side of the airfield and the personnel were accommodated in tents. The squadron was now part of No.16 Group and the new task was to carry out shipping strikes and to attack coastal targets. The Army officers seconded to No.53 from the School of Army Co-operation at Andover had to brush up on ship recognition on arrival!

Nine "SA9" patrols and a recce of Boulogne harbour were flown on 5 July without incident. In approximate terms, the SA9 patrol area ran north-east out over the North Sea from Manston to a point some 50 miles off Den Helder. F/L Bartlett was returning from an attack on a canal near Amsterdam in L8789/J in the early hours of 7 July and was unable to find Detling in bad weather. He landed on the disused airfield at Ramsgate and the aircraft was damaged when it hit several anti-invasion obstructions. Detling was some 600 feet above sea level, perched on top of the North Downs and prone to low cloud and fog. It was to prove to be a difficult airfield to find. P/O H M Newton returned from a raid on vessels at Ostend in R3678/Y at 2330 and bounced on landing in heavy rain. The aircraft tipped up on its nose.

W/C Edwards was returning from a raid on Leidam Island on 13 July in L9474/L and was unable to obtain any bearings. He ran out of fuel at 0245 and the crew abandoned the aircraft near Bulpham, Essex. All landed safely. It should be noted that the wop/ag now had control of the radio. It was mounted on a shelf behind the turret and was completely out of sight when he was in the turret. It needed both hands to tune it and each hand was encased in many pairs of gloves! It is hardly surprising that obtaining bearings was sometimes difficult.

S/L Murray, who had become S/L Ops, was posted to the School of Photography on 14 July and S/L D C Oliver took over. Six aircraft took off at 2135 to bomb oil storage tanks near Ghent. F/O Panton in N3551/E got caught in the searchlights and was shot down by flak. He and his observer, Sgt A E Farrow, were captured. Sgt L H Stride, wop/ag, was killed. After his release from Stalag Luft III at the end of the war, F/O A D Panton went on to become Air Commodore Panton CB OBE DFC and was to put his new-found skills to good use when he commanded the RAF Police! On 18 July F/O J E Mahony set off in R3661/A for a recce of Flushing but failed to return. He and Sgt D A Keetley (obs) were

reported missing and Sgt G E Exton (wop/ag) was killed. It is believed that they were shot down by a Bf 109 of 6/JG 54 into the mouth of the River Scheldt.

The oil refinery at Vlaardingen near Rotterdam was attacked on the night of 20 July. Six aircraft took part and several direct hits were made on the storage tanks which blew up and caught fire in a most satisfying manner. Despite heavy flak, all aircraft returned safely. P/O D B Starky, Sgt H W Hunt and Sgt B Moriarty went missing in R3836/X on SA9 patrol on 25 July. They had been shot down and killed by a German convoy near Ameland. P/O J C Mallon found the flare path at Detling obscured by low cloud on his return from a raid in R3660/K on 31 July. He landed across the line of the glim lamps, ran off the airfield and collided with a sand-bag emplacement. Unable to find Detling, P/O Ritchie in PZ-P ended up at Weston Zoyland in Somerset!

S/L Oliver led seven aircraft on an attack on Emden harbour on 3 August. The weather was rapidly deteriorating and two were unable to locate the target. P/O H C Corbett and crew in L9475/V made an attack on the airfields at Schiphol and Haamstede instead. Sadly, they didn't make it home. Contact was lost at 0105 on 4 August and the last bearing put them north of Bircham Newton and out to sea. He and Sgt S E Riddington (obs) were killed and Sgt K W Crane (wop/ag) reported missing. S/L Oliver in L8794/T was unable to find Detling and couldn't get any bearings either. He ordered the crew to bail out when they ran out of fuel at 0110 and all landed safely between Farnham and Petersfield. The aircraft crashed on heath-land near Bordon. Three others landed at Bircham Newton and one each at Wyton and Wittering.

P/O P J Coleson and crew took off at 1024 on 11 August on a "Dundee" patrol (Dunkirk to Dieppe) in T1816/K but were reported missing. P/O Coleson became a POW, Sgt I Inskip was never found and P/O G M Bardolph (wop/ag) was badly injured and taken to the German Naval Hospital at Chateau des Dominicaines near Hardinghen where he died on 17 August. F/L M G Stevenson in R3911/W met what he believed to be three Do 215s whilst on an SA9 patrol. One of them attacked from behind and the other two got on either side. Fire was returned by Sgt Robbie Roberts and one peeled off with smoke coming from both engines. The Blenheim's undercarriage had been damaged so a crash-landing was made at Manston at 2000. F/O I S Jameson and crew were returning from a bombing raid on barges anchored in the Zuider Zee during the early hours of 13 August and were unable to find Detling. The aircraft, T1937/E, was abandoned at 0145. All landed safely, although P/O Jameson ended up

T2043/PZ-M in late 1940 with twin-gun dorsal installation without cupola. (Flambards)

hanging inverted from some hop-pole wires in the dark. The aircraft crashed at Conghurst, near Hawkhurst, Kent.

For 53 Squadron, 13 August was to prove to be a disastrous day. At 1600, just as the airmen were having tea, 86 Ju 87s of Lehrgeschwader I led by Hauptmann von Brauchitsch, dive-bombed the airfield, supported by Bf 109s which strafed everything in sight. One bomb penetrated the heavy roof of the Operations Block. The Station Commander, G/C E P M Davis AFC, was killed instantly as was S/L D C Oliver (No.53's S/L Ops.) and F/O H M Aspen (No.53's Signals Officer). Only three people came out of the Operations Block alive. Out on the airfield, seven of No.53's ground crew lay dead and another eight were wounded. Two wop/ags, Sgts D J Roberts and K W Vowles were also wounded. Over 20 aircraft had been destroyed, including five of No.53's Blenheims which caught fire after being hit by incendiary shells. They were loaded with bombs which exploded. The raid only lasted a few minutes but a huge amount of damage had been caused. This day was later to be known as "Adler Tag".

On a happier note, DFCs for S/L W B Murray and F/L A C Brown and DFMs for Sgts B J Brooks, G H Cooper, R A Latham and W P Whetton were announced on 14 August. Despite the events of the previous day, it was possible to fly three SA9 patrols this day. The airfield at St Omer was the target on 22 August. W/C Edwards and six others set off just before midnight and were able to start several fires and cause a great deal of damage. The flak was fierce and P/O Dottridge, flying T2132/L, was hit in the port wing while escaping at low level. This caused the wing to lift and the starboard wing tip to hit the ground. He managed to keep the aeroplane flying until his observer, Sgt Freddie King, came to

help him on the control column. The two of them managed to get the Blenheim back home at reduced speed and landed safely. F/L Stevenson in PZ-R was wounded and P/O Muspratt in PZ-D had his starboard wing damaged. P/O Dottridge was awarded the DFC and F/S King the DFM later in the year.

F/O S C Rochford, Sgt W Briggs and Sgt D Brook were killed in T2035/F returning from a "Hookos" patrol (night patrol from Hook of Holland to Ostend) on 24 August. They hit two houses near Dover and the aircraft burst into flames. Blenheim T2046/J failed to return from a Hookos on 28 August and P/O W E Fitzpatrick, Sgt J Bann and Sgt H Dunnington were posted missing. They had made an attack on the seaplane base at Schellingwoude near Amsterdam. The Luftwaffe made a high-level bombing attack on Detling on 30 August and AC2 B Stone was killed. AC1 Jones and AC2 Johnson were injured and R3909 was damaged. Detling was attacked again at 0900 next morning by Bf 109s and Bf 110s. The fuel dump was set alight and the main electrical power cable to the airfield was cut. No.53 suffered no losses during the raid but this last day of August was nevertheless to end in tragedy. Five Blenheims set off to attack the refinery at Vlaardingen again. Despite heavy flak, W/C E C T Edwards in T1940/D pressed home his attack and was able to bomb the target before being shot down in flames behind the Shell refinery by the guns of Flakgruppe 261. The CO, Sgt L L Benjamin and Sgt J T Beesley were all killed. No.53 had lost a very brave and well-respected leader.

The Luftwaffe attacked Detling twice on 1 September, at 1600 and 2300, and set the Officers Mess alight. About 30 Do 17s made a high-level bombing attack at 1800 on 2 September and put the airfield out of action for three hours.

35

```
                NO. 53 SQUADRON FLYING PROGRAMME

                            7.6.41

                          AVAILABLE

 P.   P/O. HENRY        SGT. GELLARD        SGT. DAVY
 E.   P/O. ABBOTT       SGT. POOLE ✳        SGT. TEMPLETON ✳
 Y.   P/O. JACOB        SGT. SOAMES         SGT. NEAL
 T.   P/O. WILLIAMS     SGT. SEWELL✳        SGT. BROWN ✳
 A.   P/O. HEWSON ✳?    SGT. DAWSON ✳?      SGT. McCORKELL ✳?
 R.   W/C. GRANT        P/O. COATES ✳       SGT. G/SCOTT
 L.   F/O. CUNDY        SGT. FABEL          SGT. GRAHAM
 F.   P/O. HILDITCH     SGT. JAYNE          SGT. McKECHNIE
 X.   P/O. WALTON ✳     SGT. CULNANE ✳      SGT. ALLGOOD ✳
 U.   P/O. BUCK ✳       SGT. WOOD ✳         SGT. COOK
 L.   P/O. MOIRA        SGT. CARSON ✳       SGT. GRAHAM
 O.   P/O. DOBSON       SGT. KYLE           SGT. HALL
 V.   P/O. TYRRELL      SGT. CRAMP          SGT. HALL
 D.   P/O. BOLTON ✳     SGT. CORRIE ✳       SGT. KIRCHER ✳
 Z.   F/O. BANNISTER✳   SGT. DENSHAM ✳      SGT. FULLER ✳
 M.   P/O. FRANCIS ✳    SGT. WHITLEY✳       SGT. HOPPER ✳
 F.   P/O. OLDWORTH     P/O. THORNE ′       SGT. JENKINSON ✳
 S.   P/O. ALCOCK       SGT. JARVIS✳        SGT. DENNISS
 K.   P/O McLENNAN ✳    SGT. TAYLOR ✳       SGT. ROBERTS ✳

                    NOT AVAILABLE. Spare

      P/O. BONN ✳       SGT. PERKINS         -
      P/O. GAY          SGT. POWELL✳?       SGT. LEVERINGTON ✳

           ON PASS UNTIL 12.30 hrs 8.6.41.

      P/O. STEVENS      SGT. LANSDALE       SGT. GRIFFITHS ✳
      P/O. BUNCE        SGT. HAISELL        SGT. DIGGLES

                          ON LEAVE.

      P/O. G/HEYGATE✳   P/O. TROUP ✳        SGT. NAYLOR ✳
      F/L. ALDRIDGE     SGT. KING ✳         SGT. FENNELL✳

                            SICK.

      P/O. BLAKELY      SGT. COLE            -
      P/O. STIGNER        -                  -
        -               SGT. POWELL✳        SGT. DAVY
        -                 -                 SGT. OWEN
        -               P/O. HOOD            -

 AVAILABLE AIRCRAFT.              U/S AIRCRAFT.

 A.D.E.F.H.P.K. O.S.T.V.Y.R.M.X.  G. Carew Ch. U. Revs.
                                  Z. 40 hour.

 NOTES.  1. Pilots not to use cockpit heating.
         2. D.G.F.B.J.U.V.Y.L. have single rear gun.
         3. D.X.B.F.C.U.J.K. are not fitted for twin cameras.
         4. B.U.F.J.Y. no scare gun.
         5. All aircraft have I.F.F.
         6. S.U.V.K.J.Y. in knots.

                      DISTRIBUTION.

 C.O. (2 copies)    Adjutant    S/Ldr. Flying (2 copies)
 Flying Room (2 copies)   Armoury   "A" Flight   "C" Flight
 F/O Ellis    File
```

No. 53 Squadron's flying programme for 7 June 1941

Yet another high-level attack was made on the 4th and Bf 109s strafed on the 5th. No.53 suffered no losses in these attacks. S/L W B Murray DFC returned to the squadron on 7 September as CO with the acting rank of W/C. P/O Mallon returned from a recce of the Calais area next day to report that there was a convoy of 15-20 enemy ships heading north east off Cap Gris Nez. Five aircraft were sent off immediately to make an attack. They soon realised that the convoy was very well protected by aircraft. P/O Wigmore was prevented from reaching the ships by nine He 113s (sic) and three Bf 110s. P/O Dottridge shook off two He 113s (sic) and then made his attack. P/O Maurer was chased by five Bf 109s with yellow noses after dropping his bombs. Two Blenheims were shot down into the sea by Bf 109s; F/L I H Bartlett, Sgt R E Aldridge and Sgt E D Sheldrick in R3779/Z and P/O R G Hall, Sgt J D Randall and Sgt M B Conacher in T2042/H were all killed. On 19 September, P/O C F Tibbits, Sgt R W Grace and Sgt E Harrold in T2045/F went missing on a Dundee patrol. P/O Tibbits, a New Zealander, was on his first operation with No.53.

F/L A C Brown and F/L W S G Maydwell were promoted to S/L on 23 September. Dick Maydwell later went

on to command 14 Squadron equipped with Martin Marauders, during which time he shot down an Me 323 six-engined powered glider, a Ju 90 four-engined converted airliner and an Italian S.M.82 three-engined transport. He retired as G/C Maydwell DSO DFC.

P/O A K Gatward joined No.53 on the same day and he was to stay with the squadron until May 1941. Having served a very tough apprenticeship with the squadron, he went on to become a very successful Coastal Command Beaufighter pilot. At noon on 12 June 1942, he and his observer Sgt G Fern flew a No.236 Beaufighter at very low level down the Champs-Elysées in Paris dropping French *tricolores* as they went. They then sprayed the Gestapo HQ in the Place de la Concorde with cannon fire before returning safely to Northolt. He went on to command No.404 Squadron (RCAF) and ended the war as G/C Gatward DSO DFC and Bar.

Six crews were briefed to attack Den Helder docks on 27 September. The raid was cancelled when the second aircraft, flown by P/O P J E Ritchie, hit a tree on take-off in bad visibility at 0100. Sgt R H Trafford (wop/ag) was injured and T2221/J was wrecked. Rotterdam was the target on 30 September and P/O S R Bevan-John, Sgt S Macquire and Sgt H A Shaw in T2044/G failed to return. Sgt Shaw was never found.

P/O K A Faulkner crashed in flames near Manston in R2771/A at 2330 on 5 October returning from a Hookos. His observer, Sgt A R S Hall was killed and P/O Faulkner and Sgt G B Fielder (wop/ag) were seriously injured. P/O J C Mallon, Sgt W P Whetton and Sgt A T Shackleford in T2036/K were shot down and killed on 8 October near Gravelines. P/O Mallon, a New Zealander, had been on No.53 since May and had completed 43 operations. On 21 October, P/O H J W Meakin was returning from an SA9 in R3699/U. The aircraft had been damaged by flak and it became uncontrollable as he neared Detling. The crew bailed out and P/O Meakin was injured. Sadly, the Blenheim crashed into two houses in Dernier Road, Tonbridge, killing two and injuring sixteen. P/O Eric Plumtree was sent on an SA9 in T2132/R on 27 October. He was to try out the new Mk XI bomb sight. An attack was made on shipping at Den Helder but then a running battle with three Bf 110s of ZG 76 developed during which he and his crew, Sgt Wood and Sgt P M Kinsey, were badly injured. The aircraft was badly damaged but he was able to escape and landed at Martlesham Heath. He was awarded the DFC and Sgt Kinsey the DFM two days later. P/O Plumtree eventually retired as an Air Vice Marshal. Later in the day, seven aircraft were sent to attack a convoy off Calais. Once again, a heavy escort was present and all seven were attacked by Bf 109s. P/O R L Buckley, Sgt C Henderson and Sgt P E J Neale were shot down and killed in L8789/E.

Le Touquet airfield was attacked on 4 November and P/O R E Maurer in T1992/S was set upon by a yellow-nosed Bf 109. The chase ended some ten miles south of Dover, by which time the hydraulic system had been damaged and a wheels-up landing had to be made back at base. Uffz Rolf Klippgen of 9/JG 53, rather optimistically claimed a victory. The U-boat base at Lorient was the target for 7 and 8 November and all aircraft came back safely. On 20 November, No.53 moved to Thorney Island and was once again to share an airfield with No.59. S/L Maydwell was awarded the DFC and Sgt D J Roberts the DFM on 23 November. A raid on the oil installations near Ghent was made on 26 November. Flak was heavy and two aircraft and crews failed to return; P/O M M Barbour, Sgt A Cowling and Sgt G A Hinton in N3630/N and P/O R E Maurer, Sgt I S

Macaulay and Sgt B L Bembridge in V5371/T.

P/O P E Gibbs in T2218/W was returning from a strike on gun emplacements at Cap Gris Nez on 5 December in bad weather and gale force winds. The radio was u/s and he was unable to find Thorney Island in the dark. He tried to land at one airfield but the lights were switched off as he made his approach! The crew eventually had to abandon the aircraft near Occold in Suffolk and two of them were injured. Next day, P/O S R E Weatherley took V5420 up on an air test. He made his approach during a heavy squall and hit a tree on finals. He and Sgt H S Parrott were killed and the wop/ag, Sgt S McAndrew, was seriously injured. T2395/N crashed at Deal on 7 December returning to Manston from a Hookos patrol after striking a barrage balloon cable in bad weather. P/O A K Steel and the observer, Sgt W R Hemsley were killed and Sgt D Robson was seriously injured. P/O P J Cundy and crew in V5399/G were attacked by two Bf 109s on 27 December near Berck-sur-Mer. His wop/ag, Sgt Jack Hill was badly wounded. Peter Cundy went on to fly Liberators with 120 Squadron and sank U 628 whilst serving on 224 Squadron. He retired as W/C Cundy DSO DFC AFC TD.

On this same day, the German cruiser Admiral Hipper slipped unseen into Brest for repairs. This event was to signal a big change in No.53's operations and was to lead to particularly heavy losses both in crews and in aircraft. However, it was to be a few days before she was known to be in Brest. Seven Blenheims taxied out in darkness at 0630 on 28 December to make an attack on Lorient. There was a long delay before take-off clearance was given and engines were starting to overheat. L9043/O stalled and crashed immediately after take-off and the bombs exploded. F/L J D Steuart-Richardson DFC, Sgt J L Maguire and Sgt K W V Vowles were killed. The crews who followed had to undergo the sobering experience of flying over the resulting conflagration.

Eleven of No.53's personnel were Mentioned in Despatches in the 1941 New Year's honours list for their part in the fighting in France. Seven aircraft were sent to attack Flushing docks on 1 January and all returned safely. The Hipper had now been spotted by PRU aircraft and No.53 was ordered to mount its first attack on 4 January. Nine aircraft took off at 1530 and R2773/V did not come back. P/O P E Gibbs, Sgt H S Wall and Sgt H G W Martin were killed. Having attacked the cruiser in dry-dock, P/O G R H Newton in V5398/E was set upon by what he thought was an He112. The fuel system was damaged and Sgt K G Hughes, his wop/ag, was wounded so he tried to land at Haldon aerodrome, near Teignmouth. As soon as the aircraft flashed an "SOS", the lights were turned off and he was forced to crash-land almost out of fuel and was injured in the process. Nine aircraft went to Brest again on 9 January; V5370/G, flown by P/O J P Lucas, crashed into the sea near Selsey on return and Sgt H V Jackson (wop/ag) was killed.

Six aircraft got ready to go to Brest on 10 January. P/O Reg Alcock could not get the engines of his Blenheim to start up, so he and his crew made an unseemly sprint to get into the spare aircraft. V5518/H had been on maintenance and had not had an air test, but all seemed to be in order except that it seemed to be more difficult than usual to move the levers which selected the hot air for the carburettor intakes. He arrived overhead Brest, little realising that both hot air selectors had frozen open in the "cold" position. When he closed the throttles to make his attack, both engines stopped! He had just decided that he might as well carry on with the attack when a parachute flare, dropped by a Bomber Command aircraft, appeared above him. This made things very easy for the flak guns and just after he had dropped his bombs, a shell exploded inside the port wing which opened up the leading-edge into a huge airbrake. He had decided to ditch the aircraft just outside the harbour when one of the engines burst into life, rapidly followed by the other! The aircraft was very difficult to control but he managed to get to St Eval and landed a lot faster than normal because of the damaged wing. Towards the end of the runway glimlamps and with little prospect of stopping, he swung the Blenheim off to the left and into the darkness with the hope that nothing would get in their way. When daylight came, it was revealed that they had described a complete circle through a host of Beauforts, two squadrons of Swordfish and one of Albacores without hitting any of them!

Seven aircraft were briefed to go to Brest on 4 February. P/O G F Marriott in Z5765/A crashed immediately after take-off and all of the crew were seriously injured. Sgt E L Strudwick and Sgt G T Hadnam later died of their injuries. P/O C P Morris, Sgt G W F Ashwin and Sgt I R W Clark in T2283/F failed to return and were killed. Eight aircraft set off for Cherbourg at 1840 and T1992/X, flown by F/L B B StG Daly, Sgt J L Jones and Sgt R H Trafford went missing. This was F/L Daly's first operation since returning to the squadron after having been shot down and badly injured by a Hurricane in France. He had been offered an "easy" tour as an instructor at No.2 School of Army Co-operation at Andover but had insisted on coming back to No.53.

A move to Bircham Newton took place on 8 February with the aircraft following along two days later. Sorties were flown to Ostend and the Dutch coast. Four Blenheims were damaged when the Luftwaffe bombed the airfield on 16 February. A move to St Eval was ordered on 18 February and the ground party arrived there on the 20th. Due to bad weather, the aircraft didn't arrive until the 23rd. The Hipper was attacked again by seven aircraft on 24 February and all returned safely. F/L R M Mottram was awarded the DFC and Sgts R W Gellard and W E Williams the DFM on 25 February.

Convoy escorts and sea patrols were flown for the first ten days of March but ten aircraft attacked the Hipper on 11 March. P/O D K Plumb, Sgt R H S Maton and Sgt C McL Calder in P4850/V went missing. It was thought that the Hipper might be getting ready to sail so two aircraft were sent off later in the day to observe Brest harbour from a safe distance. This exercise was repeated on 12 March with three aircraft. The PR Spitfires at St Eval were unserviceable on 14 March and No.53 was asked to send a Blenheim to Brest on a photo-recce sortie. The chances of a Blenheim returning safely from the most heavily defended target in the world in broad daylight were not good and so it was to prove. P/O G R H Newton volunteered and took off at 1330 in V5399 with Sgt C Whitehill and Sgt J R Miller. They did not return and all were killed. They had fallen victim to a Bf 109 flown by Olt Walter Hückner of 6/JG 77 who shot them down near St. Renan. Nine Blenheims went off to Brest on 15 March and T2132/G failed to come home. P/O W H Leedam, Sgt F P H Oatley and Sgt W E Williams DFM were posted missing.

W/C G W P Grant was posted in on 19 March to take over as CO from W/C W B Murray DFC. Eleven aircraft attacked the submarine base at Lorient on 20 March and all returned safely. On 22 March, the battle cruisers Scharnhorst and Gneisenau put into Brest. The harbour was getting crowded! P/O B S Bannister and crew flew a recce over Brest at last light on 23 March in T2396/U. They returned to St Eval safely but found bad weather over the airfield. A fast landing was made, since they had a full bomb load on board, and they slid off the airfield into a mud shelter.

P/O Greville-Heygate in N6195/Z and P/O R Walton in T2332/O set off on a recce of the French coast on 27 March. The former found the ancient five-funnelled French battleship *Condorcet* (which had been decommissioned in 1931) off Lorient and dropped two 500-lb bombs from 5,000 feet, due to the flak being put up. P/O Walton made an attack on a 3,000-ton vessel but his bombs fell astern. He then machine-gunned the ship. Three other Blenheims went to look for enemy ships off Ushant. As they flew towards the Ile de Batz, three Bf 109s were seen taking off from Morlaix. The Blenheims kept formation until the Bf 109s attacked, selecting one aircraft each. Only P/O B S Bannister in PZ-K was able to escape. P/O J M Fothergill MC, Sgt T P O'K K T Coady and Sgt P R Parker in V5865/P and P/O R N Philpott, Sgt C A C Goad and Sgt F G Manning in T2332/O were shot down and killed. T2332/O crashed near Cléder and the two Blenheims were claimed by Uffz Bockmann and Olt Heinz Deuschle of II/JG 77. The "Big Ships" in Brest were also visited by six aircraft and all came back unscathed although P/O Jacob and crew in PZ-J had a mild altercation with a Hurricane on landing at St Eval.

On 30 March, P/O Walton and crew in T2222/D set off at 0605 on an anti-shipping patrol off the French coast. They dropped two 250-lb bombs on the *Condorcet* from 700 feet at 0802 but the bombs fell 30 yards from the ship. An anti-submarine vessel was spotted in the Baie de Bourgneuf half an hour later. One 250-lb bomb was dropped from 400 feet and it made a direct hit in the centre of the ship just forward of the bridge. There was a terrific explosion followed by a fire. The ship was then machine-gunned by the air gunner and when last seen, it was well and truly alight and sinking fast. The remaining bomb was dropped on a merchant vessel at 1000 but it fell ten yards from the ship.

Sea patrols and convoy escorts became the order of the day for the first week of April although Brest was visited on 6 April by three aircraft. P/O E L E Nicholson, P/O H A L Stone and Sgt P M Kinsey DFM failed to return from a convoy escort in T2398/E on 7 April. P/O Greville-Heygate and crew were sent to carry out a daylight reconnaissance of Brest on 9 April. They were successful in photographing the harbour and had dropped their bombs when the aircraft was hit by flak in one wing and an engine was put out of action. They were then attacked by two Bf 109s but were able to escape into cloud and returned to base safely. P/O I F Anderson, Sgt H H Walker and Sgt E A J Fabian were all killed when V5862/Y crashed immediately after take-off from St Eval on the same day.

P/O D A G Blakely diverted to Exeter in Z5879/L on 12 April and had his aircraft badly damaged in an air raid after landing. On his way to a patrol off the French coast on 16 April, P/O R C L Reade lost an engine and was forced to land V5518/H in a field at Longdowns near Penryn. He and Sgt J D O'Connell were killed when the aircraft hit a dry-stone wall. His wop/ag, Sgt R H W A Camm, was seriously injured. Sgt A F Brownlee (wop/ag) was killed in a bizarre accident whilst on flare-path duty on 17 April. He was struck by an operational aircraft which had returned in an emergency. Blenheim V6302/W failed to return from an anti-shipping patrol on 18 April. P/O E W Thomas, who had almost completed his tour, and Sgt S G Capel were posted missing. Sgt D H Trotman was killed. V5649 was damaged on 19 April whilst taxying across a road to dispersal when it collided with a taxi! N6195/Z, flown by P/O A F Buck was

badly damaged in a landing accident on 28 April.

Throughout May, daily raids were made on targets in France. Attacks on Brest, St Nazaire and Lorient in particular continued and no aircraft or crews were lost in action. St Eval was often a target for the Luftwaffe and AC1 D D Mackay was killed during such a raid on 11 May. V5649 was damaged as were four Hudsons, a Beaufort and a Whirlwind. W/C "Tubby" Grant in V6301 hit a raised gun-pit while trying to land in atrocious weather on 26 May. The Blenheim was a write-off but no one was injured. DFCs were awarded to P/O B S Bannister and P/O C E Greville-Heygate on 17 May.

The heavy cruiser *Prinz Eugen* arrived in Brest harbour on 1 June having escaped from the naval action during which the battleship *Bismarck* had been sunk on 27 May. Five aircraft set off to attack St Nazaire on the night of 10/11 June. P/O Bunce and crew in PZ-Y were unable to find the target but bombed a factory on the banks of the River Loire instead. The flak was heavy and just after the bombs had been released, the aircraft took a direct hit which put the starboard engine out of action. The aircraft twice went out of control and P/O Bunce warned the crew to prepare to bail out. Fortunately, he was able to regain control and they eventually managed to reach St Eval after a three-hour flight on one engine and with only twenty gallons of fuel remaining. This was largely due to the efforts of Sgt D Diggles (wop/ag), who had managed to get the radio working again and obtained a constant supply of bearings. Sgt Diggles was awarded the DFM later in the year. On its return from St Nazaire, V5933/U flew into some high ground at Brown Willy on Bodmin Moor in bad weather and P/O N D MacLennan (RCAF), Sgt D C Taylor and Sgt W M Roberts were killed.

P/O D M Bolton, Sgt K E Corrie and Sgt G K Kircher went missing in V5647/S from a convoy escort on 23 June. Later in the day, V6125/F failed to return from a "Bust" (anti-shipping) patrol. P/O E Hewson, Sgt A R Dawson and Sgt W G McCorkell had become POWs. Three Blenheims and crews were lost on 26 June. P/O L J Francis, Sgt R A Whitley and Sgt J StC Hopper in V6309/E failed to return from a Bust patrol. P/O D T Herrick GM, Sgt G F W Gahagan and Sgt G L Wells in V6087 and P/O C E Greville-Heygate DFC, P/O G Troup and Sgt C H Naylor in V6122/Y failed to return from a U-boat patrol.

P/O D T Herrick had been captured but died of his injuries on 30 June. He was a native of New Zealand and had been awarded the George Medal when he was learning to fly Tiger Moths at No.1 EFTS at Taieri. He witnessed a visiting Oxford, NZ275, crash on take-off on 21 June, 1940 and catch fire. Several crew members escaped but LAC Herrick, as he was then, realised that the pilot, S/L J H Kitson RAF was still in the aircraft. He and a Corporal fireman dived into the blazing wreckage in the full knowledge that a bomb was on board and got the injured pilot out. Later, the fuel tanks of the Oxford exploded. Sadly, the pilot died of his injuries shortly afterwards. Dennis Herrick had five brothers. S/L M J Herrick DFC & Bar and P/O B H Herrick were also killed in action with the RAF. Lt T D Herrick DSC & Bar and Lt L E Herrick served with distinction in the Royal Navy. The government of New Zealand would not allow the remaining brother, J L Herrick, to volunteer for overseas service in order to ensure that at least one brother survived the war to run the family farm. He had to settle for service in the NZ Territorial Army!

CHAPTER 9

CONVERSION TO

HUDSONS

A Hudson of No.53 displays its portly shape while flying from St.Eval. (Philip Jarrett collection)

No.53 moved to Bircham Newton on 2 July and it was learned that the squadron was to be re-equipped with Lockheed Hudsons. Crews were sent to No.1 OTU at Silloth on 6 July for conversion. In the meantime, some anti-shipping patrols were flown from the new base with the remaining Blenheims. These were flown without further loss and the last Blenheim sortie took place on 23 July. A lot of lives had been lost during No.53's Blenheim operations but it has to be said that many pilots reckoned the aircraft to be very agile and capable of taking a lot of damage.

The first batch of Hudson Mk.Vs started to arrive on 10 July. They were powered by two Pratt & Whitney R-1830 Twin Wasps of 1,200-hp each. Later on, No.53 also flew some Mk.IIIs which were fitted with 1,200-hp Wright R-1820 Cyclones. The new aircraft were fitted with ASV (Air-to-Surface Vessel) radar and this meant that an extra wop/ag had to be carried. It had proved necessary to change radar operators frequently since it was very difficult for them to concentrate on a flickering radar tube for long intervals. The Hudson was variously described by the pilots as being sedate and matronly. It certainly was a much more comfortable aircraft to fly in. As events were to prove, it was also capable of taking a lot of punishment and still getting the crew home safely.

The first Hudson loss came on 10 August when P/O A F Buck and crew in AM672/P attacked a German convoy in the vicinity of the Friesian Islands. They were shot down by the patrol vessels *V 1506*, *V 1509* and *V 1512*. Buck, Sgt L H Wood and F/L I P Magrath were killed. F/S T E Stepney was never found. P/O Tom Waters was following immediately behind in PZ-B and had to bank sharply to avoid the debris of P/O Buck's aircraft. The port wing tip hit the sea and was badly damaged in the process. To his great surprise, he discovered that the aircraft was still controllable, so he returned to the convoy and pressed home an attack on a large motor vessel before setting course for base. He was awarded the DFC on 30 August.

Detachments to Limavady and St Eval became the order of the day and by 13 September, eight aircraft were operating from St Eval. P/O Gay and crew took off from there on 14 September in AM777/G for an anti-submarine sweep in the Atlantic. They became uncertain of their position on the way back and found themselves right in the midst of the flak barrage at Brest! The Hudson was hit, and since only 30 gallons of fuel remained, the order to abandon the aircraft was given. Sgt J M Powell (obs) and Sgt S Tyson (wop/ag) were captured and became POWs in Stalag 357. P/O T M Gay, who had the advantage of being a fluent French speaker, managed to escape through France and Spain to Gibraltar. Sgt Archie Graham (wop/ag), who had the advantage of being a fluent Glaswegian speaker, managed to beat him home by four weeks!

S/L K Aldridge in PZ-X made No.53's first attack on a U-boat on 21 September. P/O Moira in PZ-K attacked another on 3 October but both attacks were inconclusive. The 250-lb depth charges used at the time were filled with Amatol (ammonium nitrate and TNT) and were pretty ineffective when used against a U-boat, unless they were dropped extremely close to the hull. Things got better later on in the war when the Amatol filling was replaced by Torpex (an improved explosive containing powdered aluminium). On 19 October, No.53 moved to St Eval.

F/L L J M Bunce and crew were returning from a U-Boat sweep in AM651/V on 27 October when the starboard engine seized and caught fire, possibly caused by a night-fighter. Three hundred gallons of fuel were jettisoned and all surplus equipment was thrown overboard to lighten the aircraft. As they came up to the coast at dawn, the port engine also failed and it became obvious that they would not be able to clear the cliffs which had appeared ahead. The blazing Hudson was ditched near The Manacles in Falmouth Bay. F/L Bunce and Sgt W C Cleaver (wop/ag) were able to escape through the cockpit hatch and managed to swim away from the aircraft which was almost surrounded by burning petrol. Three quarry-men working on the shoreline had witnessed the whole event and came to the rescue in a small boat owned by their foreman, Mr Frank Curnow. The two survivors were soon transferred to a Royal Navy mine-sweeper and taken to naval hospital in Falmouth. It was later learned that they had ditched on the edge of a minefield. F/S F D King DFM (obs) and Sgt E Leverington (wop/ag) were never found.

The unmistakable silhouette of a Hudson on patrol. (The late W/O V. Udberg)

No.53's first success in the war against the U-boat came on 30 October. P/O Henry and crew in PZ-H picked up a blip on their ASV radar and found a U-boat on the surface at 4800N 0910W which they attacked with three 250-lb depth charges (DCs). Just as the DCs exploded, an aircraft appeared below them. It turned out to be Catalina Z/209 which also attacked with two DCs. They had damaged *U 81*, a Type VIIc commanded by Klt Friedrich Guggenberger who was forced to return to Brest for repairs.

P/O Horsey and crew were on a U-boat search on 2 November in PZ-J when they came across a friendly convoy. Shortly afterwards, three He 115 floatplanes appeared flying in line astern, possibly mine-laying or looking for something to torpedo. The crew of the Hudson opened fire on the rearmost He 115 and soon all three were involved in the skirmish. In the end, hits were made on all of the enemy aircraft but they were last seen heading for home in vic formation.

Several other U-boat attacks were made during November and December but none of them was conclusive. On 12 December, P/O C Thomas, Sgt L Griffiths, Sgt R Smith and P/O F C Taylor failed to return from a U-boat patrol off Brittany in AE656/V. On this same day, some 60 aircrew were posted from No.53 Squadron for overseas duties under the command of S/L Peter Lilly. They flew out to Singapore with 18 Hudsons and became part of No.62 Squadron. They were to suffer terrible losses during the Japanese invasion a few weeks later. The survivors eventually made their way to India and formed No.353 Squadron with Peter Lilly as CO. Those who remained with No.53 were posted to Limavady on 17 December where the process of rebuilding the squadron began immediately.

Some patrols were flown from Limavady but little of interest took place and there were no losses. AM806 flown by F/S R C Kelly was wrecked during take-off on 3 January 1942 but no one was hurt. No.53 was ordered to North Coates on 18 January. The forward party was flown there on the 19th and 20th in three Handley Page Harrows. Anti-shipping patrols were once again to become the order of the day. W/C J R Leggate arrived on 23 February to take command. The very next day, P/Os D A Ray, R D Fairbairn, K S Davies and F S Knight in AM563/X failed to return from a "Rover" patrol. It was later learned that P/O Knight was in Stalag Luft III but the others had been killed.

Hudson AM877 crashed near Donna Nook lifeboat station just after take-off in bad weather at 0210 on 9 March. The observer, Sgt C S Milne (RCAF) was killed, and the pilot, Sgt R Walbancke was injured. Sgt Ralph Guthrie (RAAF) and crew were on patrol off Esbjerg in AM584/Y on 25 March and were attacking a 7,000-ton merchant vessel when they were badly-damaged by flak. Sgt Guthrie managed to get the badly damaged Hudson back across the North Sea and crash-landed at Donna Nook. Sgt R Rayner (wop/ag), who had been badly injured by shrapnel, was pulled from the wreckage by fellow wop/ag, Sgt Vic Udberg, and taken to hospital. Hudson III T9417, flown by Sgt R W Kennard (RAAF), crashed and caught fire on take-off from Manby on 28 March but no-one was hurt.

Sgt Dickie Thornhill and crew in AM549/F attacked a German convoy off the Friesian Islands on 8 April. The aircraft was badly damaged by flak and the petrol tanks were holed. It was realised that they had no chance of getting back to England so they made a decision to head downwind and try to reach Sweden. Unfortunately, they found themselves under

40

Badly damaged by flak off Esbjerg, Sgt Guthrie (RAAF) managed to get AM584/Y back and crash-landed at Donna Nook.
(The late W/O V. Udberg)

heavy fire over the German garrison at Sylt and a ditching became inevitable. As they hit the sea, two Bf 109s appeared overhead but did not open fire. Three of the crew swam ashore and then it was realised that the observer, Sgt Dave Moran (RCAF), was still on the sinking Hudson and couldn't swim. One of the wop/ags, Sgt Murray May (RAAF), bravely went back into the freezing water and delivered him safely to shore. They were promptly captured by the Germans and taken to Hamburg and then on to Stalag VIIIB, Lamsdorf. F/S Jack Diamond was the fourth crew member. In January 1945, they were involved in a horrendous 500-mile forced march as the Germans pulled back from the advancing Russians. The weather was appallingly cold and their ordeal lasted until April, when they finally fell into the safe hands of the Allies.

These anti-shipping sweeps from North Coates were proving to be pretty dangerous affairs. F/O A N McLintock, F/S J Hanna, Sgt J B Melvin and Sgt D R I Morgan in AM560/L failed to return on 11 April and F/S D G S Corden, Sgt A R Clouston, Sgt H Cliffe and F/S G N Moore (RCAF) went missing in AM803/V during the night of 16/17 April. Hudson V AM542/J is believed to have fallen victim to Lt Lothar Linke of II/NJG 2 when it was shot down to the north west of Texel on 22 April. P/O G G Shore, P/O S G Goatley, Sgt J M C Jenkinson and F/S R H W A Camm were posted missing.

Sgt Hastie and crew in PZ-X were on a Rover patrol off the Danish coast when they found three merchant vessels at 0032 on 27 April. The rearmost vessel was attacked from below mast height with four 250-lb bombs. Two direct hits were observed followed by heavy black smoke and the bows

of the vessel were seen to be on fire. This was the MV *Inga*, a Danish ship of 1,494 tons. She had her engine and steering-gear put out of action and help was sent for. The Danish tug *Björn* was sent out from Esbjerg to take her in tow but was unable to find the stricken ship. Sgt Guthrie and crew in PZ-D found the *Inga* some 35 miles south of the Horns Rev light at 2146 and attacked with four 250-lb bombs. One of these made a direct hit on the stern and the *Inga* finally sank shortly after noon next day. The patrol vessel *V 1206* was in the vicinity and 80 to 90 rounds were fired at it. Fire was returned and AM527/D was hit by flak. Sgt Rayner (wop/ag) was injured by shrapnel in the back, both arms and ear.

Five Hudsons attacked a convoy off Ijmuiden on 4 May. F/S K M Nichols, Sgt S E Smith, Sgt A W Newhouse and Sgt C Pottas were shot down by flak and killed in AM530/Q. 2Lt C L Summers (USAAC), an additional crew member, was also killed. The second largest ship in the convoy, the MV *Taarnholm* was attacked and damaged by P/O Puckridge and crew in PZ-X. They received a report that P/O M G Gummer and crew in AM565/W were pressing home an attack, although they had already been hit and had smoke coming from the starboard engine. P/O Puckridge then spotted PZ-W ditching near the convoy. Hudson M/59 took a photograph of the four crew on the wing of the ditched aircraft. P/O Gummer managed to get as far as Amsterdam where he met a Dutchman, Jan Van Duijn, who offered to hide him on his boat. Unfortunately, P/O Gummer was picked up by the Germans whilst waiting for a chance to get on to the boat and so found himself in Stalag Luft III. Sgt T McDamm (wop/ag) was also captured and incarcerated in Stalag VI. Sadly, F/S J B Jones (obs) and Sgt D E Round

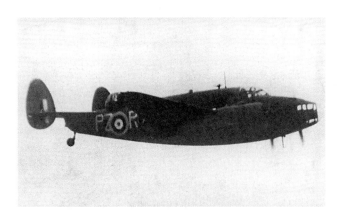

Hudson PZ-R en route from Limavady to North Coates. (The late W/O V. Udberg)

Hudson AM540/C crash-landed at Langam after being damaged by Bf 110s. (F/L G.R.G. Johnson)

(wop/ag) were never found.

Hudson AM683/Y was shot down at 0354 attacking a convoy on 8 May off Terschelling. The aircraft crashed on land just 300 yards from Den Helder but F/S C J Wyllie (RCAF), a British Latin American Volunteer from Argentina, F/S A T Thompson, Sgt W J Rowe and Sgt W R McLeod were all killed. On the same day, P/O J P Rickards (RAAF) and crew in AM540/C were set upon by Bf 110s. Sgt K Whitnall (wop/ag) was badly wounded during the encounter and Sgt J Smith (wop/ag) was shot in the leg. They escaped after a running battle but not before the aircraft had been seriously damaged. On the way home, they stumbled into a British convoy and sustained even more damage! P/O Rickards, who had been shot in the hand, was able to make a crash-landing on the airfield at Langham.

These low-level attacks on German convoys were proving to be very costly. The number of aircraft and crews lost was out of all proportion to the small number of ships actually sunk. Medium and high-level attacks had proved to be pretty ineffective due to the lack of an accurate bombsight. The C-in-C, Coastal Command, ACM Sir Philip Joubert de la Ferté, was coming to the conclusion that these

sort of attacks would have to be abandoned when news came through that No.53 was to be transferred to St Eval on 17 May.

F/S Jesty set off for St Eval from North Coates on 16 May in advance of the main party. He was flying AM521 and, as he neared Cornwall, the weather deteriorated rapidly. He was forced to land at St Merryn but slid off the wet grass airfield and crashed into an AA gun emplacement. He was unhurt but six airmen were injured.

Towards the end of May, ACM Sir Philip Joubert offered to let the C-in-C of Bomber Command, AM A T Harris, have the use of 250 Coastal Command aircraft and crews for his planned operation to bomb Cologne with 1,000 aircraft. As part of this force, six of No.53's Hudsons were painted black in preparation. The first three were actually airborne and heading for the advance base at Bircham Newton when the recall signal was received. Fortunately, the Admiralty had successfully objected to the plan.

A U-boat attack was made by S/L Hilditch in PZ-D on 29 May and two more attacks were made by Sgt Henderson in PZ-O and P/O Handasyde in PZ-D on 1 June but all three were inconclusive.

F/S 'Robbie' Roberts DFM, P/O Ralph Guthrie (RAAF) and Sgt 'Ginger' Smith. (The late W/O V. Udberg)

Visit of Lord Sherwood and Lord Cowdray to North Coates, 9 May 1942. (via F/L C. Waldrop)

CHAPTER 10

OFF TO THE

CARIBBEAN

V9232/PZ-A comes to grief at
Guantanamo Bay NAS, Cuba.
(The late W/O V. Udberg)

On 26 June, news was received that No.53 was to proceed to the USA at the end of the month. Some 20 Hudsons and crews were to fly out to the US Naval Air Station at Quonset Point, Rhode Island. The main objectives were to familiarise the Americans with ASV radar and anti-submarine procedures and also to reinforce the rather inadequate resources currently facing the U-boat menace on the other side of the Atlantic.

No.53's Hudsons were painted white all over for this operation and the first three aircraft left St Eval on 5 July and flew to Quonset Point via Prestwick, Reykjavik, Bluie West One, Goose Bay and Montreal. W/C Leggate, flying FH421/S, arrived at the new base on 9 July. The ground echelon arrived on 15 July, having set sail from Greenock for Halifax, Nova Scotia and then completed the journey by rail. The first convoy escort was flown on 23 July and the first anti-submarine patrol on the following day. These patrols went as far as the St Lawrence River to the north and New York harbour to the south.

Although some of the squadron were already flying operations from Quonset Point, others were still on their way across the Atlantic. P/O A A Morris (RAAF) and crew set off from Reykjavik for Gander in AM844/K on 25 July. Due to bad weather, they were unable to reach Gander and a forced landing was made in a large clearing four miles from Deer Lake, Newfoundland. There were no injuries but it proved impossible at the time to salvage the aircraft.

By 31 July, 15 Hudsons had arrived at Quonset Point and four more were on the way. It was learned that No.53 was to proceed to Edinburgh Field, Trinidad for anti-submarine duties together with servicing personnel from US Navy squadron VP-82. There was a lot of U-boat activity in the Caribbean at this time and one of their major tasks was to try to sink ships carrying bauxite to the USA for the manufacture of aluminium.

The first Hudsons headed south on 1 August and were routed via Cherry Point, Miami, Guantanamo Bay and San Juan to Trinidad. Initially, the squadron was based at Waller Field since the new aerodrome at Edinburgh Field had not yet been completed. The groundcrew were transported there in two US Navy R4Ds.

The move did not pass without incident. On 4 August, P/O R Guthrie (RAAF) was ordered by Air Traffic Control at Guantanamo Bay to land on a runway which proved to be too short for a fully-loaded Hudson. He slid off the end of the runway in V9232/A and went down an embankment. The first anti-submarine patrols were flown on 10 August. Two days later, F/S Jack Badger and crew in AE650/T were coming off patrol and heading for Zandery Field, Dutch Guiana. They did not have a lot of fuel and were quite put out when the Americans extinguished the airfield lights because they thought that they might be the enemy! After a while, the lights were put on for a few minutes to allow a Douglas B-18 to land. F/S Badger tried to memorise where the lights had been but landed off to one side of the runway and hit a road-roller! The aircraft was wrecked but no one was hurt.

On the same day, F/O Puckeridge and crew had just departed from Beane Field, St Lucia in V9096/P when the starboard engine caught fire. Despite the heavy load, he was able to land back again without further damage or injury.

Two U-boat attacks were made on 15 August. S/L Hilditch and crew found *U 108*, a Type IXB commanded by Kkapt Klaus Scholtz on the surface. He attacked with four Mk.VIII Torpex DCs but the U-boat escaped damage. F/S Henderson and crew in AM795/E attacked a diving U-boat to the north of Puerto Rico with three DCs. Some damage was caused to *U 217*, a Type VIID commanded by Olt zur See Reichenbach-Klinke. Unfortunately, F/S Henderson swung off the wet runway whilst landing at Waller Field during a storm the next day and AM795/E was wrecked.

More U-boat attacks were made on 16 August. P/O Kennard in AM789/H attacked Type IXC *U 510*, commanded by Kkapt K Neitzel, at 0753N 5352W. Extensive but superficial damage was caused and the U-boat was able to continue with the patrol. F/S Sillcock (RAAF) in AM797/W also damaged Type IXC *U 509*, commanded by Kkapt Wolff, to the east of Martinique. Type IXC *U 66*, commanded by Klt Friedrich Markworth, was attacked by P/O Rickards in FH433/C on 20 August but no damage was caused. During their nightly radio conversations, the U-boat captains were speculating that radar-equipped aircraft were now loose in the Caribbean and this was bad news indeed!

No.53 finally moved from Waller Field to Edinburgh Field on 22 August. By now, some Hudsons had had their turrets removed in order to improve their performance. Since attacks by Luftwaffe aircraft were hardly a feature of operations in the Caribbean, it seemed to be a sensible course of action. P/O J F Handasyde swung during a night take-off from the new airfield on 26 August and AM789/H was

Another view of V9232 shows how the starboard propeller has cut through the fuselage.
(The late W/O V. Udberg)

wrecked. F/S Sillcock (RAAF) in AM797/W found a U-boat in the process of surfacing at 0921N 5325W on 27 August. He attacked immediately with four DCs and caused such extensive and serious damage that Kkapt Beucke was forced to take Type IXC *U 173* back to base for repairs.

F/S Jack Badger and crew in FH433/C came across a submarine on the surface south of Barbados on 29 August. The crew had been briefed that a US Navy submarine was in the vicinity, so they thought that this was it. As they flew past, they were amazed to realise that it was a U-boat. The two wop/ags, Sgts Bill Cleaver and Dil Thomas were able to note that some of the U-boat's crew appeared to be sun-bathing on the deck! They attacked on the next pass with four DCs but did not cause any damage. It has not been possible to identify this U-boat, but Type IXC *U 162*, under the command of Fkapt Wattenberg, was in the area. She was sunk on 3 September by HMS *Pathfinder*, *Quentin* and *Vimy* to the north-east of Trinidad.

This crew was sent back to Quonset Point to collect a Hudson to replace the one they had lost at Zandery on 12 August. On 14 September, they set off to do an air-test in the new aircraft, V9108, but the port engine failed at 20 feet. The aircraft swung, crashed and caught fire. The crew escaped without injury but lost all of their kit. Sgt Bill Cleaver decided that it must be time to get married to his girl-friend June, and so became the only 53 Squadron member to marry an American lady in America during the war whilst on duty!

Tragedy struck No.53 on 15 September. P/O G T Risbey (RAAF) was circling low over Edinburgh Field in AM727/D trying to land in a rain storm when the aircraft struck a tree and crashed. He, P/O J W P Walker (RAAF), Sgt A M Parkin, Sgt N F Brassington and AMM3C W M Boots, (USN) were all killed.

Type VIID *U 217* received more attention from 53 Squadron's Hudsons on 20 September. F/S Hank Jesty in FH271/F found the U-boat on the surface at 1102N 5705W at 1210 and made an immediate attack with four DCs but caused no damage. F/O Puckridge in V9096/P found her on the surface again, just a few miles away from the previous position, at 1629 and made an attack. *U 217* submerged but almost immediately came back to the surface and started firing back with flak. This attack was more successful and damage had been caused to the port electric motor, both hydroplanes, the rudder, the order-transmission system and the bed-plates of both compressors which had been cracked.

P/O J Rickards and crew in FH433/C attacked a U-boat on the surface to the east of Trinidad on 22 September. They had damaged Type IXC *U 512*, commanded by Klt Wolfgang Schulze. She was later sunk by the crew of a B-18A of the 99th Bombardment Squadron, USAAC on 2 October. P/O Rickards was awarded the DFC on 19 October.

Hudson V9105/K was lost on an air-test on 28 September. The aircraft was found in the jungle three miles south of Rio Clara, Trinidad and had struck the ground in a vertical attitude. P/O A A Morris (RAAF), AMM3C G M Nobes (USN), PFC J H Fischer, PFC SL Shipes and Pte Smith (USAAC) were all killed.

W/C Jimmy Leggate and crew in FH421/S attacked a U-boat on 9 October off Paramaribo. Type VIIC *U 332* commanded by Klt Heinrich Liebe was slightly damaged. The observer on the CO's crew was a very interesting Free-Frenchman, Capt Philippe Livry-Level. He was a wealthy

The crew escaped unhurt when V9108 lost an engine on take-off at Quonset Point NAS, Rhode Island, on 14 September 1942.
(US Navy)

industrialist who had escaped to England via Lisbon and then tried to enlist as a pilot. However, since he was 45 years old and had already served in the 1914-1918 war and the 1939-1940 campaign in France, he was unsuccessful. Philippe promptly knocked 15 years off his real age and was accepted for navigation training! After serving a tour with No.53, he went on to fly with No.161 at Tempsford under the command of the famous W/C Pickard DSO DFC. By something of a coincidence, he was crewed up with Jimmy Leggate's youngest brother David and together they flew many clandestine missions into Occupied France. He also took part in the famous raid on Amiens jail on 18 February 1944 and during his time with the RAF, he was awarded the DSO and DFC and Bar.

Lt Col Williams (USAAC) and crew in FH433/C found a U-Boat some fifty miles behind a convoy to the east of Trinidad on 17 October. Their attack caused slight damage to Type IXC *U 67* under the command of Klt Müller-Stöckheim. W/C Leggate took Ed Murrow, the American journalist, with him in FH356/U on 4 November. They found a U-boat to the west of St Vincent which they attacked with four DCs. According to the graphic description in the newspapers the following day, they had sent it straight to the bottom. In fact, Type IXC *U 160* commanded by Klt Lassen was only shaken-up!

On 10 November, F/S R R Sillcock (RAAF) and crew in V9253/L found a U-boat on the surface at 1010N 5904W which they promptly attacked. She was *U 505*, a Type IXC commanded by Klt Peter Zschech. One of the depth charges struck the deck in the vicinity of the 37mm flak mounting and exploded prematurely, carrying away the gun and wrecking the outer plating of the conning tower. Debris was thrown up and some shrapnel struck one of the Hudson's fuel tanks which exploded right in front of an astonished U-Boat crew. Fragments from the Hudson were later found embedded in the wooden deck planking of the U-Boat. F/S Sillcock, Sgt P G Nelson (RNZAF), Sgt R Millar, Sgt W Skinner and S1C H L Drew (USNR) were all killed. *U 505* was eventually captured

intact by the US Navy off West Africa. She was towed to America and is now on display at the Museum of Science, Chicago.

Type IXC *U 129*, commanded by Klt Witt, was attacked on 17 November off Martinique by F/O Barnett and crew in FH433/C but no damage was done. P/O Underhill and crew in FH356/U attacked Type IXC *U 163*, commanded by Kkapt Engelmann, in the same area the next day but once again, no damage was caused.

On 19 November, news was received that No.53 was to return home via Quonset Point. In fact, Air Ministry had been trying to get the squadron back since 4 October and had suggested that they could no longer supply replacement aircraft and ASV radars from United Kingdom stocks. Since the Americans had no Hudson aircraft available, it was suggested that Lockheed Venturas might be used as replacements. In any event, the aircraft left for NAS Norfolk on 23 November and the sea party left for New York for embarkation on 8 December. By 12 December, the sea party had sailed and the aircraft were at Quonset Point ready to leave. The sea party arrived at Davidstow Moor on 31 December and this was to be No.53's base for the time being.

New Year's Day 1943 was celebrated on what was surely the bleakest operational base in the United Kingdom. Davidstow Moor was almost 1,000 feet above sea level and it was a pretty gloomy place. Certainly, it was something of a shock after the warmth of Trinidad! W/C Leggate arrived on 14 January after his Atlantic crossing and three others arrived next day. The squadron Hudsons were afterwards ferried to No.3502 SU at Gosport for maintenance and modification.

W/C Jimmy Leggate was posted to HQ 19 Group on 4 February. He was later awarded the DSO and promoted to Group Captain. No.53 had been lucky to have him as its CO and he was highly regarded by all who served under him. The new CO was W/C H R A Edwards AFC who was the brother of W/C E C T Edwards, killed near Rotterdam on 31 August 1940. Like his brother, he was a well-known pre-war air race pilot.

CHAPTER 11

THE DREADED

WHITLEY

F/Sgt Jack Badger's crew at Houlton, Maine, in January 1943, returning from Trinidad. Left to right; F/S Badger, F/S Bill Cleaver, Sgt Dil Thomas, P/O John Woodrow-Davies. (F/L W.C. Cleaver)

No.53 moved to Docking on 11 February and it was announced that the squadron was to be re-equipped with Armstrong Whitworth Whitley Mk.VIIs. This news was received with dismay since the Whitley could hardly be considered to be an improvement on the Hudson. Two Hudsons turned up at Davidstow Moor on 13 February trying to find the squadron! Hudsons AM797/W and AE509/Z made it to Docking on 18 February. These two aircraft had crossed the Atlantic non-stop from Gander to Prestwick in 8 hours 15 minutes.

The first two Whitleys, BD424 and BD425, arrived from No.502 on 28 February followed by Z9381, Z9519 and EB332 the next day. The new aircraft were dogged by poor serviceability which was partly caused by an acute lack of spares. There was even a dire shortage of copies of the Pilot's Notes. S/L K A Aldridge DFC, who had already served with No.53 on Blenheims and Hudsons, was posted back from HQ Coastal Command as OC "C" Flt.

Docking was a satellite airfield of Bircham Newton and most night operations were flown from there since the airfield at the parent unit was not considered to be big enough. For some strange reason, it was decided to move 53 Squadron to Bircham Newton on 17 March. As if to prove the point, Sgt J Milligan in BD425/O had to swing on landing to avoid going off the end of the airfield. The undercarriage collapsed and the aircraft was badly damaged.

Welcome news was received on 23 March that the squadron was to be re-equipped with Consolidated Liberators. Meanwhile, Whitley flying continued and on 26 March, EB331/U flown by Sgt W G Kirby and crew failed to return from a navigation exercise in the North Sea. A search for survivors was mounted and an air-sea rescue launch found the body of Sgt V C Matthews (wop/ag) next day. A medical examination gave the cause of his death as "due to splinters, presumed caused by enemy action". Sgt Kirby, Sgt I D Bradley, Sgt C J H MacKenzie, Sgt K Stainton and Sgt S Westwood were never found.

The last crew to return from Trinidad finally arrived on 8 April! F/S Badger and crew had ferried Hudson FK633 to Prestwick for No.301 FTU. S/L Maxwell and crew flew the first Whitley "Hoden" patrol on 10 April in LA796/B. The object of these operations was to try to find and attack German E-Boats. The patrols were flown at night and lasted 6 hours or so. F/L D H Sutton had an engine catch fire at 300 feet after take-off in EB332 on 13 April but was able to land

safely on the airfield. Two days later, he was returning from a navigation exercise when he ran out of airfield at Bircham Newton in Z9519/N. The undercarriage collapsed and the Whitley was badly damaged. DFCs were awarded to S/L T C P Maxwell on 16 April and S/L A E Hilditch on 19 April.

P/O Len Harman, P/O Cam Underhill, Sgt Sonny Hale in front of Hudson T9461/O. (F/L F. Nuttall)

CHAPTER 12

WELCOME TO THE

LIBERATOR

Liberator EW303/Y being flown on a training flight by S/L G.P. Watson on 2 February 1945. Nos.1 and 2 propellers are feathered.

No.53 was declared non-operational on 20 April and ordered to proceed to Thorney Island. Everyone bade a grateful farewell to the unloved Whitleys! Nine crews were sent to the No.1 OTU detachment at Beaulieu on 24 April for Liberator training and by 29 April, the ground move to Thorney Island had been completed.

The new aircraft was the biggest machine that No.53 had flown so far. It was powered by four Pratt & Whitney R-1830 Twin Wasps and had a wingspan of 110 feet. The Liberator had a very long range and its introduction into Coastal Command service had been vital in plugging the gap in air cover for convoys which had existed in mid-Atlantic since the outbreak of war.

The squadron strength by 23 May had reached three Liberator Mk.IIIs and seven Mk.Vs. No.53 became operational again on 20 June and three aircraft were sent each day to St Eval on detachment. F/O C W J Harradence made the first Liberator U-boat attack on 30 June in BZ750/R but the DCs hung up and heavy flak forced him to retire. On 1 July, F/O R T Merrifield and crew in BZ730/O met a convoy consisting of "three U-boats and two Narvik-class destroyers" off the north-west coast of Spain. It is now believed that there were probably only two U-boats and that they were Type IXD-1 *U 180* commanded by Fkapt Werner Musenberg and Type IXC/40 *U 530* commanded by Klt Kurt Lange. The former was carrying gold bullion and Japanese officers from the Far East. As they swung in to make an attack, they were bounced by four Ju 88s and so began a running battle which lasted for 45 minutes before they were able to escape. A contemporary intelligence report stated that one of the Ju 88s had ditched in the sea and that one had crash-landed in Spain but it has not been possible to confirm this so far. What is known is that Ju 88C-6 W/No.360383 F8+PX of 13/KG 40 flown by OLt H Horstmann force-landed at La Albericia, Santander on this day. It was reported to have run out of fuel and it later served with the Spanish Air Force after repairs. F/O Merrifield and F/O G F Wood (RAAF) (wop/ag) were awarded DFCs and F/S R Niven (wop/ag), the DFM on 8 July.

Two U-boats were spotted on the surface at 4440N 1040W on 3 July at 1212 by W/O Len Esler (RCAF) and crew in BZ731/D but they had disappeared before an attack could be made. The crew returned to the area later and at 1436 found another U-boat on the surface at 4450N 0950W. Eight DCs were dropped and six were seen to explode along its port side. The U-boat disappeared leaving patches of oil on

the surface. Five or six of the U-Boat's crew were seen to be still on the deck when the DCs exploded. In fact, Type VIIC *U 648* commanded by Olt zur See P Stahl, escaped without damage.

F/S W Anderson (RNZAF) and crew were on a "Musketry" patrol in BZ751/G on 5 July. They had passed their PLE (Prudent Limit of Endurance) and were heading for home when they sighted three U-boats at 4338N 0913W. An attack was made on one of them but the first run had to be abandoned when the U-boat took violent evasive action. On the second run, the DCs hung up! Fortunately, all went well on the third run and eight DCs were dropped, right on the mark. *U 535*, a highly-prized Type IXC/40 auxiliary tanker commanded by Klt Helmut Ellmenreich, went straight to the bottom.

She was on her first patrol. Throughout the action, *U 535* and the other two, *U 536* and *U 170*, had put up a great deal of flak and the Liberator was damaged in the wings, fuselage and tailplane. One of the beam gunners was wounded.

Further U-boat attacks were made on 7 July. F/O K C Boulter and crew in BZ749/P met Type VIICs *U 566* and *U 709* in very poor weather at 4602N 0937W and set up an attack on the latter, which was commanded by Olt zur See Karl-Otto Weber. During the run-in, flak put No.4 engine out of action and they had to break off and head for home. Later in the day, F/O R T Waite and crew in BZ731/D made an unsuccessful attack on Type VIIC *U 267*, commanded by Klt Otto Tinschert, but failed to inflict any damage.

F/O J F Handasyde and crew in BZ716/B were on patrol in the Bay of Biscay on 8 July when they were set upon by seven Ju 88s at 1640. A running battle, which lasted for 45 minutes, then ensued. The first attack put No.4 engine out of action and the second one killed one of the beam gunners, F/O J Witts, and seriously wounded the other, F/S H A Pomeroy. Despite collapsing several times from the effects of his injuries, F/S Pomeroy managed to man his gun throughout the engagement. F/O Handasyde eventually managed to find some cloud cover and escaped. One Ju 88 was seen with smoke pouring from an engine but it apparently made it back to base at Kerlin Bastard near Lorient. The Ju 88s were from V/KG 40 and four of its crew members were wounded in this action. They were Lt Lothar Wolf and his observer Uffz Hans Melzer in one Ju 88C6 and Uffzs Karl Lenz and Otto Trutt, who were observers in two other Ju 88s. F/O Handasyde was awarded the DFC and F/S Pomeroy the DFM on 20 July.

A Royal Navy Avenger with 'invasion stripes' joins F/O Boulter's BZ870/A. Both were taking part in the 'Cork' patrols that protected the western flanks of the invasion convoys. (F/S E.J.R. Grant)

F/L J A Dewhirst and crew in BZ731/D failed to return from a "Musketry" patrol on 18 July. An SOS was received at 1205 while a fix was being sent on the radio, but nothing further was heard. They are believed to have fallen victim to Ju 88s of V/KG 40. (NB: as the Liberator carried such a large crew, a complete casualty list is given in the Roll of Honour at Appendix V).

On 24 July, 89 NCOs and Airmen were posted out to form No.8053 Servicing Echelon under the new Coastal Command "planned flying and maintenance scheme". The CO was compelled to make the comment that "the splendid squadron spirit which was the basis of the glory of the 'Few' had suffered another blow". On this day, LAC H D Brown was killed by an oncoming train at Bedhampton station.

F/L G F Davey and crew took off from Thorney Island at 0300 in BZ740/F on 28 July. The aircraft crashed into high ground near Tisbury, Wiltshire, half an hour later on the way to the patrol area. The Liberator caught fire and the DCs exploded. There were no survivors.

One of the most famous U-boat actions of the war took place on 30 July. Admiral Dönitz had ordered his U-boats to cross the Bay of Biscay in groups of three in broad daylight and to rely on their combined firepower to fight off attackers. F/O W J Irving (RCAF) and crew in BZ730/O found just such a U-boat pack at 4542N 1100W at 0945. They realised that they could not possibly tackle all three so they shadowed them at a discreet distance and summoned help on the radio. Unfortunately, the first position that they sent out was inaccurate but this was quickly put right by a Sunderland of No.228 Squadron, the first of five other aircraft which homed

to the scene. The Second Support Group, led by the famous Captain "Johnny" Walker CB DSO in HMS *Kite* was also on the way. The U-boats concerned were Type XIV "milch cow" ocean-going supply submarines *U 461* and *U 462* and Type IXC *U 504*.

Halifax S/502, flown by Dutchman F/O A van Rossum, damaged *U 462* badly enough with a 600-lb anti-submarine bomb to prevent her from submerging. F/O Irving decided to press home an attack on *U 461* which put up a very heavy flak barrage. Unfortunately, his DCs missed but F/L D Marrows (RAAF), flying Sunderland U/461, saw him making his attack and sneaked in behind him. Before Kkapt Wolf Stiebler and his crew had realised what was happening, F/L Marrows had straddled the U-boat with his DCs and it went straight to the bottom. So it was that U/461 sank *U 461*!

The Second Support Group was now within gunnery range and hits began to register on the stricken *U 462*. Olt zur See Bruno Vowe came to the conclusion that, since he could neither dive nor escape on the surface, he might as well scuttle his U-boat. Klt W Luis and crew had taken *U 504* down by this stage and tried to quietly sit it out but fell victim to HMS *Kite*, *Wild Goose*, *Woodpecker* and *Wren*. Not only had all three U-boats been sunk but several other U-boats were sitting off the Azores out of fuel and waiting in vain for the arrival of the two "milch cows" to refuel them. Admiral Dönitz was soon to revise his tactics.

In the meantime, F/O Irving had realised that BZ730/O was so badly damaged that he and his crew stood no chance of reaching home. No.4 engine had been hit and the flying controls were almost ineffective. He gradually struggled up to

48

600 feet and headed for the nearest land at Cape Finisterre, which he reached at 1430. He then set off down the Portuguese coast hoping to reach Gibraltar. As he neared Lisbon, the aircraft was almost out of fuel so the crew got rid of their secret equipment, smashed the bomb-sight and tried, without success, to blow up the IFF (Identification Friend or Foe) equipment. They duly landed at Portela airfield and were met by three Bren-gun carriers filled with troops. It was soon noticed that their guns were not loaded! F/O Irving tried to set the aircraft alight but the fire was put out by a fire-tender. The British Air Attaché was allowed to take them to the Bristol Hotel and they were released from internment and flown home to United Kingdom on 9 August.

F/O G F Wood (RAAF), who had earned his DFC on 1 July during an encounter with four Ju 88s, was killed in a tragic accident on 13 August. Whilst on attachment to Central Gunnery School, he was flying in Wellington IA P9228, which was engaged in a mock combat with Spitfire IIA P7530, when the two aircraft collided and crashed near Lakenheath.

A submarine "similar in silhouette to a Spanish C.2" was found off Cape Priorino by W/C "Jumbo" Edwards and his crew in BZ754/A on 16 August. They made two attacks without causing any damage. Inaccurate flak was fired back and the submarine finally went into El Ferrol harbour and anchored alongside two large naval vessels. Five Ju 88s attacked P/O Winter and crew in BZ741/Q on 30 August but he was able to escape into a cloud. W/O McPherson and crew in BZ788/D were set upon by three Ju 88s and an Me 410 on 8 September. The mid-upper gunner hit the Me 410 just before the Liberator found some cloud-cover. They were attacked again on leaving the cloud and the aircraft was hit but no one was injured. W/C Edwards found a dinghy containing eleven survivors from a Sunderland crew on 17 September and was able to remain at the scene until they were rescued by a ship.

Liberator BZ720/N, flown by S/L Tony Spooner DSO DFC, was on patrol to the west of Lundy Isle on 21 September when five Bf 110s of II/ZG 1 pounced. Sgt I R W Thomson (RNZAF), the starboard-beam gunner, was hit in the leg and Sgt I R Heays (RNZAF), the port-beam gunner, was hit in the back by a 20mm cannon shell and later died. The aircraft was badly damaged and two engines were hit. Although it was thought that one Bf 110 had "probably been shot down", no German claims or losses were attributed to this action.

On 25 September, No.53 moved to Beaulieu. F/L J Rintoul and crew set off on a "Percussion" anti-submarine patrol in BZ753/S on 4 October. A message was received at 1034 that they were being attacked by four enemy aircraft and a Liberator of 224 Squadron later reported seeing them being shot down into the sea. There were no survivors. Two inconclusive U-boat attacks were made by F/O Cooper and crew in BZ778/G on 14 October.

During October, the squadron's Liberators were fitted with Leigh Lights by Scottish Aviation at Prestwick. This powerful light was the invention of S/L Humphrey Leigh, a staff officer at HQ Coastal Command. On the Liberator, it consisted of a steerable 61cm carbon-arc lamp which was mounted beneath the starboard wing outboard of No.4 engine. It was powered by seven 12-volt accumulators which were, in turn, kept charged by the aircraft's electrical system. For the first time, it became possible to illuminate U-boats on the surface at night. Needless to say, it also gave the U-boats an excellent target to aim back at! Neither did it do anything to improve the aerodynamic qualities of the Liberator.

F/O D R Cooper and crew were all killed on 15 November when BZ817/L crashed immediately after take-off from Beaulieu. Worse was to come on 20 November. S/L K A Aldridge DFC and crew took off in BZ816/N at 1530 to escort convoy SL139. Nothing further was heard from this aircraft. They had been shot down and killed by Type VIIC U 648 commanded by Olt zur See P Stahl. S/L Ken Aldridge was a long-serving squadron stalwart who had flown the Blenheim, Hudson, Whitley and Liberator since joining No.53 for the first time in 1940.

Liberator BZ818/C, flown by S/L Spooner and crew, set off at 1834 to escort the same convoy. At 0100, they received an order to land at Gibraltar at the end of their duty. The No.2 engine failed at 0435 and its propeller refused to feather, so causing a tremendous amount of aerodynamic drag. All movable objects, including the DCs and the Leigh Light, were jettisoned and they only just managed to reach Gibraltar with dry tanks at 1000.

W/C Edwards and crew set off in BZ819/A at 2312 to escort convoy SL139. At 0425 on 21 November, they made an unsuccessful attack on Type VIIC U 648 and the aircraft was hit by flak. This U-boat was sunk by HMS *Bazeley* and *Blackwood* on 23 November. They left the convoy at 0800. Three engines failed simultaneously at 1400 while flying at 300 feet and a ditching became inevitable. The CO spent ten minutes extricating a dinghy but found that he was the only survivor. He was rescued after seventeen hours by HM Trawler *Lincolnshire* some five miles from Longships, near the Scilly Isles. W/C R T F Gates AFC took over as CO on 30 November.

No.53's first successful use of the Leigh Light was made by W/O Anderson and crew in BZ873/S during an inconclusive U-boat attack on 10 December. S/L George Crawford AFC and crew had better luck on 13 December. They took off at 0015 in BZ814/B and although the radar was partially unserviceable, a contact was made seven hours later at 4545N 0938W. They illuminated a fully surfaced U-boat with the Leigh Light. A good attack was made with six DCs despite a heavy flak barrage which damaged the aircraft. Two bodies were seen on the surface after the explosions had subsided. They had sunk Type VIIC U 391, commanded by Olt zur See Gert Dültgen. She was on her very first cruise and had been spotted earlier by F/L J Burton and crew in BZ793/R. They had been unable to attack successfully due to a failure of the intercom system. S/L Crawford was awarded the DFC on 22 December.

He and his crew found four German destroyers on 23 December and their aircraft was promptly hit by flak. They began to shadow the enemy ships from a discreet distance and reported their presence to HQ. The destroyers were trying to link up with the blockade-runner *Alsterufer* which was coming from the Far East and the information from the Liberator was of great help to the Royal Navy. A force consisting of HMS *Glasgow* and *Enterprise* sank four out of a total of ten destroyers and the *Alsterufer* was sunk on 27 December by a Czech Liberator of 311 Squadron, also based at Beaulieu. S/L Crawford had to land with a burst tyre but no one was injured.

No.53 moved to St Eval on 3 January 1944. On the night of 6/7 January 1944, F/O Hall and crew illuminated Type VIIC U 275 under the command of Olt zur See H Bork, which sent up an intense flak barrage. The Leigh Light, No.3 engine, the generator panel and the intercom system were all put out of action, making an attack impossible. At 0005 on the same night, F/L LeMaistre and crew in A/53 attacked a U-boat with four DCs. A further attack was made at 0027 with another four DCs. During the second run-in, the aircraft received heavy flak damage. Type IXB *U 107*, commanded by Lt zur See Karl-Heinz Fritz, was able to dock at Lorient with only minor damage.

On 16 January, five aircraft were detached to Ballykelly to help combat an increased U-boat menace in the Western Approaches. S/L Crawford and crew were preparing to start engines there on 20 January in something of a hurry, when the auxiliary power unit of BZ793/R caught fire and the fuselage was badly damaged.

F/L D A Bell and crew took off from St Eval in BZ795/F for a "Percussion" patrol at 2230 on 3 February. At 0811 on 4 February, a flash report was received stating that the aircraft was about to attack a U-boat, but nothing further was heard from them. It is now known that they had attacked Type VIIC *U 763*, commanded by Klt Ernst Cordes, with DCs and scored several hits with machine-gun fire on the conning tower. Despite very heavy flak, they had pressed home a second attack but were shot down. The Liberator blew up when it hit the water and none of the crew were seen to get out. *U 763* went on to bag Halifax R/502 the next night.

F/O R S H Browning and crew set off from St Eval in BZ878/T at 1853 on 4 February to patrol an area to the west of Ireland but failed to return. Although it cannot be known for certain, it is now thought possible that they had fallen victim to Type VIIC *U 390*, commanded by Olt zur See Heinz Geissler, which reported attacking an aircraft approaching from the west at 5040N 1900W on 5 February at 0635.

P/O Esler and crew in BZ815/D made an unsuccessful attack on Type VIIC *U 763* at 0135 on 5 February. They then spotted a second and then a third U-boat which they reported to HQ. Their aircraft sustained a lot of flak damage but they got home safely. Two U-boats were attacked on the same run by S/L Spooner and crew in BZ788/G on 9 February. They had just attacked the first U-boat with six DCs when the navigator suddenly spotted another behind the first. With a great deal of quick thinking, they were able to drop two DCs on the second one. The first U-boat was Type VIIC *U 608*, commanded by Olt zur See Wolfgang Reisener. It was severely shaken-up but not damaged. It has not been possible to identify the second one. The same crew in BZ873/S repeated this remarkable feat on another two unknown U-boats on 18 February.

P/O Esler and crew in BZ815/D homed-in on a radar contact at 0200 on 20 February. As they got closer, the contact split into two. When the Leigh Light was switched on, a large vessel was illuminated which put up intense fire destroying No.3 engine. The Liberator was very difficult to control and a landing was made at base with the nosewheel still retracted. It transpired that they had found two Royal Navy ships! The mid-upper gunner was slightly wounded by splinters. An armourer at Ballykelly caused a lot of damage to BZ781/A on 25 February when he accidentally set off the 0.5" port-beam gun inside the fuselage.

Two enemy destroyers were found by F/L LeMaistre and crew in B/53 on 9 March and they began to shadow them from a discreet distance. P/O McPherson and crew came along in U/53 and were positioning "up-moon" when they were attacked by light and heavy flak. Several Fw 190s then appeared on the scene so they were forced to retreat. They came back later but were immediately attacked again by an enemy aircraft which appeared out of a cloud with its guns already firing.

On 6 April, F/O C Allison and crew in BZ769/N found Type VIIC *U 618*, commanded by Olt zur See Kurt Baberg, on the surface. Intense 37mm and 20mm flak put the bomb doors out of action so an attack was impossible. The aircraft was extensively holed and one of the beam-gunners was wounded in the leg. Another U-boat was attacked by F/L W J Irving and crew in BZ781/A at 0305 on 10 April. The flak was so intense that the first run had to be abandoned. On the second run, the DCs hung-up and the nosewheel was hit. During the third run, a shell exploded in the bomb-bay which put the hydraulic system and the flight instruments out of action. They landed safely at base with no flaps, no brakes and a flat nosewheel! The U-boat concerned was Type VIIC *U 821* under the command of Olt zur See Ulrich Knackfuss.

The night of 16/17 April was to prove pretty disastrous for 53 Squadron. F/L F M Burton and crew took off in BZ945/O at 2152 for an anti-submarine patrol in the Outer Bay (of Biscay) area. A flash report was received from them at 0349 but nothing further was heard. They had been shot down at 4620N 1130W by Type VIIC *U 993* commanded by Olt zur See Kurt Hilbig. The aircraft crashed in flames and a Liberator of 311 Squadron reported seeing the fire and the subsequent explosion. The U-boat crew saw no survivors, so dived at 0358 and continued with their transit to Lorient.

F/L G Roberts and crew in BZ800/H had followed at 2215 for a patrol in the Western Bay area. They sent a flash report at 0457 but nothing further was heard. They had been shot down by Type IXC *U 546*, commanded by Klt Paul Just, at 4645N 1035W. There were no survivors from either of the two Liberators.

A U-boat was found off the Spanish coast at 0252 on 20 April by F/L C McA Forbes and crew in BZ793/R. Unfortunately, their DCs fell astern. The same crew began an attack on what they believed to be a U-boat at 0159 on 26 April off La Rochelle. They attacked three times but, on each occasion, the DCs steadfastly refused to release. In the end, flak damage set No.3 engine alight so they set off for base. They were also attacked by an enemy aircraft on the way home but managed to escape. This same crew, flying BZ873/S, found three U-boats at 0406 on 3 May at 4542N 0807W. They made determined attacks on Type IXC/40 *U 846*, commanded by Olt zur See Berthold Hashagen, but without result. This U-boat was sunk next day by Wellington M/407. F/L Forbes was awarded the DFC on 21 May.

A rather embarrassing incident took place on 7 May off the north Cornish coast when F/O G W Winter and crew in BZ873/S spotted a submarine on the surface. They had been advised of the presence of a British submarine in this area and assumed that this was it. They later discovered that they had flown past a U-boat! The first two Mk.VI Liberators, EV895 and EV953, were collected from No.51 MU Lichfield on 8 May. The main difference was the addition of a Consolidated A6A nose-turret. (Later Mk.VIs had Motor Products A6B nose and tail-turrets). One of No.53's ground crew, Sgt D L Coleman, was thrown from a tractor at St Eval on 15 May and died of his injuries next day.

F/O G A Bowman and crew set off from St Eval for a patrol of the Inner Bay in BZ873/S at 2056 on 20 May. A flash report was sent and then cancelled at 0128 on 21 May when north of the Gironde, but the aircraft failed to return. It is not yet known what happened to this aircraft and only one crew member was ever found. F/S G Harrison (wop/ag) is buried at Bilbao.

At 2316 on 5 June, F/L LeMaistre and crew in BZ774/J left St Eval on what was to be the first of many "Cork" patrols flown by No.53. These patrols were designed to provide a constant radar coverage of the area between the

No.224 Squadron shared St.Eval with No.53 and one of its Liberator VIs, EW309/S, was photographed from F/L E.B. Le Maistre's EW291/Z on 25 August 1944. (F/S L.C. Hatch)

French coast and the south coast of Ireland, thereby making it very difficult for U-boats and enemy surface vessels to attack the Allied fleet which was about to set forth on the Normandy invasion. In fact, these patrols were very effective and remarkably little Allied shipping was lost due to enemy action during D-Day.

F/O McPherson and crew in BZ871/E spotted two U-boats south-west of Ushant escorted by two destroyers and four minesweepers. The U-boats submerged immediately and shortly afterwards, a strike force of Beaufighters was seen heading towards the convoy. A solitary Ju 88 appeared but made off into cloud when it spotted the Beaufighters. The patrol orders forbade the Liberator crew from making an attack on surface vessels.

S/L George Crawford DFC AFC and crew set off for the Western Channel area in BZ778/M at 2357 on 6 June. Luck was about to run out for this illustrious crew for nothing further was heard from them. They had been shot down by a U-boat but it has proved to be impossible to identify which one. Liberators M/53, B/224 and M/224 were all shot down by U-boats during the night of 6/7 June. It is thought likely that B/224 fell to *U 415*. *U 256* also reported shooting down a Liberator, but it cannot be determined which one. Only one crew member from M/53 was ever found and F/S R A O'Kane (RNZAF) (wop/ag) is buried in France.

Three U-boats were found on the surface at 0426 on 7 June by F/L J W Carmichael and crew in BZ944/L. They had no way of knowing that S/L Crawford and crew had just been shot down by one of the U-boats in the area. An attack was

made on Type VIIC *U 963*, commanded by Olt zur See K Boddenberg, which was damaged. When he realised that the U-boats were going to stay on the surface and fight, F/L Carmichael held off for a bit. At 0513 he made another attack and damaged Type VIIC *U 256* commanded by Klt E Brauel, which went some way towards evening-up the score for the night. Both U-boats were forced to return to Brest for repairs. During the attack on *U 256*, No.3 engine was put out of action and a shell exploded in the bomb-bay but the crew was uninjured. On his return to base, F/L Carmichael was immediately promoted to Squadron Leader to replace S/L Crawford.

At 0628 on 7 June, F/L J Burton and crew in BZ820/U found a U-boat at 4820N 0650W which they attacked. Strikes on the conning tower from the aircraft guns were seen. Three aircraft appeared and these were at first thought to be hostile but turned out to be Mosquitoes. When the Liberator returned a few minutes later, only an oil patch was visible.

S/L J W Carmichael and crew in BZ818/C took off at 2130 on 13 June for a "Cork" patrol. Just before their departure, S/L Carmichael had received a telegram from his brother, who had escaped from prison camp, to say that he was coming down to St Eval for a visit. A flash report was received at 2355 from the aircraft, which was south-west of Ushant, announcing an imminent U-boat attack. Nothing further was heard from them and the aircraft failed to return. They had fallen victim to Type VIIC *U 270* commanded by Olt zur See Heinrich Schreiber. On 14 June, S/L Carmichael was awarded the DFC and his navigator, F/S J T McKeown,

Armourers with flame and smoke floats at St.Eval

A flight mechanic working on a Liberator rudder, St.Eval

the DFM. As something of a supreme irony, S/L Carmichael never got to see his DFC or his brother.

A U-boat attack was made by F/L G G Potier DFC and crew in BZ944/L at 4913N 0538W on 18 June. Although a growing oil streak was in evidence afterwards, the U-boat was undamaged. This was Type VIID *U 218* commanded by Klt Richard Becker. It was around this time that No.53 started to find U-boats equipped with schnorkels. This device allowed the U-boat to remain submerged at periscope depth and to run on the main diesel engines whilst "breathing" through the schnorkel. Needless to say, this made the task of finding U-boats much more difficult.

F/O Esler and crew in BZ870/Q illuminated a schnorkel on the night of 24/25 June to the north-east of Ushant but were unable to attack before losing contact. F/L R T Waite and crew were on patrol in the English Channel in BZ875/V on 6 July. A schnorkel leaving a trail of smoke was spotted by the flight engineer using a pair of binoculars from the starboard beam. Several runs were made but the bomb-doors refused to open properly and the DCs kept hanging-up. Nevertheless, the crew eventually managed to drop six DCs but the attack was inconclusive.

It was around this time that No.53 began to carry the "Mk.24 Mine". This was the official cover-name for the acoustic homing-torpedo then coming into service amid great secrecy. It worked by homing on to the cavitation noises produced by the propellers of a submerged U-boat. The weapon was delivered to the aircraft hidden by a screen and

only a few of the crew were supposed to know what it was. Once on board, it was there for all to see since the front fuselage of the Liberator was connected to the rear by a catwalk which ran right through the centre of the bomb-bay! Various crews used different nicknames for this weapon, including "Donkey", "Fido", "Oscar" and "Wandering Annie".

The sono-buoy was also coming into service. This device made it possible to "listen" to a submarine after it had submerged. It was normal to drop a pattern of five sono-buoys and these were colour-coded Purple, Orange, Blue, Red and Yellow, or "POBRY" for short. By listening to each buoy in turn, it was theoretically possible to establish which way the submarine was headed and this allowed an attack to be made. The sono-buoy equipment came under the code-name "High Tea" and the first known squadron exercise with it took place on 31 July.

On the previous day, F/O S J Houghton and crew in EW302/G were on patrol in the West Channel when they were summoned to the scene of a possible U-boat by Liberator B/224 flown by F/L Wales. This aircraft had come across an oil slick and had dropped some sono-buoys, receiving a positive result with the second one. They had then attacked with a homing torpedo but this had failed to produce anything conclusive. On establishing that G/53 did not have any sono-buoys on board, B/224 dropped a marker for them to aim at, so enabling F/O Houghton to drop another homing torpedo.

Depth charges ready for loading at St.Eval

The 53 Squadron records state that "The U-boat was sunk the following day by an Escort Group (sic) after a hunt instigated by reports from these two aircraft. It was the first occasion that a U-boat had been sunk as the result of evidence of a British aircraft obtained by means of the Sono Buoy". The only U-boat in the area was Type VIIC *U 333* and she was indeed sunk by HMS *Loch Killin* and *Starling* on 31 July some 50 miles away. Although it cannot be completely discounted, the balance of evidence now available makes it more likely that the two Liberators actually attacked a wreck releasing oil rather than *U 333*.

Also on 31 July, F/O J Osborne and crew in EW306/U were on a homing exercise when the aircraft hit the sea off Trevose Head. Four of the crew were killed and four were injured, some of them badly. The survivors were picked up by a passing Walrus and then transferred to a launch.

By the beginning of August, the U-boat bases at St Nazaire, Brest and Lorient were in danger of being captured by the Allied advance and No.53 was involved in mopping-up operations in the Bay. W/C "Crasher" Gates was on his last operational flight with the squadron on 9 August in EV877/C when he spotted an oil slick at 4630N 0308W. The shape of a U-boat was seen ahead of the slick and he attacked with six DCs. This produced oil and persistent green bubbles. He set off to fetch surface vessels of the Second Support Group and Sunderlands Z/228 and Y/10 also homed-in and stayed in the area. W/C Gates was credited with sinking Type VIIC *U 608*

commanded by Olt zur See Wolfgang Reisener, which was in the process of evacuating from Lorient. The U-Boat was finished off by HMS *Wren*.

Contractors had been busy installing a "FIDO" system around the main runway at St Eval. This consisted of pipes and petrol burners which ran the complete length of the runway. When it was necessary for aircraft to operate in foggy conditions, the entire system was lit up and the fog was literally burned off, creating a clear "tunnel" above the runway. Needless to say, it consumed thousands of gallons of petrol and was very expensive to run but it was to save many lives in times to come. F/L J Burton made the first operational landing using "FIDO" at St Eval in EW295/S on 4 August and F/O S J Houghton made the first Coastal Command night take-off using the system in EV877/C on 6 August. His second pilot wore dark glasses in case the captain was blinded but this proved not to be the case.

F/L G G Potier DFC and crew flying EW302/G set off at 2213 on 14 August and were off the west coast of France on the way to their patrol area when they picked up a radar contact at 2356 at 4722N 0439W. The Leigh Light was switched on and a fully-surfaced U-boat was illuminated. The gunner in the front turret opened fire and scored several hits on the conning tower. An explosion took place just behind the conning tower and then a large red glow appeared to the left of it. Fire was returned from the U-boat but six Mk.XI DCs were dropped on it and all went quiet. They had badly damaged Type VIIC *U 618* commanded by Olt zur See Erich Faust. A Wellington arrived at 0230 on 15 August and illuminated the scene revealing oil streaks. Vessels of the Third Escort Group arrived at 0534 and the U-boat was finished off by the frigates HMS *Duckworth* and HMS *Essington*.

W/C Gates was awarded the DFC on 18 August and posted to HQ Coastal Command as a Group Captain on 21 August. The new CO was W/C N B Littlejohn OBE, who had previously been flying with No.547. Awards of the DFC were made to F/L W J Irving (RCAF), F/L K L Fogden, F/O D Destonis (RCAF) and W/O I R W Thomson (RNZAF) on 22 August.

On 27 August, F/L C McA Forbes DFC and crew in EV899/W were investigating numerous small radar contacts in the vicinity of Ile de Batz. It was a pitch-black night and at 0300, a wing-tip hit the sea and the aircraft crashed. F/L Forbes, Sgt B A Coombes (wop/ag) and Sgt E R Steer (wop/ag) were thrown clear and managed to get into a dinghy despite their injuries. They were spotted at 0725 by F/L Bob Dobson and crew in EW295/S and then picked up by HMCS *Minas* and taken to hospital in Cherbourg. The other seven crew members were never found.

The SS Irish Willow *proclaims her neutrality, 22 July 1944*

CHAPTER 13

NORTH TO

REYKJAVIK

Reykjavik airfield on 2 January 1945.
(F/O L.H. Ding)

Anti-submarine patrols continued to be flown in the Bay for the first week of September but there was little activity. No.53 was ordered to Reykjavik in Iceland on 7 September. The U-boats were now being forced to use bases in Norway and Germany and the squadron was needed to help cover the sea area between Scotland and Iceland. On this same day, F/L G G Potier was awarded a Bar to his DFC. F/O J S Wilkinson was awarded the DFC on 9 September.

Seven Liberators of "A" Flight left St Eval on 12 September and flew to Bishops Court and then on to Reykjavik the next day, with "B" Flight following along one day later. The first sorties from Iceland were made by "A" Flight on 15 September. The runways at Reykjavik were too short for a fully-loaded Liberator to take off from, so the aircraft had to be flown over to nearby Meeks Field and, after the crew had been briefed at RAF Geck, they took off from Meeks and landed back at Reykjavik at the end of the operation. The "B" Flight aircraft did not arrive from Bishops Court until 19 September.

It immediately became evident that the squadron's Liberators did not like the Icelandic climate when serious carburettor-icing problems were encountered. The CO finally grounded the aircraft on 22 September until a solution could be found. Nevertheless, when news came in that a convoy, consisting of SS *Yukon*, a merchant vessel employed by the U.S. Navy, and a single destroyer escort was overdue, S/L G P Watson OBE DFC and crew volunteered to take EV877/C despite the grounding and try to find them. They found the ships at 1626 sailing towards Reykjavik but at 1804, the *Yukon* was struck by a torpedo or a mine. Despite this, she still managed to limp into port. Several other aircraft were then sent out to make sure that no U-boats were in the vicinity. Despite their efforts, it is now known that the ship was hit by a torpedo fired from Type VIIC *U 979*. Carb-icing problems persisted however so a total grounding order was made on 25 September.

The turbo-superchargers on earlier model Liberators had been controlled manually. Those on the new Mk.VIs were electronically-controlled and with cruise power set when flying at at low level, insufficient turbo-boost was being created to heat up the intake air in the carburettors, even with the intercooler shutters fully closed. Various experts and

company representatives were sent for and W/C Littlejohn flew daily air tests, but it was not until 7 October that the problem was solved and the aircraft returned to service. The CO, who had been unwell for some time, was admitted to hospital and S/L Henley, a Newfoundlander, took temporary command in his absence. Four anti-submarine patrols were flown every night, mainly to the south-west of Iceland and escorts were provided for the convoys passing through the area. F/L Dobbie (RAAF) and crew were unable to lower the nose-wheel of EW300/K on 23 October but managed to land at base without causing too much damage. The DFC was awarded to F/O C K McPherson on 10 October.

During the month, several training sorties were made during which practice attacks were made on "Mount Litvin", a large rock off the Icelandic coast. Its proper name was Geircugladrangur and it is believed to have got its nickname from an unfortunate pilot who had attacked it one night thinking it was a U-boat! The radar return was very similar and the rock even looked something like a U-boat, so this made it a very useful training aid. Three Liberators were scrambled on 3 November to join Canso X/162 (RCAF), also based at Reykjavik, which had made an attack on a schnorkel at 6200N 1800W. Nothing was found however and the weather got so bad that all three had to divert to Stornoway. On 8 November, W/C A R Holmes (RCAF) was posted in from No.547 to take command.

F/L W G Payne and crew in EV895/H set off at 0110 to search for a U-boat suspected to be lurking off Gardskagi but nothing further was heard from them. F/L Potier and crew in EW297/O were on the same patrol and at 0247 reported that they were circling a fierce fire burning on the sea. The fire was so intense that the heat could be felt at 1,000 feet. This crew was convinced that a vessel was ablaze in the middle of the conflagration and reported seeing it founder at 0350. The fire was still burning when they left the scene at 0627.

F/O Dumbell and F/O Poulter in Anson I LT199/D made a search later in the day for survivors. At 1300, they found a Liberator nose-wheel floating in the sea at 6405N 2207W and directed a surface vessel to retrieve it. One theory given at the time was that EV895/H had struck the target being investigated, but no vessel was reported as missing. It was not to be a good day for EW297/O either; the port-outer

KH129/J crashed on landing in filthy weather at Reykjavik, 29 May 1945. F/L G.J. Earnshaw and crew alongside.
(F/O Ian Little)

engine failed after taking off from Meeks Field at 1855 and F/O J A Withers was unable to maintain height. A belly-landing was made back at Meeks but no one was injured.

On 13 December, S/L Watson ferried Liberator I AM923/W from Meeks Field to Prestwick. This aircraft was one of the original batch of coastal Liberators given to 120 Squadron to operate in the second half of 1941 and it had been struck off charge after a landing accident at Reykjavik on 18 October, 1943. It would seem that some of the groundcrew had carried out a gradual rebuild of AM923, probably as a form of therapy, since there wasn't a lot to do at Reykjavik!

Anti-submarine patrols and convoy escorts continued to be flown throughout December but only one possible sighting of a schnorkel was made and attacked by F/O Withers in EW300/K during an armed transit flight from Meeks to Ballykelly. A No.162 (RCAF) Canso was reported missing on 20 December and F/O Dumbell, flying Anson LT199/D, found the wreckage near the west shore of Kleifarvater. There were no survivors.

January 1945 saw No.53 converting to new Liberator VIIIs. A training detachment was set up at Ballykelly and the first of the new aircraft, KH178 and KH180, arrived in Iceland on 20 January. The Liberator VIII had an Emerson nose-turret fitted and the mid-upper turret removed. There were also internal differences. F/L Potier set off on an armed transit flight to Ballykelly in EV879/D on 27 January. Although the flight was uneventful, there was an element of drama involved in that he was also on the way to his wedding and it was doubtful if he would get there in time! He just made it by the skin of his teeth. F/O Withers and crew in EW300/K left Leuchars on patrol at 1612 on 31 January. At 1943, a schnorkel was found at 6048N 0346W but it had

disappeared before they could make an attack. Unfortunately, they were not carrying sono-buoys.

F/O H Nixon and crew in EW300/K returned from a patrol on 9 February to find both Reykjavik and Meeks Field obscured by heavy snow. Having jettisoned the DCs south of Eldy Rock, they started to circle Meeks in the hope that they might find a break in the weather. The runways were obscured by snow and could only be seen when exactly overhead. No.2 engine failed due to a lack of fuel at 1125 followed rapidly by No.4 so a final circuit was made and a crash-landing made diagonally across the runways. Although the aircraft was a write-off, no one was injured.

At 0035 on 1 March, S/L Watson and crew in EW289/T were on escort duty to convoy UR155 when they picked up a radar contact and then visual evidence of a possible U-boat. As they manoeuvred to make an up-moon approach, they were blinded by three flares fired by one of the vessels in the convoy and were unable to make contact again. Sadly, the Panamanian steamer *Alcedo* had been torpedoed half an hour earlier. The U-boat concerned is thought to have been Type VIIC *U 1022*. F/L Potier and crew in EW293/M made an inconclusive U-boat attack on 2 March.

This same aircraft was written off during a night take-off at Meeks Field on 3 March. F/L M D Deloford DFC was directed to the wrong runway and hit a snow bank. One of his navigators, F/O F W Snapes, was killed outright and the other, F/O J Yates, died of his injuries on 6 March. Two squadron aircraft collided in the dark overhead convoy UR156 on 9 March. The Nos.1 and 2 propellers of EW303/Y flown by F/O J C Rowley struck the belly of KH341/N flown by F/L A R Wilcox and almost severed the bomb-bay catwalk. Although there were no injuries, one of the crew in KH341 was struck a glancing blow on the boot by the tip of a

F/O H. Nixon's crew alongside the wreckage of EW300/K at Meeks Field, Iceland, on 9 February 1945 after force-landing in a blizzard short of fuel. (S/L H. Wallbank)

propeller! The captain's case, containing his diversion kit, was cut through and his mackintosh bisected. F/O Rowley was able to restart the No.1 engine of EW303/Y despite a damaged propeller and both aircraft were diverted to Tain where they landed safely.

Another inconclusive attack was made on a possible U-boat by F/L G Earnshaw and crew in KH388/B on 13 March. No.18 Group took over responsibility for all anti-submarine operations on 29 March and it was decided to concentrate on daylight patrols since there was a better chance of spotting schnorkels. The Leigh Lights were removed from the aircraft. The added responsibility of flying long-range meteorological flights was given to No.53 on 31 March whilst No.251, also based at Reykjavik, converted from Hudsons to Fortresses.

F/O D I McGillivray (RCAF) and crew in KH180/Q carried out an inconclusive attack on a schnorkel at 6052N 1150W on 10 April.

F/O H Lewis and crew had been sent to collect EW303/Y from Tain after repairs had been made following the collision with KH341/N on 9 March. They were carrying out an air test on 16 April after Nos.1 and 2 engines and propellers had been changed. Something went badly wrong whilst feathering and un-feathering drills were being carried out for control was lost and the aircraft spun into Helmsdale Bay. Two WAAFs had gone along for the ride and they were

found by the crew of RAF launch 2587. LACW W Hutchinson and LACW M MacLean was seriously injured. Sadly, LACW Hutchinson later died. The crew was never found.

Ice patrols in the Denmark Strait started on 17 April. F/L H E Addington (RCAF) and crew in KH413/U followed and plotted the ice-edge almost as far as 71°N when it became obscured by thick fog. The war in Europe ended on 7 May when Germany capitulated. A great sense of relief was felt by all but anti-submarine patrols continued in order to escort surrendering U-boats to port and to keep watch for any "pirates" who might be reluctant to surrender. Several U-boats made their way to Reykjavik and squadron crews were able to visit the sort of ships that they had been chasing since 1941.

S/L Watson and crew took off in KH132/K at 2116 on 15 May to carry out a special met flight. They flew to 7215N 2015W before returning to Meeks, where they briefed the crew of the Lancaster *Aries* which then departed to fly over the geographical North Pole and back. F/L Earnshaw and crew were uninjured when KH129/J was written off in a landing accident at Reykjavik on 29 May. On this same day, F/L Nixon and crew in KH413/U made what was to be the last of No.53's operational flights in Coastal Command.

Reykjavik under snow in January 1945. KH413/U in centre

No.53's headquarters at Reykjavik

KN743/Y, flown by F/L Davies and crew, made No.53's last troop-carrying flight (and Liberator flight), arriving back at Upwood from India on 16 June 1946

CHAPTER 14: INTO TRANSPORT COMMAND

While the war in Europe was over, the war against Japan in the Far East was still raging. No.53 was to transfer to Transport Command and its first task was to ferry troops out to India. The main air party arrived at the new base at St Davids on 1 June and the CO and the Adjutant flew to HQ Coastal Command the next day for a briefing. Some 48 crews of five were to be formed (captain, 2nd pilot, navigator, flight engineer and wireless operator/air gunner) and the existing aircraft were to be stripped of guns for training pending delivery of Liberators modified for trooping. In the original plan, sixteen crews were to come from No.228, nine from No.210 and ten from No.172. No.53 was now under the command of No.301 Wing, Transport Command.

It was also decided that the Commonwealth personnel could go home and this included W/C A R Holmes (RCAF) and S/L T G Dobbie (RAAF). S/L G E R Pearl was posted in to replace the latter on 9 June. W/C D MacKenzie was posted in from No.547 on 23 June to take over from W/C Holmes who was posted to 426 (RCAF) Squadron. F/L C Grayson and crew in KH183/D were killed on 8 July when the aircraft crashed and burnt out at Emlych Farm shortly after take-off from St Davids.

The war in the Far East ended when Japan surrendered on 14 August. This of course meant that No.53 was going to be kept very busy fetching troops back from the conflict. The squadron was now well into the swing of its new role and the problems associated with trooping were slight when compared with the war years. These problems were usually confined to fairly frequent engine failures and taxying accidents on poorly-lit airfields. Such an event took place at Castel Benito, Libya on 17 August when Liberator KK322 struck Stirling V PJ991 whilst being marshalled-in. On 25 August, No.220 Liberator KL348 taxied into KH198 at Mauripur, India.

On 17 September, No.53 moved to Merryfield from St Davids. By 1 October, all transport training had been completed and No.53, along with other transport squadrons, set about moving 10,000 troops from the European theatre to India. The European terminal was at Melsbroek, near Brussels and at either Chakulia or Poona in India. The outbound leg was flown via Castel Benito, Cairo West, Shaibah and Mauripur. The return flights carried troops proceeding on home leave or repatriation and routed via Mauripur, Habbaniya, Lydda and Castel Benito to Merryfield.

F/L J T Barrett was taxying at Palam, Delhi in KH279 when a fault in the hydraulic system caused the starboard undercarriage to collapse on 21 October. Stirling V PJ976 of 158 Squadron was hit by the port wing tip of KH146 in a taxying accident at Mauripur on 5 November. F/L L Mielecki and crew were killed on 22 November when KH126 crashed at White's Farm near Broadway Pound, Somerset shortly after take-off from Merryfield. The twenty-two passengers on board also perished.

No.53 moved to Gransden Lodge, where a passenger and freight terminal had been established, on 10 December. F/L W H Spencer (RNZAF) had an unpleasant experience on 27 December when the No.2 engine on KH346 quite literally blew-up and then caught fire. He did well to get his aircraft and passengers down safely at Istres airfield in the south of France.

January 1946 was a fairly typical month and 1,358 passengers and 314,139 lbs of mail and freight were flown in 820 flying hours. F/L W G Stonehouse managed to land KG848 safely back at Gransden Lodge on 7 February when No.1 engine caught fire just after take-off. The squadron disbanded on 28 February but was re-formed on 1 March at Upwood by re-numbering No.102 Squadron. The new CO was W/C D F Hyland Smith DFC AFC.

Fairly long delays occurred at Mauripur during April, mainly due to a lack of troops to be brought home. It was becoming obvious that the operation was running down and crews began to be posted from the squadron for conversion training on the Avro York. The last trooping flight left for India on 31 May flown by F/L Davies and crew in KN743/Y. The CO was posted on 3 June and S/L S A Sharpe took over until 13 June when he handed over to F/L D H Phillips. Liberator KN743/Y came back from India on 16 June and No.53 disbanded again on 15 June.

CHAPTER 15

RE-FORMED WITH

DAKOTAS

Dakota IV KN700/T over Salisbury Plain, September 1947. (S/L L. T. Bennett)

No.53 was re-formed at Netheravon on 1 December 1946. This was brought about by re-numbering No.187 Squadron which was equipped with Douglas Dakota IV aircraft powered by two 1,200-hp Pratt and Whitney R-1830 Twin Wasps. The new CO was W/C P Fleming and the squadron was now under the command of No.46 Group, Transport Command. The squadron establishment was increased to 32 crews and the main tasks were glider towing and transport-support duties such as parachuting and supply-dropping in support of the Army. The standard glider in use at Netheravon at this time was the Airspeed Horsa II flown by pilots from "N" Squadron, Glider Pilot Regiment. It was a commonly held belief that some of the older Dakotas stretched by three inches on take-off as they took the strain!

During December, a fair amount of overseas route flying was also carried out. Because there were no night flying facilities and little in the way of radio equipment at Netheravon, crews had to be transported by road to other bases such as Abingdon and Northolt before and after flights. By the end of the month, some 93 return flights had been made to airfields in Germany, the most common destinations being Bückeburg, Übersen and Gütersloh.

The Transport Command Examining Unit (TCEU), otherwise known as the "Trappers", inspected the squadron during January 1947 and S/L Smith was awarded a coveted

The wreckage of KN439 which crashed while approaching Utersen airfield on 20 December 1947. (S/L L. T. Bennett)

"A" Category. He was then quickly posted to TCEU! On 24 January, seven crews were detached overseas for route flying duties. On 16 March, Dakotas KN446 and KN508 were damaged when their picketing points gave way during a gale. Heavy snow fell during March and when it finally melted, Netheravon was unusable due to water-logging. Nine further crews were posted overseas and only sixteen remained on strength by the end of the month.

A very successful transport-support practice camp course was held at Netheravon between 15 April and 17 May. During the period 934 parachute descents were made and several mass glider lifts were carried out. No.4053 Servicing Echelon were commended for the high degree of aircraft serviceability achieved throughout the exercise. Overseas route flying duties re-commenced after the practice camp and one aircraft ventured as far as Wadi Halfa and Khartoum.

Dakota KN700 suffered an engine failure after take-off on 4 July at Netheravon but F/L D A Templeton was able to land safely. Horsa II RX804 was struck off charge on 7 July when it was found that the entire empennage was loose due to wood shrinkage. Next day, W/C G H Gatheral took over as CO and W/C Fleming was posted to HQ Transport Command. F/O D Hanson was landing in KN383 after a glider tow on 15 July when the starboard tyre burst. He was just able to keep the aircraft straight and so avoided further damage. Scheduled services were also started during July to Bückeburg, Berlin and Warsaw. The flights to Berlin and Warsaw carried diplomatic personnel and mail and were, at that time, the only link with the communist countries. Initially, they departed from Croydon but later left from Blackbushe.

Thirteen Dakotas set off for Abingdon on 6 September to take part in Operation *Longstop*. The object of the exercise was to demonstrate the use of aircraft in the close-support role. After two weeks of training, a mass assault was made on Netheravon on 23 September by British and French troops dropped from around 40 Dakotas, including 12 from No.53. They then returned to Abingdon to pick up more troops which were air-landed at Netheravon under the watchful eyes of the Chief of the Air Staff. F/L F W Wincott was flying KN701/N during the exercise when the starboard engine failed at a critical moment. He was able to land back at Abingdon and was awarded a Green Endorsement for his troubles.

Horsa II TL356 made a spectacular arrival at Netheravon on 2 October. It touched down rather early and left its

Netheravon airfield in September 1947. (S/L L.T. Bennett)

KN590/H at Netheravon, September 1947. (S/L L.T. Bennett)

undercarriage on the wrong side of the airfield boundary! Happily, the pilots were uninjured. P2 W J Hall had a nasty moment when the starboard engine of KN701/N over-sped immediately after take-off during a night flying sortie at Abingdon. The propeller refused to feather but he was able to land safely, despite the drag caused by the wind-milling propeller. During October, the squadron carried 298 passengers, 34,671 lbs of mail and 193,623 lbs of freight.

On 8 December, half of the crews were posted out to No.18, which was in the process of reforming at Netheravon as a Dakota squadron. On 10 December, squadron aircraft carried out a shuttle service between Netheravon and No.53's new base at Waterbeach. The move had been completed by the end of the next day. W/C Gatheral was posted out to become OC Flying Wing at Waterbeach and S/L M B Cooper took over as CO. Nos.18 and 62 also moved into Waterbeach with their Dakotas at the same time. Route flying began again on 17 December and all flights originated from nearby Oakington, which had all the necessary route handling facilities. Oakington was also home to the Dakotas of Nos.27, 30 and 46 which had moved in during the previous month.

F/L R H Pitman DSO had now joined 53 Squadron. Bob had flown two tours on anti-shipping operations during the war and had successfully torpedoed four large enemy ships, all of which had been sunk. He had also led a formation of 39 Squadron Beaufighter Xs which had sunk the 51,000 ton Italian liner *Rex* at Capodistria on 8 September 1944. This had put paid to the plan to use the liner as a block-ship in Trieste harbour. Bob had also been fortunate enough to return to base safely in aircraft damaged by enemy fire on no less than nineteen occasions. F/L Pitman went on to fly the

Hastings and the Beverley with No.53.

Disaster struck on 20 December when Dakota KN439 crashed while trying to land at Ütersen, near Hamburg. F/L Gordon Cremer and crew had picked up several Mosquito pilots at Wahn, destined for Ütersen. An intermediate stop had been made at Bückeburg and F/L Cremer was making the final turn-in from a BABS instrument let-down in bad weather when the port engine failed and control was lost. The aircraft landed on soft, level ground short of the airfield and caught fire. The 2nd pilot, F/O C Hore, was injured when he was thrown through the windscreen. Although the aircraft was burnt out, F/L Cremer, F/L G L Graham, S2 Les Bennett and all of the Mosquito pilots were able to escape with cuts and bruises.

A new route to Fayid in the Suez Canal Zone started during January 1948. The round trip took 38 flying hours and four days to complete, routing via Istres in the south of France and Castel Benito in Libya. Apart from route flying, transport-support and glider towing sorties were also flown from Waterbeach. S/L P C Lemon DSO DFC took over as CO on 1 June. Little did he realise that No.53 would be involved in the biggest airlift operation that the world had ever seen by the end of the month.

In Berlin, relations between the Russian authorities on the one hand, and the British, American and French authorities on the other had been deteriorating for some time. All surface routes to Berlin were closed by the Russians on 24 June. HQ No.46 Group immediately put Operation *Knicker* into action. Eight Dakotas, including two flown by No.53 crews, left for Wunstorf on 25 June and were immediately put into action flying supplies to Gatow for the British forces

Dakotas lined up at Netheravon, September 1947. (S/L L.T. Bennett)

in Berlin. W/C Gatheral went with them and set up a Transport Wing HQ at Wunstorf. Another eight Dakotas went to Wunstorf on 28 June.

It was originally thought that the Russians would only close the surface routes for a few days, but it soon became apparent that this was not going to be the case and that a much larger airlift capacity would have to be provided. An extra 38 Dakotas were flown out on 29 June and Operation *Knicker* became Operation *Carter Paterson*. Within a few days, this was changed to Operation *Plainfare* when some wag pointed out that Messrs Carter Paterson had been a famous **Removal** firm before the war and that this might just send the wrong message to the Russians!

Nos.38 and 47 Groups were also ordered to supply transport aircraft and the first twelve No.47 Group Avro Yorks arrived at Wunstorf during the first week of July. By then, some 50 Dakotas from Nos.30, 46, 53, 77, 238 and No.240 OCU were based there and the airfield was reaching saturation point. The AOC No.46 Group, Air Commodore J W F Merer, visited Wunstorf on 5 July to see the operating problems at first hand. The Transport Wing HQ was moved to Bückeburg on 19 July and all Dakotas were moved to Fassberg on 29 July to make room for more Yorks.

The weather was pretty bad at this stage of the airlift but the Dakota fleet was still managing to make over 100 trips per day to Berlin. Each Dakota carried a payload of 5,500 lbs at the beginning of the operation but this was soon increased to 7,500 lbs by raising the permissible landing weight and by discarding all surplus equipment. The Dakotas moved to Lübeck on 22 August to make room for USAF C-54s at Fassberg. The new airfield was only two miles from the Russian Zone, so great care had to be taken on take-off and landing.

By now, No.53 and all the other Dakota squadrons taking part in the Berlin Airlift had really ceased to exist as autonomous units, except in an administrative capacity. Crews took the first aircraft which became available and a common pool of aircraft and men had rapidly evolved. Nevertheless, it is of great credit to the squadron that none of its crews were involved in an accident during Operation *Plainfare*.

After flying 113 Plainfare sorties, F/L K H Miles and his navigator, F/O J D Beacham, were recommended for the award of the AFC and this was duly ratified on 10 December. F/L Don Hanson was also awarded the AFC on the same day. No.53 disbanded as a Dakota squadron on 31 July 1949.

KN632/W of No.53 Squadron. (A. Thomas collection)

CHAPTER 16

THE HASTINGS

ARRIVES

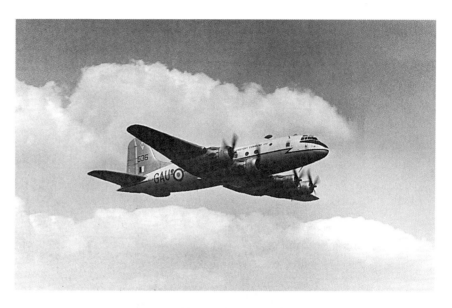

*Hastings TG536/GAU with its squadron
number in a diamond on the fin.
(Philip Jarrett collection)*

No.53 reformed at Topcliffe next day equipped with Handley Page Hastings C.1 aircraft. In fact, the squadron was immediately detached to Schleswigland to take part in Operation *Plainfare*. The initial 20 crews were posted in from Nos.47 and 297, who were already operating from Schleswigland. S/L J P Trant was posted in from Dishforth on 2 August to take command.

The Hastings had a wing span of 112 feet 9 inches and was powered by four Bristol Hercules 216 engines. The Hercules was a fourteen-cylinder, two-row, sleeve-valve, radial engine and each produced 1,800-hp. The aircraft had a maximum take-off weight of 81,000 lbs (later increased to 83,000 lbs when external fuel tanks were fitted) and it was equipped with a tail-wheeled undercarriage.

Between fifteen and twenty flights a day were made to Gatow and Tegel carrying coal. No less than seven engine failures were recorded during August and F/L Wheeler and Sgt Webb (Glider Pilot Regt) experienced airframe vibration in TG504 on 26 August. This was caused by a faulty rudder spring-tab. By the end of the month the squadron had carried 6,080,000 lbs of coal to Berlin.

The Airlift was now gradually running down and this made it possible to post some crews back to Nos.99 and 511 at Lyneham on 26 September, leaving some 14 crews at Schleswigland. The amount of coal carried during the month fell to 3,482,752 lbs. F/L D J Harper and crew of 53 Squadron flew the last sortie of Operation *Plainfare* on 6 October. The squadron detachment moved to Wunstorf the following day and was kept on standby just in case trouble flared up again. It was now possible to carry out some badly-needed training from Wunstorf. Hastings TG567 flown by P2 McLaren was damaged when it was struck by lightning during a navigation exercise on 14 November. The detachment was posted back to base at Topcliffe from Wunstorf on 13 December.

Hastings TG516 flown by F/L D J Harper was damaged when No.1 engine caught fire before take-off at Topcliffe on 10 February 1950. Two unserviceable aircraft had been left behind at Wunstorf and the last of these arrived back on 11 February. During the month, route flying as far as Singapore had re-commenced. F/L D W Barnard had a nasty moment on 21 April when the rear-top panel of No.2 engine on TG504 broke loose in turbulence and hit the leading edge of the tailplane whilst over Iraq, but he was able to land safely at Habbaniya. S/L Trant was detached to Hornchurch on 27

April for duties in connection with a dock strike.

Engine failures were still happening frequently. Strange as it may seem nowadays, the Hastings force at this time used re-cycled oil in its engines. An Oil-Cooler Flushing Unit was set up at Lyneham and the engine oil-coolers were fitted with back-pressure gauges. When the back-pressure reached a certain value, the cooler needed flushing. This was fine if the aircraft was at Lyneham but not quite so handy if it happened to be at Mauripur!

The oil-cooler shutters were also inefficient and "coring" was a common occurrence. This phenomenon was caused by the cooler getting too cold which allowed the oil in contact with the matrix to solidify. This drastically cut the flow of oil passing through the cooler, rather like a mechanical version of the narrowing of the human arteries. Consequently, the temperature of the remaining oil flow escalated to dangerous levels. Coring was fairly common when the aircraft was forced to climb into cold air, such as was necessary to cross over the Massif in France, for example. Eventually, new oil-shutter seals were developed and this helped ease the problem enormously, but not before the Hastings had become known as the finest three-engined transport in the RAF!

Routes were flown to Fayid, Singapore and to Nairobi during July. Flights to Iwakuni in Japan, in support of the British forces involved in the Korean War, were added in October. F/L G C Doak left Habbaniya in TG530 on 28 November. Sixteen minutes after take-off, he was horrified to note that the oil temperature on all four engines had exceeded limits. He was able to return to Habbaniya using reduced power and a complete oil change cured the problem. Routes were flown to Korea in December.

It had been decided to shut down the Singapore slip-schedule for Christmas so Hastings TG574 was sent off to act as the "sweeper". It had already "swept-up" four complete slip-crews and three passengers on its way from Singapore through Negombo, Karachi and Habbaniya when F/L G Tunnadine and crew climbed on board at Fayid on 20 December. They had hoped to make their next refuelling stop at Castel Benito but had to make an unscheduled stop at El Adem. They finally left El Adem at 1958 and set course for Castel Benito climbing up to 8,500 feet before setting cruise power. The co-pilot, F/L S L Bennett, went back to rest on the crew bunk since he was expected to fly the aircraft on to UK from Castel Benito. His place on the flight deck was taken by S/L W G James of 99 Squadron.

TG529/GAB airborne from Abingdon for Watchfield DZ with two jeeps loaded on the 'heavy beam' under the fuselage.
(F/L A. MacLean)

Some 42 minutes after take-off, at 3205N 2120E, there was a loud bang and a great deal of violent shuddering. A blade had come off of No.2 propeller and had sliced through the fuselage, severing all of the tail control rods. It had then struck F/L Bennett, who was resting on the bunk and taken his right arm off. The three remaining blades on the No.2 propeller were now hopelessly out of balance so the entire engine was torn from its mountings and fell off, taking the port undercarriage and a large section of the wing leading edge with it.

Graham Tunnadine was desperately trying to keep the aircraft flying straight and level but had an almost impossible task on his hands. The flight engineer, Sgt P E Walker, had quickly established that there was no hope of repairing the severed tail control rods so the only primary flying controls left undamaged were the ailerons. First of all, the captain had to prevent the nose from getting too high otherwise the resulting stall would be impossible to recover from. He tried having the movable baggage and equipment in the cabin moved forward but there wasn't enough of it to have the desired effect. Next, he got the slip-crews to move fore and aft until the aircraft was flying level.

He was then able to keep the aircraft reasonably straight by using the ailerons and asymmetric thrust from the remaining three engines. Just how long the engines could put up with this sort of punishment was another question. The signaller, Sgt G J Bain, had sent out a Mayday call which was answered by Benina, the RAF airfield near Benghazi. Although they had not expected any aircraft that night, they told Sgt Bain that they could quickly lay out a flare path and provide fire equipment and medical services, so it was decided to attempt a landing there.

S/L T C L Brown, a senior medical officer from Abingdon who was travelling as a passenger on TG574, had immediately gone forward to look after F/L Bennett. He tried to move him from the wrecked bunk area but found that he was trapped by wreckage. He made the brave decision to stay with the seriously injured co-pilot, fully realising that he would be in great danger when the Hastings crash-landed.

F/L Tunnadine had eased the aircraft down to 6,000 feet by the time they arrived overhead Benina and his plan was to make a belly-landing by putting power on at the last moment, in the hope that this would be enough to raise the nose. He then descended to 1,000 feet by moving the slip-crews around again and positioned the aircraft on to final approach. Two slip-crew members stayed on their feet in order to make last-minute trim changes before diving into the nearest seats just before impact.

The wreckage of TG574, Benina, 20 December 1950.

Hastings C.2 WD491/GAF at Lyneham in 1957. (Andrew Thomas collection)

They almost made it to the airfield but TG574 struck gently rising ground just a few hundred yards short of the runway. The aircraft bounced for another 100 yards, the starboard wing struck the ground and the Hastings ended up on its back at 2155. Thanks to the use of rearward-facing passenger seats, everyone in the cabin survived with only minor injuries. It was a different story at the front of the aircraft. The nose was smashed in and F/L Tunnadine, S/L James and the navigator, F/S I A Johns, were dead. Sgt G J Bain was seriously injured and died on 24 December. Sgt Walker and the AQM, Sgt W A Slaughter, were injured.

Sadly, F/L Bennett had died of his injuries and S/L Brown, who had bravely sat on the floor holding him in his arms, was seriously injured. He was happily to recover and was awarded the George Medal. The crew of TG574 were each awarded the King's Commendation for Valuable Service in the Air. Many at the time considered this to be miserly recognition for such a magnificent piece of flying.

No.53 moved to Lyneham on 9 February 1951. The Singapore slip-schedule started up again on 15 February. Crews were drawn from Nos.53, 99 and 511 and it took three and a half days for an aircraft to make the round trip; *inshallah!* Close to 1,000 hours were flown by the squadron during March.

On 25 April, Dr Mohammed Mussadecq took over the government of Iran and announced his intention to nationalise the assets of the Anglo-Iranian Oil Company. There had been serious rioting in Abadan and several people had been killed, including two British employees. It was felt prudent to have a Hastings force standing by in the Middle East in case it became necessary to fly troops to the area. To this end, the Singapore slip was suspended on 25 May. S/L Jackie Trant left for the Canal Zone next day to take charge of the coming detachment and F/L D J Harper took over as temporary CO. By June, seven squadron crews were on standby at Fayid and

Kabrit for Operation *Barming* and this was increased to twelve crews in July.

Flights from UK to Australia in support of the coming atom-bomb test programme began during August. The usual destinations were Laverton and Mallalla in Australia. One crew spent several weeks at Mallalla and the captain had a whale of a time flying the Mustangs of the resident RAAF squadron. F/L E S Davis took over as temporary CO on 8 August handing over to F/L H Baker on 8 September. Eleven crews were still in the Canal Zone in September and they were getting thoroughly bored by being on a seemingly endless standby. In the end, the problems in Iran were peacefully settled by negotiation.

Several crews were sent back to Lyneham on leave at the beginning of October but the peace was not to last. With a near-perfect sense of timing, the Egyptian government suddenly decided to repeal the Anglo-Egyptian Treaty of 1936 which allowed British forces to be based in the Canal Zone. Serious civil unrest broke out immediately.

Six crews set off from Lyneham on 17 October for Cyprus and moved the 16th Airborne Brigade from there to Fayid. Eight crews moved two squadrons of the RAF Regiment from Lyneham to Fayid on 20 October. The aircraft returned to Lyneham with families being evacuated from the Canal Zone. F/L Templeton positioned seven slip-crews to Castel Benito on 23 October to prepare to move the 19th Infantry Brigade to Tripoli starting on 26 October. To say that No.53 was somewhat stretched at this time would be something of an understatement.

Further elements of the RAF Regiment were flown from Castel Benito to Fayid on 8 November and towards the end of the month, the 3rd Infantry Division, with elements of REME, were flown from Lyneham to Nicosia. The aircraft continued to Fayid and returned with families. By the beginning of December, six aircraft a day were leaving for

Hastings C.2 WD488/JAM.

Fayid. A tragic accident happened at Lyneham on 7 December. Hastings TG608 was being used for continuation training and LAC Wren was detailed to check the tyres after a series of landings. The engines were running and somehow or other, he made contact with No.1 propeller and was killed.

In March 1952, two crews were sent to Abingdon to carry out heavy drops of jeeps and guns. A heavy beam was fixed to strong-points underneath the fuselage of the Hastings and to this was attached either, two jeeps, or one jeep and a field gun, fitted with parachutes. Having this sort of load hanging underneath did absolutely nothing for the performance of the aircraft and an engine failure on take-off would have had catastrophic consequences. It is interesting to note that it was this requirement to carry external loads on the heavy beam and the space needed to load them underneath the aircraft, that dictated the extremely nose-high attitude which the Hastings adopted when stationary. In fact, the cockpit was over twenty two feet above the tarmac. This made doing a decent landing in a Hastings a rather demanding exercise, as anyone who has ever seen one make a series of quite spectacular bounces would willingly testify!

Three crews were sent out to Kasfareet in the Canal Zone on 3 May with aircraft fitted with heavy beams to join other Hastings and Valetta aircraft taking part in Operation *Leapyear*. This involved flying at night from Kasfareet in formation and making dawn drops at Mafraq in Jordan. Formation flying and supply-dropping was still flown in vic formation at this time. Keeping station in a vic formation at night was one thing, but managing to do it with the additional handicap of having two jeeps hanging underneath was another. W/C Jimmy Brodie MBE AFC once made the observation that when power was applied to catch up, the aircraft responded like a dead donkey and when it was

necessary to slow down, it behaved like a young stallion after a mare! Kasfareet airfield had to be closed for repairs after the exercise. Extensive ruts had been made in the tarmac of the taxiways and runways by the heavy aircraft which had taken part in the operation.

S/L B H Worts was posted in to take command on 12 May. Route flying continued throughout the year and most months saw a No.53 Hastings en route to Australia. Several flights were also made to Canada, the usual destination being Dorval near Montreal.

Crews were "spread" along the Singapore slip-route in preparation for Operation *Fast Run* in February 1953. The plan was to fly troops out to the Far East as fast as possible, but before it could get under way, the North Sea caused extensive flooding to parts of East Anglia and all available aircraft were needed to ferry sandbags to the affected areas. After two weeks, the slip-crews were brought home again and *Fast Run* was cancelled.

Trouble in Kenya was escalating and the Governor, Sir Evelyn Baring, requested that more troops be sent out in April to assist with the Mau Mau campaign. No.53 spent much of the month flying The Buffs out to Nairobi. A special flight was made to Moscow on 20 April to collect internees who had been held during the Korean War. Likewise, another flight went to Japan to collect released POWs from the same war.

Several squadron aircraft were at Abingdon on 22 June taking part in a transport-support exercise. They lined up on the runway for a stream take-off. At 0822, it was the turn of Hastings WJ335 flown by F/L J Dodds and crew. The aircraft made a short take-off and climbed at a steep angle to 300 feet, then stalled and had almost recovered when it struck the runway in a nose-down attitude and caught fire. The crew of

F/L Owen loading a jeep on WJ328 at Changi, August 1953.
(F/L S.H.Guy)

An engine change for Hastings C.2 WJ333 at Darwin, May 1954.

six were all killed and it was later learned that the elevator control-locking mechanism had somehow or other been inadvertently left engaged.

S/L Barney Worts led a detachment consisting of ten crews and five aircraft to Changi, Singapore on 1 July. F/L Angus Maclean and crew were the last to leave Lyneham but promptly lost partial use of two engines due to oil-cooler trouble and had to make a fairly tense GCA recovery back into Lyneham, which was covered by low cloud at the time. After repairs, this aircraft made it to Changi on 4 July. The primary object of the exercise was to move part of the Malayan Regiment to Hong Kong via Saigon. Flights were also made to Iwakuni, Negombo, Cocos, Rangoon, Bangkok, Car Nicobar and Labuan.

Hastings TG564 was destroyed by fire in a landing accident at Kai Tak airport in Hong Kong at 0815 on 27 July. Because of the surrounding terrain, the approach to the old runway at Kai Tak was particularly difficult and windshear was often present. The starboard undercarriage of the aircraft, flown by F/L S E Judd, struck a store hut some 200 yards short of the threshold. The aircraft came to rest just off the right side of the runway. It caught fire and was burnt out, partly assisted by the Kowloon Fire Brigade which used water on a fire that was being fuelled by petrol and oil! F/L Sid Judd was seriously injured. The Changi detachment returned to Lyneham during the second half of August.

Eight flights were made to Eastleigh, Nairobi, in association with Operation *Warden* during September. It is also interesting to note that continuation training for the squadron's 2nd pilots on Chipmunk aircraft began around this time. Some 108 hours of such flying were recorded during August and another 60 in September. The Chipmunks, WB558, WE660 and WB685, were also used by Nos.99 and 511 pilots. A special flight to Hawarden to collect Vampire spares, which were urgently needed at Oldenburg and Wahn, was made in November.

F/L D Thomas was taxying in at Lyneham after a flight from Luqa in TG509 on 15 January 1954 in high-wind conditions. The aircraft was hit by a fierce gust of wind in excess of 50 knots and despite the efforts of the two pilots, the aircraft weather-cocked through 90°. On the way round, a sharp crack was heard and the rudder cables broke, allowing the rudder to turn through 180°, causing serious damage. Five Operation *Fast Run* flights were made to Singapore during the month and two of these were extended to Iwakuni.

Two special flights to Oakes Field in the Bahamas were

made during February. One routed via Lajes and Bermuda and the other via Lajes, Gander and Goose Bay. March saw one aircraft venture as far as Barbados and two were sent to Gibraltar to pick up some of the survivors from the troopship *Empire Windrush* which had caught fire and sunk in the Mediterranean. Another four Operation *Windrush* flights were made during April. Four special flights to the Bahamas and one to Bahrain were flown during May. S/L A B J Pearson AFC took over as CO on 1 June. Scheduled services to Fayid were also becoming a regular feature of No.53's task with 15 return flights being flown during June, 20 in July and 26 in August.

F/L R H Pitman DSO had now rejoined No.53 for a second tour on the Hastings, having completed a quick refresher course at Dishforth. During the course, he and his crew had almost ended up on the Great North Road when a flapless landing didn't quite work out as planned. While they were waiting for a tug to pull the aircraft off the grass and back on to terra firma, an RAF "Queen Mary" recovery truck carrying two wrecked Gloster Meteors, pulled up on the road. The driver walked over to the perimeter fence and told "Uncle Bob", as he was now affectionately known, that he would come back for them in the afternoon!

The squadron went to Abingdon in September for transport-support training with No.1 Parachute Training School and the 16th Independent Parachute Brigade. Over 1,000 troops were dropped and 25 flights dropped panniers. In addition, jeeps were dropped on 11 occasions. The training continued into October when a similar number of troops, panniers and jeeps were dropped.

One Singapore flight was extended to Fiji in January 1955 to return some Fijian soldiers who had been wounded during the anti-bandit operations in Malaya. Ten crews and five aircraft were detached to Changi in February, returning to Lyneham on 12 March. Two squadron aircraft ferried the groundcrew and equipment of No.217, which had been on a detachment to Malta with its Lockheed Neptunes, back to Kinloss in April. Transport-support training took place again at Abingdon during May. Nearly 900 troops were dropped, 63 supply-dropping flights were made and 26 jeeps were dropped from 13 flights.

Serious unrest in the West Aden Protectorate meant that ten crews and five aircraft had to be sent out to Fayid on 29 June to become part of a force required to fly troops to Aden. Elements of 51 Brigade, including the 1st Battalion Seaforth Highlanders, were moved there for the forthcoming

The crew escaped when TG564/JAZ crashed at Kai Tak, Hong Kong, on 27 July 1953. (Alan Day)

operation. Flights to Fayid continued during July and one aircraft ventured as far as Lagos, Nigeria, in August.

Fifteen flights in support of Operation *Brazen* were made to Nicosia during October. Colonel George Grivas, a regular Greek officer, had entered Cyprus from Greece in secret during 1954 to organise the EOKA movement which had *Enosis*, the union of Cyprus with Greece, as its goal. By the middle of 1955, this campaign had grown into a series of particularly vicious terrorist attacks and the British forces on the island were becoming more and more involved in trying to eradicate the terrorists. By the time that Cyprus had gained its independence in 1960, 105 servicemen, 50 policemen and 240 civilians, 26 of whom were British, had been killed by EOKA.

In the 1956 New Year's Honours list, the MBE was awarded to W/O Allardyce. No.53 flew twelve special slip schedules to Cyprus during January carrying the 1st and 2nd Airborne Battalions. The situation in the Suez Canal Zone was continuing to deteriorate and it was decided in February to keep seven crews on standby in Nicosia on a rotational basis. This standby continued throughout the months of March and April until it came to an end on 12 May. The crews were returned to Lyneham next day.

Hastings WD491 was damaged on 18 June when the port wing tip hit some trees 200 yards short of the runway at Lyneham during a training detail. It is recorded that the starboard wing had been raised in order to avoid a motorcycle on the road which crossed the approach path! The captain was able to overshoot and then landed safely after a normal circuit.

F/L Andy Wilson was awarded the AFC in the Birthday Honours list. At the time, he was detached to Pearce, Western Australia with TG610 and was flying in support of the atom bomb tests being held on the Monte Bello Islands. He and his crew were flying when news of the award came through and so were unaware of the honour. As they neared Pearce for landing, Andy announced that the aircraft had suffered a complete hydraulic failure. This was going to make for a rather tricky landing. The detachment commander called Andy on the radio and told him that, if he could keep his tailwheel exactly on the runway centreline, he would immediately award him the AFC!

S/L A Brown DFC took over as CO on 1 July. It is of interest to note that an Anson C.19 was also now being used for training 2nd pilots, in addition to the Chipmunks.

Throughout June, three crews were kept on a 20-hour standby at Lyneham for possible duty in Cyprus. This continued into July and it looked like things were coming to a head when President Nasser of Egypt nationalised the Suez Canal on 26 July. The canal had been built by the British and the French and had been owned by these two powers since its opening in 1869. King Farouk had been toppled by a military *coup d'état* in 1953 and Lt Col Nasser had come to power after a second *coup* in 1954. He had never been a particular friend of Britain and France and had become even less well disposed towards the two countries when they refused to sell him modern weapons. He had then turned to Czechoslovakia and was soon equipped with modern Soviet aircraft and arms.

The entire squadron was now on standby while the politicians tried to decide what to do about the loss of their canal. Normal route flying and training was disrupted but concentrated support training started on 16 August. The situation continued throughout September and October until three crews were finally sent out to Nicosia at the end of the

Hastings C.1 TG604/GAC at Blackbushe in 1956. (MAP)

month in order to be ready to take part in a possible airborne invasion of the Canal Zone. The British part in the operation was to be carried out using a fairly large force consisting of Hastings and Valetta aircraft

The three aircraft, captained by F/L T C Waugh, F/L L V Dale and F/L W I Warmington, finally dropped elements of the 3rd Battalion, The Parachute Regiment on to El Gamil airfield, Port Said at first light on 5 November. As soon as the troops had secured the airfield and its perimeter, the honour of landing the first Hastings there fell to F/L Dale and his crew. A great deal has already been written about why this operation was a debacle from the political point of view. From the air-support point of view, it also revealed the folly of not having an adequate heavy-drop capability. A few Hastings fitted with heavy beams had been provided but the normal fighting vehicle used by the Parachute Regiment at the time was the Austin Champ and the Hastings could only carry

jeeps. This meant that the troops had to go into battle with war-surplus vehicles and with which they were unfamiliar. The French forces on the other hand, were supported by rear-loading Nord Noratlas aircraft and were supplied with all of the equipment that they needed. Although Egyptian resistance only lasted about 24 hours, British casualties stood at 22 dead and 97 wounded. F/L Waugh and crew flying WJ332 landed at El Gamil on 4 December to collect the dead Parachute Regiment soldiers. Their bodies were taken to Blackbushe for burial at nearby Aldershot.

No.53 Squadron was still on standby in December and special flights were made to Nicosia to replace aircraft and crews and to return casualties recovering after the Suez operation. A special effort was made to get everyone home for Christmas and this was accomplished by Christmas Eve despite a surfeit of fog in UK. The time had come for the squadron to convert on to Beverleys.

The wreckage of TG564 at Kai Tak. (Alan Day)

TG556/B at Topcliffe in 1950. (A. Thomas collection)

CHAPTER 17

TO ABINGDON AND

THE BEVERLEY

Beverley C.1 XB264/C

No.53 moved to Abingdon on 8 January 1957 and took delivery of its first Blackburn Beverley C.1 aircraft during the following month. The Beverley was a large aircraft for the day and had a wing span of 162 feet. It was powered by four Bristol Centaurus 173 eighteen-cylinder, sleeve-valve, two-row radial engines each of which was capable of producing 2,850-hp. (The author remembers once being told that anyone who could satisfactorily describe the sleeve-valve principle, without the use of a working model or a blackboard, was certainly a true genius)! It would be fair to say that the appearance of the Beverley would best be described as "purposeful" and the massive fixed nose-wheeled undercarriage did nothing to improve its aesthetic appeal. However, the aircraft had already proved itself to be extremely rugged and capable of taking large and awkward loads into tiny airstrips. The capacious fuselage was capable of carrying a payload of 44,000 lbs and, in addition, 36 passengers could be accommodated in the tail boom.

The new squadron buildings were constructed alongside the bomb dump situated in the north-east corner of Abingdon airfield. No.53 was so far from any recognisable form of civilisation that its new HQ soon became known as "Sleepy Hollow". No.47 Squadron had received its Beverleys during March 1956 and had settled into the south-east corner of the airfield. The Beverley was too big to go into any of the existing hangars at Abingdon and it was to be some time before a purpose-built hangar was built. This meant that the groundcrew had to carry out all maintenance tasks in the open, for the time being at least.

Beverleys XB291 and XH117 were damaged in a taxying accident on 11 February. In fact, XH117/Z was to have a short career with No.53. Flown by F/L N E H Gilbert, the aircraft left Abingdon as Flt.No.3052 bound for Cyprus at 1102 on 5 March. Just after take-off, a serious fuel leak developed in the vicinity of No.1 engine and because of the fire risk, the engine had to be shut down. An immediate BABS instrument let-down back into Abingdon was begun but No.2 engine also failed at 1,000 feet. The aircraft then lost height, struck a set of power cables and several elm trees before cart-wheeling into a row of houses at Sutton Wick, Drayton about two miles south of the airfield. The aircraft caught fire and F/L Gilbert, F/L R G Wilcox (nav), Sgt G M Woodhouse (sig) and Cpl J L A Spoel (aqm) were killed. F/O M J Ludlam (2nd pilot) and F/L L A Andrew (nav) were seriously injured. The aircraft was also carrying a 47 Squadron slip-crew, three of whom were killed and one

seriously injured. Eight RAF policemen and their dogs, who were travelling as passengers, also died as did two civilians on the ground. Another civilian was injured. The accident had been caused by a non-return valve in the No.1 port fuel tank which had been fitted incorrectly and this had caused the leak and the starvation of fuel to No.2 engine.

Conversion to the Beverley was completed in March and crews completed their categorisation checks during April. A Beverley detachment had been established in Aden during January and the two aircraft out there had been flown by crews drawn from Nos.30 and 47. Three crews from No.53 took over the detachment in April. The Beverleys had been sent out to supplement the airlift capacity of No.84 Squadron based at Khormaksar, which was still equipped with Vickers Valetta C.1s. For the first time, it had become possible to fly bulky items into small "hot and high" air-strips such as Dhala, which was situated near the Yemen border to the north of Aden colony. Not only was Dhala a short strip but it was situated several thousands of feet above sea level and had a mountain range right at the end of the strip. This meant that an overshoot was impossible and the Beverleys landed towards the high ground and took off in the opposite direction. The Aden detachment also operated within the Oman theatre whenever it was necessary.

A lot of continuation and transport-support training went on throughout May. F/L Stan Alden was 35 minutes into a continuation training sortie in XB264/C on 12 June when No.4 engine caught fire. This was rather inconvenient since No.1 had already been shut down for practice! The fire was quickly extinguished but not before substantial damage had been caused to the engine and the surrounding airframe. No.1 engine was re-started and a safe landing was made. During the month, one aircraft was sent to Odiham to be inspected by the Japanese Chief of Air Staff.

Three crews were sent to Oman at the beginning of August and they were soon employed in flying troops and supplies to Sharjah and then on to Firq and Fahud, as part of the operations against rebel tribesmen. F/L Herbert and crew in XB286/S flew three state coaches to the British Trade Fair being held in Helsinki on 31 August. Sgt Norman Biddiscombe, who had been F/L Dale's navigator during the Suez operation, was Mentioned in Despatches.

Beverley XH121/Z was en-route from Luqa to Abingdon at 8,500 feet on 23 September when No.4 engine caught fire some nine hours after take-off. F/L Alden was getting quite used to this sort of thing and quickly got his crew to carry out

The wreckage of XH117/Z at Sutton Wick, two miles south of Abingdon, 5 March 1957. (J.G. Perkins)

the fire drill. This was successful and the flight was continued to Abingdon using the three remaining engines.

The aircraft in Oman had suffered from a poor serviceability record so it was decided to carry out further tropical trials. To this end, XB263, XB287 and XH116 were sent out to Sharjah with a full spares and servicing back-up in October. Representatives from Blackburns and Bristols also went along. The three aircraft performed remarkably well and it was hardly surprising that the conclusion reached was that the Beverley needed experienced technicians and a good spares back-up to operate efficiently!

The year ended with XB291/X making a tour of Rhodesia and South Africa in December. The aircraft was flown by a crew led by F/L Adams and F/L Baker. The Station Commander, G/C Griffiths DFC AFC, joined them as a spare pilot. Also helping out at the sharp-end was the AOC-in-C Training Command, AM Sir Richard Atcherly. Six parachute instructors from No.1 PTS at Abingdon went along to do some jumping in "hot and high" conditions. The aircraft was demonstrated to all interested parties in the two countries and Blackburns sent along several crates of champagne to help "oil the wheels". Needless to say, lots of fun was had by one and all but no new Beverleys were sold.

January 1958 was taken up with transport-support training. During February, five Beverleys from Nos.30, 47 and 53 took part in Operation *Quickstep*. This involved moving nearly 500 men, 10 tons of equipment and 11 Land Rovers and trailers from Abingdon to Tripoli/Idris (previously Castel Benito). F/L J Adams and crew were climbing out of Nicosia in XB283/G on 17 February when No.1 engine caught fire at 3,000 feet. The fire was successfully extinguished and an immediate landing was made back at Nicosia. No.53 also took over the Aden detachment

from No.30 in February.

S/L B W Taylor DFC took over as CO on 3 March. During the month, two Beverleys from Abingdon were sent on a "flag wag" tour of Nigeria. The 53 Squadron aircraft was flown by F/L Stan Alden and crew and it carried a Scottish Aviation Pioneer CC.1. Visits were made to Lagos, Kano, Enugu and Kaduna.

A continuation of Exercise *Quickstep* required seven crews to operate a slip-schedule to Nairobi and also to Aden via Khartoum during April. The Aden Detachment ended in May since No.84 had now received its own Beverleys. A hard core of experienced crews, mainly from Nos.47 and 53, were posted out to Khormaksar to get the operation off to a good start.

Three crews were detached to Nicosia in June and the rest of the squadron started transport-support training at the beginning of July. This programme was rapidly abandoned and replaced by another detachment to Nicosia, which was to stand by there for a possible airlift of troops and equipment to Amman. One aircraft went out to Aden in August and took Folland Gnat F.1 XK768 from there to Kanpur in India. The Nicosia detachments carried on until September after which many squadron members took the opportunity to go on leave.

October was to have been a transport-support training month but this was once again interrupted by events in Jordan. There is a comment in the operations record book which is worthy of note; "Fairly early in the month our retreat from Jordan was seen to be imminent, but until a few days beforehand we had to rely on Scott Gibbons of the *Daily Mail* for details of what we were to do. Unfortunately, his dispatches from Amman proved to be as contradictory as those from other sources"! In the end, F/L Calvert and F/L McDonnell with their crews left for Nicosia on the 20

No.53 Squadron Beverleys in formation. (53 Squadron archives)

October and F/L Earland and F/L FitzRoy took another two Beverleys out next day. Between 25 and 29 October, at least four round trips to Amman were flown by each of the crews. The entry concludes; "Both groundcrews and paratroopers slaved away in an impressively non-trade union fashion and the whole operation went without a hitch. The only incident occurred when a certain aircraft was flying the United Nations-observed route over Syria. The second pilot was goggling at a pair of MiG-17s which had beat up the aircraft when his captain airily urged him not to worry as they were Hunters"!

Another detachment was sent to Aden in November and the rest of the squadron was kept occupied flying freight and aircraft, including Pioneers, Chipmunks and Whirlwinds, out to Cyprus. Two Exercise *Sunspot* flights, rotating Canberra squadrons in Malta, were flown during December and more Chipmunks and Whirlwinds were taken to Cyprus.

The task during January 1959 was curtailed to some extent by snow, frost and fog but a fair amount of transport-support training was flown and three exercises were successfully carried out. Due to sickness, some 2nd pilots had to be borrowed from No.47 in February but the squadron still managed to fly 542 hours during the month. The Russians started to impose restrictions on surface movements into Berlin again during March. Transport Command began sending aircraft, including Beverleys from No.53, down the corridors to Gatow on a frequent basis so that crews could become familiar with the corridor procedures. These flights also showed the Russians that another airlift could soon be mounted should it prove necessary.

Squadron aircraft took part in Exercise *Air Progress* held in the Far East during March. Aircraft from the USAF, RAAF and RNZAF also took part. Among other tasks, the

No.53 Beverleys carried troops from Bangkok to Korat. F/L Kirkbride and crew took part in a static display at Cottesmore in April and were inspected by the Prime Minister, Harold Macmillan. F/O Smedley did a heavy-drop at Valley watched by King Hussein of Jordan. The King later took the right-hand seat at Odiham and flew on a para-dropping sortie with F/L Scorey. Several aircraft took part in Exercise *Mayflight* a V-bomber dispersal exercise, during May. The AOC in C, Transport Command, AM Sir Dennis Barnett inspected Abingdon and No.53 on 26 May.

The staging post at Habbaniya closed on 31 May and this ended almost 45 years of RAF service in Iraq. Relations with the government of General Kassim had been deteriorating for

Sycamore HR.14 XJ384 being loaded on XB267/B

XE289/V at Nicosia, Cyprus. (53 Squadron archives)

some time but relations with Iran had been steadily improving, so staging post facilities in Teheran were now offered instead. During June, it began to look likely that Iraq was planning to invade Jordan. King Hussein made a request for British help so 5,000 troops and their equipment were quickly flown out to Cyprus and then taken on to Amman by a force of Beverley and Hastings aircraft. The troops remained in Jordan for some two months and were then flown home when the situation had stabilised.

June also saw the arrival of flight engineers on No.53. It had originally been thought that there would be no need for a flight engineer on a Beverley crew since only short-haul flying was envisaged and that his duties could easily be performed by the two pilots. However, flights of ten hours and more had become common and among other duties, the co-pilot often had to dash off to hand-pump fresh oil into the thirsty Centaurus engines during flight. It was often said that Beverley crews navigated outbound and then followed the oil slick home! It should be noted that no autopilots were fitted for the first two years of the Beverley's life, so the two pilots were kept busy. As an interim measure, a "director's chair", such as would be found in a film studio, was provided for the flight engineer to sit on. One wit even had the name "Shirley Temple" painted on the back of his chair. After a year or so, a folding jump-seat was fitted behind and between the two pilots.

The German Commander, Brigadier General Kroh, made a visit to Abingdon in July and was flown in a Beverley by F/L Henson. The flight should have included a parachute drop but this had to be cancelled owing to low cloud and rain. The idea that each squadron should devote an entire month to transport-support training in rotation was finally dropped in August. It was then policy for each squadron to carry out some of this training every month.

The largest air-transported NATO exercise to be held so far took place in Norway in September. The exercise was mounted from Bardufoss and the Beverleys were tasked with air-dropping Army vehicles on to a nearby DZ but persistently bad weather meant that they had to be air-landed instead. All aircraft had returned from Norway by the beginning of October. One aircraft transported a complete Ground Controlled Interception station out to Idris on 5 October and the Hunters of Nos.43 and 66 Squadrons were escorted home from El Adem between 28 and 31 October. The year ended with troops being dropped on to Derna airfield in Libya as part of Exercise *Martini* in December.

February 1960 saw the start of Exercise *Starlight*, a major No.38 Group airborne-assault exercise to be held in Libya. Twelve Beverleys took part and several No.225 Whirlwind helicopters were flown out to El Adem by them. A forward operating base was set up at Tmimi, a desert airstrip used by both the Luftwaffe and the RAF during the Second World War. The strip was only 2,400 feet in length and the surface was rather soft. The Beverleys frequently sank in up to their axles but carried on regardless and flew over twenty sorties on some days without difficulty. The exercise went on through March and ended with the troops being flown out of the desert to Derna.

It was around this time that F/L Peter Lewis finally managed to persuade Messrs Arthur Guinness, the famous brewing company, to "adopt" 53 Squadron. Cultural visits to the Park Royal brewery became an essential part of squadron

Paratroopers 'kitting-up' prior to boarding XB289/V at Nicosia. (53 Squadron archives)

life and the Guinness toucan became the No.53 mascot. A special squadron tie, incorporating a toucan fitted with a Beverley tail unit and a bogie undercarriage was designed and it sold like hot cakes.

The Long Service and Good Conduct Medal was awarded to M/Sig Hughes and F/S Mercer in April. The latter was thought to be the oldest serving air quartermaster in the RAF. SAS troops were dropped during Exercise *Jutefire* in Denmark and Exercise *Izarra* in France during May. A fair amount of formation flying practice was also carried out during the month.

On 22 May, XB284/H flown by W/C Taylor and crew, left for Bangui, French Equatorial Africa routing outbound via Luqa, El Adem, Khartoum and Nairobi. The return flight was made via Kano and Idris.

The Belgian Congo became Zaire when independence came on 30 June. Serious unrest broke out during July and a revolt by the indigenous Congolese population against the remaining Belgian colonial authorities spread rapidly into widespread bloodshed. Under the auspices of the United Nations, it was decided to mount an operation to evacuate Belgian nationals from the country. A Beverley detachment drawn from Nos.47 and 53 flew out to Accra in Ghana to take part in Operation *Full Cock*. Shuttle services were flown between Accra and Leopoldville carrying UN troops and their equipment outbound and women and children back. President Nkrumah of Ghana entertained the personnel of Nos.47 and 53 Squadrons and a return match was organised by the two squadrons. At one of these events, F/O Butch Bainton was heard to tell President Nkrumah that the Beverley crews had been "working like blacks"! During August, all of the remaining Belgian troops were flown out of Zaire and replaced by additional UN forces. The Beverleys of 30 Squadron, now based at Eastleigh, Nairobi, were also involved in the operation.

W/C A A J Sanders DFC AFC took over as CO on 10 August. Five days later, he was flying XB268/D on a training flight and had shut down No.1 engine for practice. Whilst carrying out a full-power overshoot, No.3 engine started to fluctuate wildly so he quickly had No.1 re-started and No.3 shut down before making a safe landing back at Abingdon. It was later learned that the No.1 cylinder on No.3 engine had disintegrated. On 20 August, F/L J J Harvey and crew took off from Colerne in XB290/W to drop one-ton containers on to a nearby DZ as part of Exercise *Stormy Petrel*. Ten minutes later, No.3 engine suffered a mechanical failure and had to be shut down. As they were only three minutes flying from the DZ, they carried on with the drop and then took the aircraft back to Abingdon.

Aircraft from Nos.47 and 53 took part in Exercise *Holdfast* based at Sylt during September. The crews were accommodated in tents and the weather was best described as being "bracing". The main part of the exercise consisted of an airborne assault on the Kiel Canal by 16th Battalion, The Parachute Regiment. The failure of No.1 engine caused F/L Hyland and crew in XB263/K to return to Abingdon whilst on a flight to Schleswigland on 25 September.

No.53 took part in Exercise *Natation* directed by No.38 Group based in Malta in October. Paratroopers were flown from Nicosia to Luqa and all were dropped at night, together with vehicles and guns, on a DZ near Bir El Chnem some 30 miles east of Idris. The weather was good to start with but it soon deteriorated into thunderstorms and sand-haze. The thunderstorms eventually reached Malta and produced one-inch hailstones. A full scale tornado and funnel cloud demolished houses and killed several civilians but fortunately just missed Luqa airfield. Some 450 troops of the 1st Battalion Royal Fusiliers from the Malta garrison were also

XH116/Y at Abingdon in September 1961 with the Abingdon Coat of Arms on the nose. (Ray Sturtivant)

moved to El Adem for six weeks of training in desert warfare.

The nose of Beverley XB289/V was damaged by fire at Luqa on 1 October while taking part in this exercise. A faulty refuelling bowser caught fire but prompt action by a fire tender saved the aircraft and another three Beverleys parked nearby. The aircraft was flown back to Abingdon after temporary repairs and then taken north to Brough for proper attention by Blackburns.

Operation *Clipkey*, which consisted of Bomber Command standby duties, commenced during December. Crews and aircraft were kept on a state of constant readiness in case it became necessary for Bomber Command to disperse its V-bomber force to other airfields. In this eventuality, Transport Command aircraft followed along with the supporting ground crews and all of the equipment needed to operate from the new bases. This even included police dogs and handlers. F/L Hugh Crawley of No.53 held the record of getting a Beverley off the ground from a standing start in 35 minutes. To a fighter pilot, this might not seem very fast but it should be remembered that the words *Beverley* and *Scramble* were not synonymous!

Three aircraft each from Nos.47 and 53 joined six aircraft from No.30 in Eastleigh, Nairobi during the month for Operation *Stunsail*. This involved moving the King's African Rifles between Kenya and Uganda. The Minister for Defence, Julian Amery MP, visited Abingdon and 53 Squadron on 13 January 1961. F/L R B Lamb and crew were returning to Abingdon from Odiham in XB286/S on 24 January when airframe vibration coupled with rudder-buffeting was experienced. It was discovered that the rear-starboard escape hatch had become detached and had caused damage to the tailplane and to the starboard fin, but a safe landing was made at Abingdon after carrying out a low-speed handling check.

Beverleys XB287/T and XB290/W, flown by F/Ls Arthur Herbert and Peter Lewis, took part in Exercise *Private Eye* in February. Elections were taking place in Nigeria and the Beverleys were used to carry Nigerian police forces and their vehicles around to potential trouble spots. A Pioneer CC.1, complete with air and ground crew, was carried out from UK and taken to Mubi, a small airstrip situated in northern Nigeria. This aircraft was to be used for observation duties around the area. Other places visited included Maiduguri, Enugu, Kaduna and Iola.

The District Commissioner in Mubi asked S/L Ken Parfit, the detachment commander, if it was possible to have his Land Rover flown to Kano for urgent repairs. This was duly done and it was taken back after the repairs had been made. The same flight carried a quantity of supplies for the District Commissioner, including his annual beer ration. Because of a sandstorm at Kano, the Beverley crew had to spend the night in Mubi and the District Commissioner felt duty-bound to lay on a party for them and anyone else that he was able to round up quickly. By the time that XB290/W finally left for Kano, his annual beer ration had been seriously depleted! Fortunately, it was possible to make good the deficit on a subsequent training flight.

The two Beverleys also flew re-supply flights to the British garrison at Mamfe, British Cameroon. The troops there were patrolling the border in case there was any trouble as a result of the coming independence of neighbouring Nigeria. No.230 Squadron was temporarily based at Mamfe equipped with Twin Pioneer CC.1s. In the end, a plebiscite was held and it was decided that the northern part of British Cameroon should join with Nigeria and the southern part with the newly-independent French Cameroon.

Because of political unrest in the region, the Government of Kenya made an urgent appeal for help during March. Operation *Oliver* was mounted in response and seven

XL130 of the Aden Detachment becomes the first Beverley to land at Beihan while ferrying Ferret scout cars. (F/L R. Kirkbride)

Beverleys, under the command of W/C Sandy Sanders, set sail for Eastleigh airfield near Nairobi. The political situation soon settled down again so it was decided to use the Beverley force to fly relief supply missions to Northern Kenya. No rain had fallen for three years and famine was sweeping the region.

A certain disaster was narrowly averted by an alert flight engineer who noticed that his Beverley had been refuelled at El Adem with kerosene instead of aviation gasolene by mistake, just before take-off! A visit by 27 Foreign Air Attaches was also made during the month and all were taken for a flight in a squadron aircraft.

Exercise *Mayflight*, a Bomber Command dispersal exercise, got under way on 10 May. Eight crews were put on 24-hour shifts, sleeping in the Customs Hall at night and living in the squadron accommodation during the day. On 22 May, F/L Lamb and crew took part in Exercise *Flat Earth*. Two hundred Royal Engineers were parachuted into Robins Lodge near Stanford in Norfolk. After some 33 hours of hard work, a 750 x 50 yard grass airstrip had been constructed. It was then tested by a Beverley landing and taking off again without difficulty. F/O J D Kirk and crew in XM105/P left Coltishall on 5 June for Abingdon. Shortly after take-off, a cylinder head on No.1 engine blew off and the engine caught fire. He was able to return safely to Coltishall and was later awarded a Green Endorsement for his efforts.

On 19 June, Britain's treaty with Kuwait, originally signed in 1899, was repealed. Within the week, Iraq was threatening to invade and the ruler of Kuwait requested assistance. All squadron crews were brought to readiness and flights to Aden were begun. These flights consisted of a twelve-hour sector to El Adem, where the crew had a welcome night stop, before flying another twelve-hour sector to Aden. These long flights were made possible by the use of Military Operating Standards, which allowed an increase in take-off weight of 7,000 lbs to 142,000 lbs.

By early July, ten UK-based Beverleys had been detached to Khormaksar airfield in Aden under the command of W/C Sanders to supplement the Beverleys of Nos.30 and 84 already in the theatre. Operation *Vantage* was mounted and flights were begun to Bahrain and then on to Kuwait. Some 7,000 troops, weapons and vehicles, including Saracen and Ferret scout cars, were carried. Overweight take-offs were once again authorised and several of these were of the "sixpence/half-a-crown variety". One aircraft lost an engine immediately after take-off from Khormaksar and it was unable to climb above 50 feet. A successful landing was made after a rather nail-biting circuit which was flown over the flat desert using the "ground-cushion" effect! Flights were also made in support of the Hunter and Canberra squadrons which had been sent to Kuwait. Although two Beverleys, one each from Nos.30 and 84, were badly damaged by terrorist bombs during the operation, the UK Beverley force survived this highly successful operation intact. Nearly 900 operational hours were flown by the No.53 aircraft and most crews exceeded 100 hours for the month.

No.53 sent four Beverleys to Farnborough to take part in the SBAC air display held in September. The formation was led by S/L E J Strangeway and troops, guns and vehicles were unloaded in two and a half minutes. The aircraft then reversed back to the runway threshold before making a short-field stream take-off.

XB287/T being refuelled at El Adem, Libya. (53 Squadron archives)

The Tana river in Kenya burst its banks in November, causing widespread flooding. Many large towns, including Nairobi, were cut off. A detachment of four Beverleys, under the command of S/L Strangeway, flew out to Nairobi on 16 November, carrying four Bristol Sycamore helicopters on the way. Eastleigh airfield was completely water-logged so operations were flown from the civil airfield at nearby Embakasi. Food was free-dropped from 50 feet in 200-lb sacks. The UK-based Beverley force dropped a total of 7,273 tons of much-needed supplies during the operation. Sincere thanks were sent to all who took part by the Governor of Kenya, Sir Patrick Muir Renison.

F/L A E Herbert, who had left the squadron in September, was awarded the AFC in the 1962 New Year's Honours List. Because of heavy snow, no flying was possible until 4 January when half of No.53 were sent out to Aden as part of Operation *Solomos* to boost the transport capability in the Middle East. Six aircraft ended up based in Bahrain and it was announced that the detachment was expected to last until mid-summer. Those who remained behind at Abingdon were able to make an educational visit to the Guinness brewery at Park Royal.

Under the pretext of having an exercise with the East German Air Force, the Russians tried to close down large parts of the three Berlin air corridors in February. Six No.53 crews were sent out to Wildenrath on 9 February to take part in Operation *Dark Bottle*. Frequent flights were made along all three corridors to Gatow airfield in order to exercise the access rights to Berlin as laid down in the Potsdam agreement. Russian aircraft came close on many occasions and it would be interesting to know what sort of a reaction

their pilots had when they first laid eyes on a Beverley!

F/L Peter Lewis and crew in XB291/X took AVM P G Wykeham DSO OBE DFC AFC, AOC No.38 Group, along with them on 15 February so that he could see the operation at first hand. The Berlin radar controller advised them of an impending interception as they flew along the northern corridor, but because of the foul weather, the Russian pilot stayed at a discreet distance. In fact, the weather was so bad that one aircraft recorded a headwind of 105 knots. Large parts of Hamburg were flooded by huge waves and many people drowned. The Beverleys helped out by flying relief supplies up to Hamburg until 19 February, when they were replaced by Hastings aircraft.

On 17 May, Beverley XL132 of No.242 OCU sustained an engine failure after take-off from Thorney Island. An uncontrollable fire developed and the aircraft crashed into Chichester harbour with loss of life. On 20 May, S/L Strangeway and crew were flying XB288/U from Denmark to Abingdon. An engine failed over the North Sea and an uncontrollable fire rapidly developed. An emergency landing was made at Amsterdam/Schiphol airport where the fire was extinguished by the fire tenders. Both events had been caused by faulty cylinder head hold-down bolts. All Beverleys were grounded until a solution could be found. In the end, the Centaurus 173s were replaced by modified Centaurus 175s.

W/C E W Cropper took over as CO on 16 July. Beverleys from both Abingdon squadrons took part in Exercise *Soft Putty* during August. This major transport-support exercise was mounted from Larissa in Greece and the crews were accommodated in tents, which had cleverly been erected by the Army in a hollow. Whether or not this was done on purpose has never been established, but it was certainly inevitable that torrential rain would fall and many a crew wakened up in the night to find their belongings floating out of the tent! Exercise *Soft Putty* ended on 20 September and was to become known throughout Transport Command as "the great Greek tragedy".

By now it was known that the squadron had been chosen to operate the new Short Belfast C.1s, which were under construction at Sydenham (Belfast Harbour). Several squadron stalwarts paid a visit to the production line and came back visibly impressed. The Belfast was even bigger than the Beverley and it was realised at this early stage that the new monster was going to present a bit of a challenge. During their stay in Ireland, the opportunity was also taken to make a pilgrimage south to the Guinness brewery in Dublin.

It was announced in December that the two Beverley squadrons at Abingdon were to have their unit establishments reduced from eight to six aircraft each. Furthermore, it was also learned that Nos. 47 and 53 were to be amalgamated into one large squadron in the not too distant future. The long-awaited air quartermaster's flying badge finally appeared during the month and Sgts Dorward, Hodgson and Jillings were among the first on No.53 to receive the AQM brevet.

It started to snow at Christmas and a fair amount of it fell over the next few days. The writer was Orderly Officer at nearby Benson on the night that the snow started and that is not a good thing to be doing when the Station Snow Plan swings into action! It also got very cold and most Transport Command airfields were put out of action for a while. Abingdon managed to get operations going again quite quickly and relief flights to drop fodder for the starving farm animals at Hallsdown Farm, Wiveliscombe in Somerset were put in hand on 5 January 1963. Benson was still closed with snow on the runways and desperate efforts were being made to get one of them cleared. This included rounding up all of the Argosy crews and sending them out on to the airfield armed with brushes and shovels. One of the Beverley crews from Abingdon just could not resist flying past them at very low level and dropping a bale of hay!

On 21 January, the 2nd Battalion Green Jackets were flown to El Adem for Exercise *Sandstorm*. F/L Lamb with G/C Sowery, Station Commander at Abingdon, acting as his co-pilot and W/C Cropper as navigator flew XB287/T on from El Adem to Kufra Oasis loaded with petrol and supplies for an Army expedition. Kufra was around 500 miles south of El Adem and it had been used as a base by the Long Range Desert Group during World War II.

On 13 April, Beverley XB268 was being flown by S/L M P Wells and crew on a night low-level cross country exercise from Idris to El Adem. Some thirty miles from El Adem, they were informed of deteriorating weather conditions there but S/L Wells could still see the runway lights clearly and so decided to carry out an ACR7 radar approach. All went well until the aircraft entered an unexpected fog bank just before the airfield. Unfortunately, the aircraft struck the ground during the attempted overshoot and it came to rest 500 yards short of the runway. F/S F Denby, the air quartermaster and SAC D E Marshall, a wireless mechanic from Abingdon, were killed. S/L Wells and the other five crew members were injured, three of them seriously.

Between 6 and 8 May, elements of the Bomber Command V-force were moved from Waddington, Coningsby and Wittering to Yeovilton, Lyneham and Machrihanish as part of Exercise *Mayflight*. The two Beverley squadrons at Abingdon were amalgamated into a larger No. 47 Squadron on 28 June. Miserable weather meant that the parade had to be held in "E" Hangar and so it was that No.53 disbanded and W/C Cropper handed over command to W/C J J Barr, OC No.47.

Shortly afterwards, the author, who was flying Argosys for No.267 at nearby Benson at the time, was rather surprised to see a freshly-painted sign carrying the No.53 Squadron badge being erected outside "C" Hangar there. The plan was that No.53 was to become the third Argosy squadron at Benson with eight aircraft under the command of W/C Maurer. The sign disappeared after a week or so and the eight aircraft were issued to the Argosy squadrons serving overseas instead.

The writer only once got the opportunity to fly a Beverley. This was during Exercise *Triplex West* which was held in Libya during October, 1963. He flew a No.47 Squadron aircraft, from the right-hand seat, to Bomba and back from El Adem. The powered flying controls made it possible to fly the aircraft by use of the finger tips and the landing on the coastal air strip at Bomba was accompanied by the usual spectacular sandstorm, created when the propellers were put into reverse. There was something of an embarrassment when a senior "Trapper" climbed on board at Bomba and sat on the flight deck for the return journey. It was quite a novel experience to be confronted by a TCEU route-checker whilst seated in the wrong type of aircraft! Good humour fortunately prevailed and despite the author's rather agricultural landing back at El Adem, nothing further was said.

XB289/V at Abingdon. (MAP)

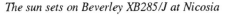
The sun sets on Beverley XB285/J at Nicosia

CHAPTER 18

THE MIGHTY

BELFAST

Belfast XR362 'Samson' on the ramp at night, Brize Norton

Slow progress was being made on the Belfast front. The first aircraft was finally rolled out of its hangar at Sydenham on 5 October wearing the civilian registration G-ASKE. Now marked as XR362, it made its first flight on 5 January 1964 in the capable hands of Denis Tayler, Short Brothers' chief test pilot. He encountered a degree of directional instability during the flight and wisely decided to land the aircraft on the larger airfield at nearby Aldergrove. The problem was solved by fitting a yaw-damper to the rudder.

The Belfast had started life on the drawing board in 1957 as the Short Britannic to be powered by four Bristol Orion turboprop engines. Short Brothers had built most of the Bristol Britannias for the RAF under licence and the proposed aircraft incorporated basic Britannia wing and tail structures, with the wings mounted on top of a large fuselage of completely new design. In its final form, the Belfast had a wing span of 158 feet 9.7 inches and a fuselage length of 136 feet 5 inches. The huge freight bay was more than 80 feet long and was 12 feet square over most of its length. At the time, the only other aircraft in the western world that could accommodate a 12-foot-square load was the Lockheed C-5A Galaxy.

The proposed Bristol Orion turboprop engines had failed to materialise and had been replaced by four Rolls Royce Tyne Mk.101s, each of which was capable of producing around 5,500-shp. The auxiliary power unit was a Mk.120 Artouste gas-turbine, housed in the starboard main undercarriage fairing. The crew entrance door was on the starboard side of the forward fuselage. Immediately opposite was a rest room containing six bunks for use when a double crew was carried. A fully equipped airline-style toilet was situated in the nose, and to the right of the crew door was a spiral staircase which led upstairs to a well-equipped galley. Behind the galley was a balcony known as the "minstrels' gallery" which stretched the width of the fuselage. To this could be attached a "stub-deck" fitted with passenger seats. The flight deck was reached through a corridor leading forward from the galley and it was quite enormous; there was some 7 feet 6 inches of head-room at the back bulkhead. It was considered to be the largest flight deck in the world at the time and one wit once remarked that evasive action on a Belfast consisted of the entire crew unstrapping and then completing two laps of the cockpit!

The second aircraft, XR363, flew on 1 May followed by XR364 on 19 August. All three appeared at the SBAC Show at Farnborough in September and gave an impressive display of disgorging 24 tons of Army vehicles after landing. XR364 was then allocated to the automatic landing trials programme. The prototype left for Spain on 15 October for "hot and high" trials at Torrejon. These included tests at the maximum take-off weight of 225,000 lbs (later increased to 231,000 lbs). These tests were continued at Nairobi in December. Belfast XR364 appeared at the Paris Air Show during June, 1965.

By now it had become obvious that the aircraft was failing to perform to specification with a shortfall of some 10-11%. The main problem was identified as being the excessive amount of drag being generated by the design of the rear fuselage. Shorts went back to the drawing board and re-designed the entire back end and this solved the problem, but not before the first five aircraft had already flown and become known as "Belslows"! All five were subsequently returned to the manufacturer and converted into "fastbacks".

No.53 reformed at Brize Norton on 1 November with W/C A D A Honley as CO. The first Belfast to be delivered to No.53, XR367, arrived on 10 January 1966 flown by Denis Tayler and S/L Andy Wilson AFC. The aircraft was formally handed over on 20 January by Mr Cuthbert Wrangham, chairman of Short Brothers, to AVM R E Craven, AOA Transport Command. RAF crews had been attached to Short Brothers throughout the development of the aircraft and now it was their turn to teach the new crews how to fly the aircraft. S/Ls Bob Reynolds, Tony Picking, "Nobby" Hall and Andy Wilson were ready to get started by the beginning of the year.

Andy Wilson had first served on No.53 in 1946 on Liberators and had later completed a Hastings tour with the squadron. He had also completed an exchange tour with the USAF on the Douglas C-133 Cargomaster, which looked rather similar to the Belfast. The C-133 had obviously made a lasting impression on Andy for he was once heard to remark that the fundamental difference between the two was that our one worked!

Brize Norton airfield was closed soon afterwards so that the runways and taxiways could be re-surfaced. For the next year, all flying took place from nearby Fairford and it was to this airfield that W/C Dan Honley delivered XR368 on 1

Belfast XR364 poses for the camera over Northern Ireland. (Short Bros. & Harland)

May. The squadron celebrated its 50th birthday with a church service and a party on 15 May. On 7 June, XR364 became the largest aircraft yet to make a fully-automated landing. The Belfast was fitted with the Smiths Mk.29 Automatic Flight Control System which was the military version of the Smiths SEP5 Triplex Autoland System as fitted to the HS-121 Trident airliner. The autoland trials consisted of over 800 automatic landings, most of which were made at RAE Bedford. The system was so accurate that the runway started to crack-up with repeated landings being made on exactly the same spot so a random scatter was fed into the system to prevent further damage.

After several months of route-proving trials to such destinations as Aden and Singapore, the first official operational flight took place in October when XR367 moved No.1310 Flight from Atkinson Field, Guyana to Fairford. The cargo consisted of three Westland Whirlwind helicopters and equipment. The aircraft routed via Barbados and Lajes in the Azores, arriving back at Fairford on 7 October. The same aircraft then took two Wessex helicopters from Odiham to Akrotiri in Cyprus. Belfast XR367 then joined XR368 and XR369 on Operation *Tiger Balm* which involved ferrying No.230 Squadron, including eleven Whirlwind helicopters, from Labuan, Borneo back home to UK at the end of the "confrontation" with Indonesia.

During May 1967, XR370 made a 12,000 mile flight to Woomera in Australia in support of ELDO, the European Space Vehicle Launch Development Organisation. The load consisted of part of the French second stage of the Europa launch vehicle, collected from Evreux and the third stage from Munich.

Transport Command was given the new title of Air Support Command on 1 August. W/C Basil Taylor, who had been OC No.53 from 1958 to 1960, was working in the Ministry of Defence at the time and saw this as a golden opportunity to find a new radio callsign to replace the old "RAFAIR" version. He was a keen student of the race horse and, in cahoots with W/C Basil D'Olivera, OC No.216, came up with "ASCOT". This was officially explained away to his seniors when submitted for approval, as standing for "Air Support Command Operational Task". The callsign is still in use to this day!

In November, XR369 and XR371 became involved in the British withdrawal from Aden. Over 400 tons of equipment were flown up to Bahrain and W/C Honley flew the last Belfast sortie carrying the field guns of the Argyll and Sutherland Highlanders. It was around this time that the author, who was flying Argosys for No.105 Squadron in Aden at the time, got his first chance to get close to a Belfast. Despite the fact that the beast had arrived on three engines, he was greatly impressed and made a vow, there and then, to do a tour of duty on 53 Squadron. It was to take another four years of Argosy flying before his wish was finally granted.

S/L M J Middlemist took over as CO on 8 January 1968. W/C Honley went on to become an Air Commodore. On 16 January, a damaged Lightning was flown home inside XR367

XR363 'Goliath' becomes airborne from Brize Norton on a humid day, hence the propeller vortices

from Darwin to the factory at Warton for repair. In March, XR362 flown by F/L Eddie Epps and crew, carried a record payload consisting of 70,682 lbs of Red Cross medical supplies from Changi in Singapore to Saigon in Vietnam. W/C J D Spottiswood took over as CO on 27 May. One Belfast went to Abingdon for the Queen's Review in June and appeared in the static park.

A new record payload of 72,365 lbs of equipment was flown back from a NATO exercise held at Schleswig in April 1969. During June, the aircraft were all named after mythological giants. The name was carried on both sides of the forward fuselage beneath the flight deck windows. On 3 July, W/C Don Spottiswood and crew flew XR370 *Ajax* with yet another record payload of 77,853 lbs from Boscombe Down to Brize Norton. The load consisted of two Abbot self-propelled guns.

The Squadron Standard was presented to No.53 on 4 July by the Chief of the Air Staff, ACM Sir John Grandy GCB KBE DSO, on behalf of Her Majesty The Queen. The Standard was received by F/L Brian Stephens. The parade took place on a bright and sunny day and Belfast XR369 *Spartacus* took pride of place in the foreground, flanked by a B.E.2c (replica), a Hawker Hind, a Dakota, a Hastings and a Beverley. Belfast XR370 made a fly-past and then took former squadron members, including Lt Col Pat Hannay OBE MC who had been the CO from 1937-1939, for a short flight around the local area.

On 28 November, S/L Crawford Simpson and crew flying XR365 *Hector,* took the first Sea King helicopter to be carried in a Belfast to Cold Lake, Alberta for cold-proofing trials. Shortly afterwards, the first Sea King for the Indian Navy was flown to Dabolim, Goa in XR368 *Theseus* by F/L Dave Ferguson and crew. A replacement Whirlwind helicopter for the Royal Navy's Ice Patrol was taken to Punta Arenas, Chile during January 1970. The Belfast routed via Porto Santo, Sal, Recife and Buenos Aires and was flown by a double crew.

In February, W/C Don Spottiswood and crew flew XR370 *Ajax* to Dorval near Montreal to collect a Boeing 747

simulator for BOAC. The simulator had been manufactured by CAE and had to be taken to Heathrow. Although it was not particularly heavy, the simulator was rather large and great care had to be taken to get it to fit into the freight bay. It is interesting to note that the alternative means of transportation was by ship and that would have meant a long delay, since the St Lawrence river is normally frozen over at that time of the year.

A *coup d'état* in Libya by Colonel Mohammer Ghaddafi deposed King Idris and the new regime made it very clear that British Forces were no longer welcome in the country. The withdrawal got under way during March and was complicated by the new rulers only allowing one aircraft movement per day. So that maximum use could be made of this restriction, XR365 *Hector* made a daily flight between El Adem and Akrotiri and frequently carried a payload of around 78,000 lbs. The final flight was commanded by G/C Jock Kennedy AFC, Station Commander at Brize Norton, and the freight bay contained the ACR7 airfield approach radar from El Adem.

Exercise *Bersatu Padu* took place during April. This was the biggest airlift exercise ever undertaken by Air Support Command. Belfasts XR365, XR366, XR369, XR370 and XR371 took part and eight return flights were made between Brize Norton and Singapore. The first aircraft was met on arrival at Changi by the new Station Commander, G/C Dan Honley!

W/C N A D Nugent took over as CO on 1 May. W/C Spottiswood went on to become an Air Vice Marshal. Various aircraft were flown back to UK for the RAF Museum during the year. Supermarine Stranraer RCAF 920 was collected from Vancouver by two Belfasts and Fairey Swordfish HS503, which had also been found in Canada, was flown home. Spitfire F.24 PK683 was returned from Changi.

Her Majesty The Queen visited Brize Norton on 12 March 1971 and was shown over a Belfast by F/L C N Murgatroyd and crew. F/L "Jacko" Jackson and crew flew XR367 from Sharjah to Masirah on 27 June. In the freight bay was a stone-crusher which was needed for construction

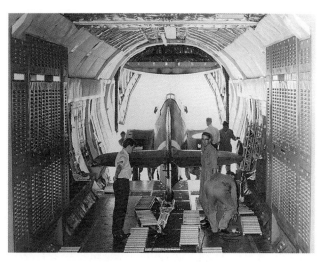

Whirlwind HAR.10 XP357 of No.230 Squadron being loaded into XR369 at Labuan with No.209's Twin Pioneers in the background

Hurricane LF686 being loaded into XR362 for delivery to the National Air & Space Museum at the Smithsonian Institution, Washington, D.C.

work at the latter airfield. It weighed 52,000 lbs and the associated equipment brought the total up to 62,000 lbs. After leaving No.53, F/L Jackson went on to fly the BBMF Avro Lancaster PA474.

One of the very few incidents involving a Belfast took place during July when XR369 *Spartacus* accidentally hit the boundary fence alongside the Bampton road whilst landing at Brize Norton in foggy conditions. Apart from causing some surprise to the car drivers who were patiently waiting at the traffic lights, little damage was done to the aircraft. Legend has it that the Station Commander gave the captain a good ticking-off and awarded him "four faults" as something of a punishment!

No.53's tenth and final Belfast was finally delivered on 3 November. This was XR364 *Pallas* which had been receiving several modifications after completion of its automatic landing trials. The withdrawal of British forces from the Arabian Gulf was taking place at this time. On 15 December, XR370 *Ajax* became the last RAF aircraft to leave Sharjah, UAE and XR363 *Goliath* was the last to leave Muharraq, Bahrain. Both aircraft carried the respective Station Commanders.

For some time W/C Neil Nugent and several of the squadron stalwarts had dreamed about getting all ten Belfasts airborne in formation at the same time. Now that XR364 had been delivered, the plan became possible for the first time. The AOC-in-C, Air Marshal Sir Harry Burton, gave his blessing and so it was that all ten took off one after the other into a gloomy sky on 23 December to join up above the clouds at 7,000 feet. Sadly, the spectacle of a complete production line flying past in formation was largely hidden from the spectators on the ground, but a Jet Provost from Little Rissington flew alongside and several photographs were taken to record the event for posterity. This was the only occasion that all ten Belfasts were to be found at Brize Norton at the same time.

From the author's point of view, 1972 got off to a splendid start. After ten years of flying the Argosy, he was posted in to No.240 OCU at Brize Norton on 3 January to commence training on the Belfast. It was a most comprehensive course and every last nut and bolt was discussed at length. Many months later, the course culminated in a "global trainer" which visited Akrotiri, Masirah, Gan, Tengah, Hong Kong, Guam, Wake Island, Honolulu, McClellan AFB, California, Charleston AFB, South

Carolina, Gander and so back to Brize having flown all the way around the world "eastabout".

On 23 March, XR367 had just landed at Brize Norton and was taxiing round behind the control tower when the local controller noticed that half of the elevator was hanging off! An elevator hinge bracket had failed and all Belfasts were immediately grounded. It was then found that the Britannia had suffered a similar problem in the past and that they had been fitted with modified brackets. By using Britannia spares, all ten Belfasts were back in the air within a few weeks.

S/L Tony Woodford and crew left Fairford on 29 May flying XR367 *Heracles* in support of a demonstration tour being made by Concorde 002, G-BSST. A 10 Squadron VC10 also went along and the tour took them to Akrotiri, Teheran, Masirah, Bangkok, Singapore, Hong Kong, Manila, Darwin, Williamtown, Sydney, Melbourne, Madras, Bombay, Bahrain and Toulouse. Almost 108 hours had been flown by the time XR367 returned to Brize Norton. S/L Woodford later went on to become an Air Vice Marshal.

W/C M J Middlemist returned to No.53 and took over as CO on 12 June. F/L Dave Ferguson took XR369 *Spartacus* to Heathrow on 30 June and uplifted a JT9 engine needed for a Pan American Boeing 747 at Frankfurt. Air Support Command was absorbed into Strike Command on 1 September and No.46 Group was re-formed at Upavon to look after the strategic transport force.

During the year, a Belfast collected Supermarine Seagull V A2-4 from Australia for the RAF Museum. This aircraft was exchanged for Spitfire XVI TE384 which was taken there on the outbound journey. The wreckage of a Fairey Battle was also collected from Iceland. No.53 also supplied airlift capacity for the withdrawal from Malta and made several flights to Belize in support of the British forces there. These latter flights usually carried Puma helicopters from Odiham or Harriers from Wittering.

One of the first major events of the year on the 53 Squadron social calendar was the Burns Supper, held as close as possible to 25 January. These suppers were momentous occasions and seats were eagerly sought after. In fact, non-squadron members often had to wait three years for a seat. The evening usually ended in riotous fashion and the medical staff in Sick Quarters soon learned to be on special standby whenever No.53 was holding such an event, just in case their talents were required!

Hunting H.126 blown-flap research aircraft XN714 being loaded into XR366 for delivery to NASA at Moffett NAS, California, 31 April 1969

A stone-crusher weighing 52,000 lbs being loaded into XR367 at Sharjah for delivery to Masirah by F/L Jackson and crew, 27 June 1971

S/L Bob Brighton with the author as co-pilot and W/C Malcolm Niddlemist as navigator, set off for West Freugh on a training flight in XR368 *Theseus* on 16 May 1973. The flight had a secondary purpose; to collect Lt Col Pat Hannay OBE MC and his car and to deliver them in some style to Brize Norton for a visit to his old squadron.

A major NATO exercise was held in California during May and No.53 was tasked with carrying several Scorpion tracked armoured reconnaissance vehicles from Germany to Moffett NAS near San Jose. Since these vehicles were very heavy, the journey had to be completed in relatively short sectors and several slip-crews were pre-positioned at points along the proposed route. As something of an illustration of how this sort of operation worked, F/L Eric James and the author picked up XR368 *Theseus* at Brize Norton when it arrived from Germany and flew it on to Gander via Keflavik and Stephenville, Newfoundland (weather diversion) on 17 May. On 19 May, XR362 *Samson* was taken on to Offutt AFB, Nebraska via McGuire AFB, New Jersey and then XR363 *Goliath* to Moffett NAS on 22 May. Next day, this crew flew XR363 back to Offutt via Buckley ANGB, Denver and then slept in the bunks while another crew took the aircraft on to Gander via Andrews AFB, Maryland. At Gander, a fresh crew got on board to fly the aircraft back to Brize Norton. The inbound operating crew then took to the bunks and F/L James and crew spent the rest of the journey on the stub-deck.

It was often said that at least one 53 Squadron Belfast was to be found on the other side of the Atlantic on just about every day of the year. Certainly, the aircraft caused great interest everywhere it went and many interesting comments were made by our American brothers. One air traffic controller asked "what it was" and on being told that "it" was a Short Belfast, made the famous reply, "Jeez, if that's a Short Belfast, I'd hate to see the long one!" An airline captain taxying past XR364 *Pallas* at Dallas/Love asked, "Say, what kind of Pallas is that? A Gin Pallas?" As often as not, the description "Charlie Two Sixty" seemed to keep most inquisitors happy.

F/L Colin Bond and the author arrived at Gander from Forbes AFB, Kansas on 10 June. The crew were told that an urgent request for help had been made to the Ministry of Defence by the Canadian Department of Transport. A new office building was badly needed at Goose Bay, Labrador and the sectioned building was sitting at St Johns awaiting

transportation by sea. Unfortunately, the sea around Goose Bay was still frozen over and looked like staying that way for the rest of the year. The crew took XR367 down to St Johns the following morning and flew the new building, weighing some 77,000 lbs, to Goose Bay later in the day. The building was complete in every detail right down to the sanitary arrangements and a flag pole!

Towards the end of June, it was time to recover the Scorpion tracked vehicles from California and return them to Germany. The author's log book shows that he operated as F/L Harley Hall's co-pilot in XR364 *Pallas* from Andrews AFB to Moffett NAS on 23 June. Then XR367 *Heracles* was flown to Washington/Dulles via Tinker AFB, Oklahoma and finally, XR370 *Ajax* to Gander before climbing into the bunks for the rest of the journey.

The Brazilian government decided to hold an international air show at San José dos Campos at the end of September. Hawkers decided to exhibit their two-seat Harrier demonstrator G-VTOL and arranged for it to be flown to Rio de Janeiro inside CL-44 Guppy N447T, operated by Transmeridian. They also asked the Ministry of Defence if they could borrow a single-seat "fighting" Harrier and this request was duly sanctioned. So it was that S/L John Colston, the author and crew, lifted off Wittering's runway bound for Sal in the Cape Verde Islands on 10 September. In the freight bay was a No.1 Squadron Harrier on its specially-designed cradle. After a night stop at Sal, the journey was continued to Recife and then on to Sao Paulo/Congonhas, where the Harrier was to be re-assembled. S/L Colston and crew returned via Rio and Sal to Brize Norton.

This wasn't quite the end of the episode though. Just as the Harrier was about to make its first flight after re-assembly, an urgent message was received to say that it had been grounded! Two recent Harrier crashes had been found to have been caused by faulty nuts on the compressor casing migrating into the innards of the engine and the Sao Paulo Harrier was unfortunately fitted with the same kind of nuts! The aircraft was therefore dismantled and taken back to Wittering in another Belfast.

No.53 was presented with the Berlin Gold Cup on 6 December at a ceremony held at Brize Norton in the presence of AOC No.46 Group, AVM Sir Denis Crowley-Milling KCB CBE DSO DFC. The Berlin Gold Cup was presented to the RAF by an anonymous German donor in grateful thanks for the help given by the transport squadrons of the RAF to

The squadron's Sixtieth Birthday Party, 15 May 1976. Brian Trubshaw flies past in Concorde G-BOAC with XR365 'Hector' in the foreground. (David Steel)

the residents of Berlin during the Airlift. The cup was presented to W/C Middlemist by the Mayor of Berlin, Herr Klaus Schutz. This award was made to the most efficient squadron in No.46 Group.

During the afternoon of 5 January 1974, XR367 *Heracles* under the command of S/L John Colston and with the author in the right-hand seat took off into a clear blue sky from Cold Lake, Alberta. As the name suggests, it was indeed very cold with the surface temperature hovering around -36°C. The scheduled destination was Gander in Newfoundland where a slip-crew was waiting to take the aircraft on to Brize Norton.

The two navigators, F/Ls Dick Stanton and John Copsey, had calculated that should the strong tail winds forecast for the flight actually appear, it would be possible to make it to Brize Norton in one hop. Since the aircraft was suffering from annoying hydraulic problems, S/L Colston decided to go along with the idea so that repairs could be made back at base. The decision on whether to continue across the Atlantic would be made approaching Gander and the slip-crew there was told to stand by in case they were needed.

It soon got dark and the author was on watch about two hours after take-off while S/L Colston had dinner back in the galley. The navigators announced that it was time to climb up from 25,000 feet to 27,000 feet and this was duly dialled-up on the automatic flight control system but nothing happened. On the third time of asking, the aircraft suddenly reared violently upwards and the airspeed died off at an alarming rate. The author tripped out the automatics and discovered, to his horror, that the control column was frozen solid fore-and-

aft! With a great sense of relief, he quickly discovered that the elevator trim control wheel was still free and working in the correct sense. At a speed approaching 120 knots, the nose suddenly lowered and a very rapid rate of descent quickly built up!

By now, John Colston had realised that all was not well and so abandoned his repast and managed to get back into his seat in the flight deck. Gradually, it became possible by experimentation to dampen down the pitch oscillations to a relatively-comfortable plus or minus 700 feet per minute. By this time, it was noticed that M/E Dave Frost had sustained a gashed forehead caused by the author's clip-board, which had been speedily discarded in his attempt to stop *Heracles* from falling out of the sky!

The surface temperature at Gander was around -25°C and it had become obvious that successfully landing a Belfast with the main elevator controls frozen solid, was likely to be a highly problematical exercise. The nearest pool of warm air was a long way away around Bermuda, so the decision was made to try to reach Brize Norton. After six or seven hours of flying the aircraft on the trim wheel, it became possible to re-engage the automatics.

Fortunately, the tail winds appeared as forecast and after a successful Atlantic crossing, a very gradual descent was begun. The elevator controls finally thawed out whilst passing over Lyneham at around 2,000 feet and a normal landing at Brize Norton was made by the author after a PAR let-down. The flight had taken 13 hours and 30 minutes and a new distance record for a Belfast of 4,303 nautical miles had been set. It was a record that the crew could well have done without!

Transport line-up at Brize Norton in 1974: Belfast C.1 XR362, VC.10 C.1 XV108, Britannia C.2 XN404, Hercules C.1 XV297 and Comet C.4 XR398

It was later discovered that the Britannia had suffered from this sort of trouble before and that the problem had been solved by fitting a simple electric fan-heater, which blew hot air over the control-runs in the rear fuselage whenever it was needed. Many of us were left wondering why nobody had thought to install such a device in the Belfast until after this and one other similar incident had occurred.

F/L Robin Gulliver, the author and crew set off for Filton in XR369 *Spartacus* on 3 April. The British Aircraft Corporation needed to have a mobile Rapier missile display unit taken out to Zurich. The unit was housed in the rear part of an articulated truck and it only just fitted into the freight bay. Because of Switzerland's neutral status, a special clearance had to be obtained to take a military aircraft into the country. The crew had to wear civilian clothes and Robin Gulliver's business suit and "accoutrements" clearly impressed the interested crew of the Aeroflot An-12 which was parked alongside at Zurich!

On 20 July, Turkish armed forces invaded the northern part of Cyprus. In the ensuing emergency, some 22,000 people from 50 nations found themselves stranded in the country. A major airlift was mounted to get them off the island using Akrotiri as the main base. No.53 flew 37 Belfast sorties, carrying urgently needed supplies on the outbound sectors. Seats were lashed down on top of the cargo so that the aircraft could be used in the passenger role on the return journey to Brize Norton.

Many of the evacuees groaned when they realised that they were destined to be incarcerated in the freight bay of a Belfast, rather than in a VC10 or a Britannia, but most of them were to be pleasantly surprised. Seats were fitted in the rear of the aircraft where it was quiet. Enough space was left in front so that the older children could go for a walk or even play football. Navigators became entertainment officers and arranged visits to the flight deck while loadmasters became adept at heating up baby bottles in the hot-cups and then putting the little darlings down to sleep in the bunks while the parents had a well-earned rest. The only near-casualty was F/L Dave Carter who almost suffered a cardiac arrest when he opened the toilet door to find a stunning Swedish blonde

lady already in residence. She did not have a stitch of clothing on and was trying to rid herself of the grime collected during her stay at Akrotiri!

F/L Tony Harper and crew took XR367 *Heracles* to Chivenor on 3 September to collect a mobile ACR7 airfield approach radar. The equipment was then delivered to Biggin Hill so that some form of radar control would be available for the popular Biggin Hill Air Fair. W/C C A Simpson AFC took over as CO on 30 September.

It was announced in the March Defence Review that the two Britannia squadrons at Brize Norton were to be disbanded during 1975. With the withdrawal of British forces from the Middle and Far East, some defence cuts were perhaps inevitable and although it would be sad to see Nos.99 and 511 disband, at least No.53 had survived the axe; for the time being at least.

A fairly spectacular Belfast incident occurred at Brize Norton on 16 June 1975. The author, who was on the third trip of his captain's conversion course, was being shown how to do a two-engined landing by S/L "Paddy" Wilson when a lot of vibration was felt shortly after touch-down. All 16 main-wheel tyres of XR367 had burst for no apparent reason and the runway was blocked for about five hours! No fault could be found by the engineers and things were beginning to look a bit black for S/L Wilson and the author when S/L Bob Brighton got through another 16 tyres during a high-speed taxying test two days later! Needless to say, the runway was blocked for another five hours. F/L Trevor Newton lost another four or five tyres during a more sedate taxying test on 20 June and only then was it discovered that there was a very obscure fault in the brake system of XR367 which made it possible for main hydraulic pressure to by-pass the anti-skid brake units.

Switzerland was visited again on 31 July when the writer and crew collected another Rapier display unit from Geneva and took it back to UK in XR370 *Ajax*. The first part of the Defence Cuts to affect Brize Norton took place on 31 August when No.511 was disbanded.

Towards the end of October, Guatemala again made territorial claims on Belize and armed intervention began to

The Disbandment Parade at Brize Norton on 14 September 1976 with Belfast XR368 'Theseus' as a backdrop. (David Steel)

look likely. It was decided to reinforce the British forces there, so No.53 put together a slip-pattern to transport three No.33 Puma helicopters and elements of the RAF Regiment with vehicles. Ferret scout-cars were also flown out for the Army. As far as can be recalled, twelve Belfast round trips were flown and every single one went without a hitch. This was particularly satisfying since the airfields at Gander and Nassau appeared to be covered in unserviceable C-130s!

The author's log book shows that he operated XR362 *Samson* to Gander with F/L Dave Carter in the right seat on 5 November. Then XR365 *Hector* was taken to Nassau on 8 November. XR371 *Enceladus* was taken to Belize and back to Nassau on 9 November as was XR362 the next day. The return flight to Brize Norton was made in XR366 *Atlas* via Bermuda on 12 November. Six Harriers from No.1 Squadron were also flown out to Belize from Wittering using air-to-air refuelling. The Harriers were to become No.1417 Flight and the Pumas, No.1563 Flight.

The year at Brize Norton ended on a sad note when No.99 disbanded on 31 December. All Britannias were flown out to Kemble and St Athan for disposal and the landscape at Brize was never to be the same again. Although unkind souls had been known to remark that the reason why the Britannias were known as the "Whispering Giants" was because they had nothing to shout about, the aircraft had given sterling service to the RAF throughout their lives and would be sadly missed.

F/L Paddy Aiken and crew in XR365 *Hector* collected another 747 simulator for British Airways from Dorval during January 1976. This one was larger than the one collected six years before and proved to be very difficult to load. It was eventually shoe-horned in with only one inch to spare on either side and was duly delivered safely to Heathrow.

The beginning of the end for No.53 Squadron was announced in the Defence White Paper published in March. The Belfasts were to be gradually taken out of service and the

squadron finally disbanded in September. The announcement was received with a great feeling of disbelief, not only by the members of the squadron but also by a lot of people in the Army who were left wondering how they were going to get their large pieces of equipment moved around by air in the future. This most miserable of months also saw the closure of Gan in the Maldives which had been one of the more attractive staging posts in the RAF.

In the meantime, unusual loads continued to be carried. The author and crew took a large vehicle which contained a complete colour TV outside-broadcast unit to Dubai on 16 April in XR369. It was only possible to get the vehicle into the freight bay by partially deflating the tyres. The owners were very pleased to see their new toy delivered so quickly and without damage but did reveal that they had paid £56,000 for the privilege. Another Belfast delivered a Commando helicopter to Doha in Qatar at the same time and the going rate for that was around £54,000. It was good to know that at least one RAF squadron was making some money for the government of the day and this was no doubt one of the main reasons that it wanted the Belfast taken out of service!

The first Belfast to be retired was XR362 *Samson* which was taken to Kemble on 27 April. Despite having the Sword of Damocles hanging over it, No.53 decided to celebrate its 60th birthday in suitable fashion. A formal lunch was held in Gateway House on 15 May for present and past members and guests and this was followed by a flying display. The fly-past included the BBMF Lancaster with a Hurricane and a Spitfire, a Belfast, a VC10, an Argosy and a Phantom. Brian Trubshaw even managed to borrow a Concorde for the occasion and gave a splendid display. A cocktail party was held in the evening and this was followed by a buffet dance which went on into the wee small hours.

Flt.No.3404 left Brize Norton on 25 May bound for Gander and then on to Washington/Dulles airport. Part of the load consisted of the Magna Carta, mounted on a stone plinth.

The Squadron Standard arriving at Edinburgh on 18 September 1976. Colour Party, left to right, was Sgt Malcolm Girling, F/L Stan Matthews, M/E John Ward and F/S Roy McMullen

This precious document was delivered safely for display in Washington DC. XR364 *Pallas* was taken to Kemble to die on 3 June and was followed by XR365 *Hector* on 19 August.

The writer took XR371 *Enceladus* to Kemble on 26 August. This aircraft was to survive and is now to be found in the Aerospace Museum at RAF Cosford. The privilege of making the last Atlantic crossing by an RAF Belfast fell to author and his crew when they arrived back at Brize Norton from Albuquerque, New Mexico, Ottawa and Gander in XR367 *Heracles* on 5 September.

The disbandment parade was held on 14 September in the presence of AVM P G K Williamson CBE DFC, AOC No.38 Group. It was a suitably wet and miserable day and the parade had to be held in the massive base-servicing hangar. Belfast XR368 *Theseus* proudly faced the parade through the open hangar doors whilst the colours were paraded by F/L Stan Matthews to music supplied by the band of the 2nd Battalion, The Parachute Regiment. It was a very sad day; No.53 Squadron had always been a very special squadron.

The next day turned into something of a wake. F/L Tomkinson, who was known to all and sundry as "Tomkinops", had arranged to fly *Theseus* to Kemble and had decided to take about 25 kindred spirits along for the ride. These included a Customs Officer and a lady Movements Officer. Air traffic control at Kemble asked him to hold off to the west of the airfield at low level while they recovered some fighter aircraft, so it was decided to visit the "Tomkinops"

abode in Dursley. The main street of that town was closely inspected in both directions from a pretty low level before returning to Kemble.

The Red Arrows arranged a bus to take everyone down to the "Wild Duck" and then the wake moved on to the home of F/L Bernie Burton, who happened to live nearby. By now, the telephone lines at Kemble and Brize Norton were humming as the good citizens of Dursley tried to find out why they had been under attack by the RAF. The only thing that saved the careers of the operating crew was that the vast majority of the callers had rung to say that they hadn't seen the RAF for years and had enjoyed the flying display! The survivors of the wake arrived back at Brize Norton at 0300 in the crew bus, which had judiciously been re-scheduled by the caring and sympathetic MT Section at Brize Norton.

On 16 September, XR366 *Atlas* made a farewell fly past around Lyneham, Upavon, Odiham, Benson and Abingdon. It had been decided to keep XR366 at Brize Norton with a crew so that it could be used as a demonstration aircraft for any potential customers. The politicians had made it clear that the aircraft was only to be seen at Brize or Lyneham, but No.53 had other ideas. The aircraft was positioned outside the passenger terminal on 18 September and the Squadron Standard, carried by F/L Stan Matthews, was paraded on board. W/C Crawford Simpson and crew with 100 squadron members and dependents on board, set off for Edinburgh!

The "powers that be" had stated that the Squadron

Standard should be laid-up in St Clement Danes in London but that did not seem to be a fitting resting place for a Scottish standard. No.53 had therefore made arrangements to lay the colours up in St Giles Cathedral in Edinburgh. Four Bulldogs from the East Lothian UAS made a fly past at Edinburgh airport as the Squadron Standard was paraded off the aircraft.

The laying-up ceremony took place in St Giles Cathedral next day, 19 September 1976. It was also Battle of Britain Sunday and the band of the RAF Regiment from Catterick, the birthplace of the squadron, was in attendance. The No.53 Squadron Standard was paraded into St Giles flanked by those of Nos.43 and 111 based at Leuchars. The lesson was read by Lt Col Pat Hannay and Mrs Alison Henderson, the widow of Major G Henderson who had been CO from 1917-1919, attended as a guest of honour. A great feeling of sadness was felt afterwards by all as they flew back to Brize Norton in *Atlas*.

No.53 Squadron members and families together for the last time before boarding XR366 'Atlas' for the return flight from Edinburgh to Brize Norton

Postscript:

Belfast XR369 *Spartacus* was flown to Kemble on 30 September leaving XR366 at Brize in the capable hands of F/L Ian Laurie and F/L Trevor Newton. The writer went off to become the RAF Liaison Officer in Colombo, Sri Lanka for a few months but was able to scrounge two more flights in XR366 on his return, the last of which took place on 25 February 1977. The chances of ever flying a Belfast again looked pretty slim but he found himself getting airborne in *Theseus*, now marked as G-BEPS, from Manston on 14 February 1978 with Trevor Newton and Colin Fielder. This was the beginning of the Belfast's career as a civilian freighter and the temptation to stay with it was very high. It is suffice to say that the lure of flying Sir Freddie Laker's DC 10s and joining the twelve other members of the 53 Squadron "Belfast mafia" already there, proved to be too strong!

The Belfast continues to give sterling service to Heavylift Cargo Airlines to this day and one of their biggest customers has been the Ministry of Defence! In particular, the aircraft was frequently used during the Falklands War and a lot of bulky items were got to where they were needed speedily, rather than having to rely on slow sea transport.

The Squadron Standard at rest in St. Giles Cathedral, Edinburgh, after the laying up ceremony

Lt Col Pat Hannay OBE MC, CO from 1937 to 1939, when he presented his claymore to the squadron, May 1973

Colour Party: Sgt Malcolm Girling, F/L Stan Matthews, M/E John Ward, F/S Roy McMullen

THE SQUADRON BADGE

During the latter half of 1939, His Majesty King George VI approved the badge of No.53 Squadron. Early in 1938, the then CO of the 1st Cameron Highlanders, Lt Col D N Wimberley MC, had put forward the suggestion that "some form of unofficial affiliation between a regiment of the Army and a squadron of the RAF might further cement those ties, already strong, between the two Services. This affiliation if agreed, would inevitably lead to those little exchanges of courtesy which go so far to add that mutual trust, respect and friendship felt by one unit for another". This is of no little interest because the Squadron Badge is based on that of the Queen's Own Cameron Highlanders to which regiment Major A P C Hannay MC, OC No.53, belonged. Great credit for the realisation of this ideal must be accorded to the Air and Army Councils for so sponsoring the original suggestion of Lt Col Wimberley and allowing it to take shape. Credit is also due to Major General N J G Cameron, who was once Colonel of the Cameron Highlanders, for his very practical help and also to the Chester Herald, Mr J D Heaton-Armstrong, who took great pains not only to further the original project but to provide a badge of which both 53 Squadron and the Queen's Own Cameron Highlanders would always feel proud.

THE SQUADRON STANDARD

The Squadron Standard was presented to No.53 Squadron by the CAS, ACM Sir John Grandy GCB KBE DSO, on behalf of Her Majesty Queen Elizabeth, on 4 July 1969. The Standard was laid-up in St Giles Cathedral, Edinburgh on 19 September 1976 and is to be seen there to this day hanging proudly alongside that of No.603 (City of Edinburgh) Squadron. The eight Battle Honours chosen to flank the Squadron Badge on the Standard are:

Western Front	1916-1918	Fortress Europe	1941
Ypres	1917	Biscay	1941-1944
Messines	1917	Atlantic	1941-1945
Dunkirk	1940	Normandy	1944

Past Commanding Officers at the Disbandment Parade, 14 September 1976
Left to right: W/C B.W. Taylor DFC, G/C A.D.A. Honley AFC, G/C J.D. Spottiswood AFC, W/C M.J. Middlemist.
(David Steel)

APPENDIX I

No.53 Squadron Commanding Officers

Captain A C Wright	17 Jun 1916	Sqn Ldr S A Sharpe	3 Jun 1946
Major C S Wynne-Eyton	14 Oct 1916	Flt Lt D H Phillips	13 Jun 1946
Major G Henderson	20 Nov 1917	Wg Cdr P Fleming	1 Dec 1946
Captain G B A Baker	19 Jan 1919	Wg Cdr G H Gatheral	8 Jul 1947
Captain F H Davies	3 Feb 1919	Sqn Ldr M B Cooper	11 Dec 1947
Major G H B McCall	11 Feb 1919	Sqn Ldr P C Lemon DSO DFC	1 Jun 1948
Major A P C Hannay MC	28 Jun 1937	Sqn Ldr J P Trant	2 Aug 1949
Sqn Ldr W B Murray	21 Apr 1939	Sqn Ldr B H Worts	12 May 1952
Wg Cdr E C T Edwards	1 Jun 1940	Sqn Ldr A B J Pearson AFC	1 Jun 1954
Wg Cdr W B Murray DFC	7 Sep 1940	Sqn Ldr A Brown DFC	1 Jul 1956
Wg Cdr G W P Grant	19 Mar 1941	Sqn Ldr B W Taylor DFC	3 Mar 1958
Wg Cdr J R Leggate	23 Feb 1942	Wg Cdr A A J Sanders DFC AFC	10 Aug 1960
Wg Cdr H R A Edwards AFC	4 Feb 1943	Wg Cdr E W Cropper	16 Jul 1962
Wg Cdr R T F Gates AFC	30 Nov 1943	Wg Cdr A D A Honley	1 Nov 1965
Wg Cdr N B Littlejohn OBE	21 Aug 1944	Sqn Ldr M J Middlemist	8 Jan 1968
Wg Cdr A R Holmes RCAF	8 Nov 1944	Wg Cdr J D Spottiswood	27 May 1968
Wg Cdr D MacKenzie	24 Jun 1945	Wg Cdr N A D Nugent	1 May 1970
Wg Cdr A Frame	17 Dec 1945	Wg Cdr M J Middlemist	12 Jun 1972
Wg Cdr D F Hyland Smith DFC AFC	1 Mar 1946	Wg Cdr C A Simpson AFC	30 Sep 1974

APPENDIX II

No.53 Squadron Stations

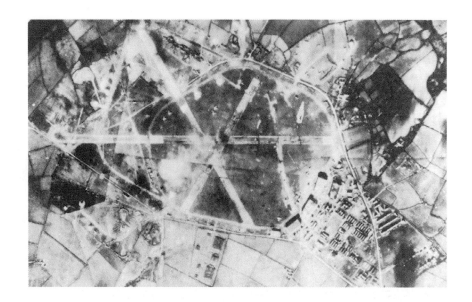

St. Eval airfield in 1943

15 May 1916	Founded at Catterick
11 Dec 1916	To Farnborough
26 Dec 1916	To St Omer
4 Jan 1917	To Bailleul
1 Feb 1918	To Abeele
21 Feb 1918	To Villeselve
22 Mar 1918	To Allonville
23 Mar 1918	To Fienvillers
25 Mar 1918	To Boisdinghem
6 Apr 1918	To Abeele
13 Apr 1918	To Clairmarais
11 Sep 1918	To Abeele East
21 Oct 1918	To Coucou
5 Nov 1918	To Sweveghem
16 Nov 1918	To Seclin
24 Nov 1918	To Reumont
28 Nov 1918	To Laneffe
18 Mar 1919	To Old Sarum
25 Oct 1919	Disbanded at Old Sarum
28 Jun 1937	Reformed at Farnborough
8 Apr 1938	To Odiham
18 Sep 1939	To Plivot
11 Oct 1939	To Poix
19 May 1940	To Crecy
19 May 1940	To Lympne
20 May 1940	To Andover
31 May 1940	To Eastchurch
13 Jun 1940	To Gatwick
3 Jul 1940	To Detling
20 Nov 1940	To Thorney Island
8 Feb 1941	To Bircham Newton
19 Feb 1941	To St Eval
2 Jul 1941	To Bircham Newton
19 Oct 1941	To St Eval
17 Dec 1941	To Limavady

20 Jan 1942	To North Coates
17 May 1942	To St Eval
5 Jul 1942	To Quonset Point, Rhode Island
1 Aug 1942	To Waller Field, Trinidad
22 Aug 1942	To Edinburgh Field, Trinidad
23 Nov 1942	To Quonset Point
31 Dec 1942	To Davidstow Moor
11 Feb 1943	To Docking
17 Mar 1943	To Bircham Newton
29 Apr 1943	To Thorney Island
25 Sep 1943	To Beaulieu
3 Jan 1944	To St Eval
7 Sep 1944	To Reykjavik
29 May 1945	To St Davids
17 Sep 1945	To Merryfield
10 Dec 1945	To Gransden Lodge
28 Feb 1946	Disbanded at Gransden Lodge
1 Mar 1946	Reformed at Upwood by renumbering No.102 Squadron
15 Jun 1946	Disbanded at Upwood
1 Dec 1946	Reformed at Netheravon by renumbering No.187 Squadron
11 Dec 1947	To Waterbeach
24 Jun 1948	Detached to Wunstorf for Berlin Airlift
29 Jul 1948	Detached to Fassberg
22 Aug 1948	Detached to Lübeck
1 Aug 1949	To Topcliffe and detached to Schleswigland
7 Oct 1949	Detached to Wunstorf
13 Dec 1949	Detachment returned to Topcliffe
9 Feb 1951	To Lyneham
8 Jan 1957	To Abingdon
28 Jun 1963	Disbanded at Abingdon
1 Nov 1965	Reformed at Brize Norton
14 Sep 1976	Disbanded at Brize Norton

A Hawker Hector of No.53 Squadron. (Philip Jarrett collection)

APPENDIX III

Aircraft used by No.53 Squadron

* Indicates aircraft lost or had an accident with No.53
+ Indicates allotted to No.53 but possibly not delivered

Avro 504A

7949, 7950, 7951, 7953, 7958, 7968, 7971, 7972*, 7977

Armstrong Whitworth F.K.3

5512, 5521*, 5525, 5526, 5529, 6193, 6207*, 6227

Martinsyde S.1 Scout

2449, 4246, 5446

B.E.2b

2771, 2781

B.E.2c

2092, 2471, 2490, 2661 +, 2662 +, 2663 +

B.E.2d

5837*

B.E.2e/B.E.2f

2569, A3057, A3152*, A3162

B.E.2e/B.E.2g

6308*,	6309,	6311*,	6313*,	6314,	6315,
6316*,	6317*,	6318,	6321,	6323,	7188,
7221,	7229,	7230,	7231,	7237,	7240,
7246,	7249,	7250,	7251,	7252,	7255,
7256*,	7257,	A2749,	A2754,	A2779*,	A2783,
A2862,	A2884				

B.E 12

6490

92

Blenheim IV L4837 early in 1939

R.E.8

A3237*, A3238*, A3240*, A3243*, A3249*, A3260*,
A3261*, A3457*, A3458*, A3463*, A3464*, A3490*,
A3538*, A3595*, A3605*, A3617*, A3619*, A3625*,
A3629*, A3684*, A3690*, A3694*, A3721*, A3771*,
A3785*, A3835*, A3838*, A3847*, A3858*, A3865*,
A3931*, A4207*, A4209*, A4214*, A4236*, A4239*,
A4269*, A4271*, A4292*, A4295*, A4303*, A4308*,
A4326*, A4376*, A4400*, A4438*, A4452*, A4495*,
A4583*, A4586*, A4591*, A4592*, A4617*, A4621*,
A4631*, A4632*, A4664*, A4679*, B791*, B841*,
B2251*, B2279*, B2282*, B3402*, B4021*, B4090*,
B4093*, B4101*, B5017*, B5037*, B5061*, B5076*,
B5887*, B6463*, B6464*, B6466*, B6564*, B6570*,
B6596*, B6598*, B6615*, B7718*, B7827*, B8097*,
B8890*, C2244*, C2259*, C2265*, C2284*, C2291*,
C2293*, C2308*, C2310*, C2311*, C2315*, C2342*,
C2345*, C2364*, C2377*, C2405*, C2501, C2503*,
C2506*, C2534*, C2545, C2549*, C2558*, C2563*,
C2567*, C2593, C2602, C2613*, C2742*, C2743*,
C2747, C2870*, C2901, C2908*, C2930, C2935*,
C3474, C4574*, C5026*, C5037*, C5083*, D4690*,
D4811*, D4825, D4834*, D4860*, D4866, D4871,
D4903*, D4943*, D4966*, D6703, D6722, D6723*,
D6799*, D6801, D6804*, D6839, E16*, E18*,
E48*, E1109*, E1112*, E1157*, F5871*, F5873*,
F5875*, F5889*, F5897, F6018, H7022, H7033,
H7262*

Nieuport 27 Scout

B6819*

Hawker Hector

K8139, K8147, K8148, K8150*, K9687*, K9688*,
K9695*, K9696, K9697*, K9701, K9702*, K9703,
K9707, K9708*, K9711*, K9712*

Avro Tutor

K4823

Vickers Valentia

K2344

Miles Magister

L8166

Bristol Blenheim IV

L4836*, L4837, L4838, L4839, L4840*, L4841*,
L4842*, L4843*, L4844, L4845, L4847, L4848*,
L4849, L4850*, L4851, L4852*, L4854, L4860*,
L4861*, L4862*, L4864, L8789*, L8794*, L8863*,
L8864, L9043*, L9190*, L9238, L9247, L9325,
L9329*, L9330*, L9331*, L9332*, L9399*, L9459*,
L9460*, L9466, L9470*, L9471*, L9473, L9474*,
L9475*, L9476*, N3551*, N3630*, N6195*, P4850*,
P6916*, P6922, P6926, P6928, P6931, P6933,
R2771*, R2773*, R3596*, R3602*, R3605*, R3633*,
R3634*, R3638, R3660*, R3661*, R3677*, R3678*,
R3679*, R3691*, R3699*, R3700*, R3703*, R3733*,

R3735*, R3779*, R3819*, R3836*, R3849*, R3909*,
R3911*, T1802*, T1816*, T1937*, T1938*, T1940*,
T1992*, T2035*, T2036*, T2042*, T2043, T2044*,
T2045*, T2046*, T2132*, T2218*, T2219, T2221*,
T2222, T2283*, T2331*, T2332*, T2356, T2395*,
T2396*, T2398*, T2431, V5370*, V5371*, V5378,
V5398*, V5399*, V5420*, V5421, V5496, V5497,
V5503, V5518*, V5647*, V5649*, V5862*, V5865*,
V5932, V5933*, V6024, V6087*, V6122*, V6125*,
V6301*, V6302*, V6303, V6309*, V6315, V6392,
V6394, Z5763, Z5765*, Z5879*, Z7313*, Z7314*,
Z7316, Z7360, Z7447, Z7451, Z7452, Z7453

Lockheed Hudson III

T9417*, T9438, T9457*, T9460, T9461, V9068,
V9090, V9091, V9092, V9096*, V9105*, V9108*,
V9129*, V9197, V9232*, V9253*, AE509

Lockheed Hudson IIIA

FH271, FH356, FH421, FH433

Lockheed Hudson V

AE639, AE643, AE650*, AE656*, AM521*, AM522,
AM527*, AM530*, AM532*, AM537, AM540*, AM542*,
AM549*, AM560*, AM563*, AM565*, AM568, AM570,
AM584*, AM603, AM623, AM631, AM641, AM647*,
AM648, AM651*, AM666, AM669*, AM672*, AM677*,
AM681, AM683*, AM686*, AM692, AM694, AM695*,
AM698, AM700*, AM702, AM714, AM718, AM727*,
AM741*, AM742*, AM757, AM777*, AM779, AM781*,
AM789*, AM795*, AM797, AM803*, AM806*, AM826,
AM827, AM844*, AM855, AM866, AM877*, AM885

Lockheed Hudson VI

FK479

Armstrong Whitworth Whitley V

P5061, Z6632

Armstrong Whitworth Whitley VII

Z9381, Z9519*, BD424, BD425*, BD677, BD688,
EB331*, EB332, EB392, EB393, LA795, LA796,
LA797, LA813

Consolidated Liberator III

BZ761, FK225, FK238, FL992

Consolidated Liberator IV

TT343* (ex 42-51350)

Consolidated Liberator V

BZ716*, BZ720*, BZ726, BZ730*, BZ731*, BZ740*,
BZ741, BZ744, BZ745, BZ749*, BZ750, BZ751*,
BZ753*, BZ754*, BZ760, BZ769*, BZ771, BZ774,
BZ777, BZ778*, BZ781*, BZ783, BZ784, BZ786,

BZ788*, BZ793*, BZ794, BZ795*, BZ796, BZ800*,
BZ803, BZ804, BZ806, BZ814*, BZ815, BZ816*,
BZ817*, BZ818*, BZ819*, BZ820, BZ870, BZ871*,
BZ873*, BZ875, BZ878*, BZ913, BZ919, BZ944,
BZ945*, FL941, FL961, FL978

Consolidated Liberator VI

BZ968, BZ985, EV877, EV879, EV883, EV895*,
EV896, EV898, EV899*, EV953*, EV954, EV988,
EV998, EW100*, EW289, EW290, EW291, EW293*,
EW295, EW297, EW300*, EW302, EW303*, EW304*,
EW306*, KG863*, KG865, KG866, KG868, KG897+,
KG901, KG902, KG905, KG907, KG908, KG914,
KH198*, KH199, KH200, KH279*, KH344, KH419,
KK254, KK373, KL593*, KL622, KL637, KL639,
KL642*, KL647, KL650, KL670, KL673, KN748

Consolidated Liberator VIII

KG848*, KG985, KH126*, KH128, KH129*, KH132,
KH143, KH146*, KH178, KH180, KH181, KH183*,
KH184, KH222, KH223, KH225, KH238, KH337,
KH340, KH341*, KH346*, KH347, KH387, KH388,
KH411, KH412*, KH413, KK322*, KL631, KL634,
KL643, KN720, KN727, KN734, KN743, KN755,
KN756, KN757, KN775, KN786, KN813, KN825,
KN831, KP129

Douglas Dakota IV

KJ866, KJ907, KJ970, KJ997, KK128, KK129*,
KK131, KK193, KN214, KN217, KN276, KN330,
KN360*, KN379, KN381, KN383, KN385, KN393,
KN415, KN423, KN424, KN425, KN434, KN435,
KN439*, KN446, KN449, KN487, KN490, KN491,
KN493, KN494, KN498, KN499, KN506, KN508,
KN512, KN523, KN541, KN551, KN552, KN566,
KN567, KN577, KN590, KN605, KN607, KN608,
KN625, KN629, KN632, KN637, KN640, KN642,
KN657, KN659, KN660, KN680, KN696, KN700,
KN701, KP215, KP217, KP223, KP233

Handley Page Hastings C.1

TG504, TG506, TG508, TG509*, TG512, TG513,
TG515, TG516, TG517, TG518, TG521, TG522,
TG523, TG524, TG525, TG527, TG528, TG529,
TG530, TG531, TG532, TG535, TG536, TG537,
TG551, TG553, TG554, TG556, TG557, TG559,
TG561, TG562, TG563, TG564*, TG567, TG568,
TG569, TG570, TG571, TG572, TG573, TG574*,
TG577, TG578, TG579, TG587, TG604, TG605,
TG606, TG607, TG608, TG609, TG610, TG613,
TG614, TG616

Handley Page Hastings C.2

WD475, WD481, WD487, WD488, WD491*, WD493,
WD495, WD497, WD498, WD499, WJ325, WJ328,
WJ329, WJ330, WJ331, WJ332, WJ333, WJ334,
WJ335*, WJ336, WJ337, WJ338, WJ339, WJ340,
WJ343

Beverley C.1 XB288/U. (MAP)

Blackburn Beverley C.1

XB260, XB263, XB264, XB265, XB267, XB268*,
XB269, XB283, XB284, XB285, XB286, XB287,
XB288, XB289, XB290, XB291, XH116, XH117*,
XH119, XH120, XH121, XH122, XH123, XH124,
XL130, XL151, XL152, XM103, XM105, XM110,
XM111

Short Belfast C.1

XR362, XR363, XR364, XR365, XR366, XR367,
XR368, XR369, XR370, XR371

Belfast C.1 XR368 and Argosy E.1 of No.115 Squadron at Brize Norton on the squadron's sixtieth birthday. The photograph was taken from a 41 Squadron Phantom FGR.2 and delivered immediately after landing

Blenheim IV T2043 shows its code letters PZ-M in late 1940. (Flambards)

APPENDIX IV

Squadron Codes

While serving with 2nd Brigade during World War I, No.53 Squadron aircraft carried a "white crescent supine" (lying on its back with the points upwards) behind the roundel and the aircraft's individual letter aft of the crescent. Instructions to remove squadron markings (except for the single-seater fighter squadrons) were issued on 22 March 1918.

The Hawker Hectors were initially painted silver over-all and carried no codes. Later, individual identification letters were added forward of the roundel.

K8139/S, K9688/K, K9703/D, K9712/U.

No.53 Squadron was allocated the letters "TE" at the time of the Munich Crisis. Although the Hectors were re-painted in a camouflage scheme, there is no evidence that they carried the new code letters. The following Blenheims have been identified.

L4837/TE-G, L4840/TE-Q, L4841/TE-N, L4843/TE-J, L4850/TE-O, L4852/TE-A, L4864/TE-P, L9329/TE-L

As soon as war was declared on 3 September 1939, the squadron letters were changed from "TE" to "PZ". This code was carried by No.53's Blenheims and Hudsons.

BLENHEIM

PZ-A:	R2771, R3661, Z5765
PZ-B:	L9459, L9466
PZ-C:	R3735
PZ-D:	L4847, T1940, T2222
PZ-E:	L4842, L8789, N3551, T1937, T2398, V5398, V6309
PZ-F:	T2035, T2045, T2283, V6125
PZ-G:	T2044, T2132, V5370, V5399
PZ-H:	P4850, T2042, V5420, V5518
PZ-J:	L8789, T2046, T2221, T2331
PZ-K:	R3660, T1816, T2036
PZ-L:	L9474, Z5879
PZ-M:	T2043
PZ-N:	N3630, T2395
PZ-O:	L9043, T2332, V6087
PZ-P:	R3679, V5865
PZ-R:	T2132
PZ-S:	T1992, V5647
PZ-T:	L8794, V5371
PZ-U:	R3699, T2396, V5933
PZ-V:	L9475, P4850, R2773
PZ-W:	L4860, R3911, T2218, V6302
PZ-X:	R3836, T1992
PZ-Y:	R3678, V5862, V6122
PZ-Z:	N6195, R3779

HUDSON

PZ-A:	V9232,	FK479	
PZ-B:	V9197		
PZ-C:	AM540,	FH433	
PZ-D:	AM527,	AM727,	
PZ-E:	V9090,	AM795	
PZ-F:	AM549,	FH271	
PZ-G:	AM777,	AM885	
PZ-H:	AM789		
PZ-J:	AM542		
PZ-K:	V9105,	AM741,	AM844
PZ-L:	V9253,	AM560	
PZ-O:	T9461		
PZ-P:	V9096,	AM672	
PZ-Q:	AM530		
PZ-S:	FH421		
PZ-T:	AE650		
PZ-U:	FH356		
PZ-V:	AE656,	AM651,	AM803
PZ-W:	AM565,	AM797	
PZ-X:	AM563,	AM866	
PZ-Y:	AE639,	AM584,	AM683
PZ-Z:	AE509		

HQ Coastal Command issued an instruction on 16 October 1942 that squadrons were to remove the squadron code from their aircraft on 1 November 1942 but to retain the third letter for individual squadron identification. It was felt that the Germans had broken the codes and now knew exactly which squadron was where. This order came too late for it to affect No.53's Hudsons but it is most likely that the Whitleys only carried single letters.

Z9519/N,	BD424/K,	BD425/O,	EB331/U,
EB393/N,	LA795/S,	LA796/B,	LA797/D,
LA813/A			

The new system soon caused chaos since stations often had several squadrons with the same type of aircraft there at any one time. Naturally enough, each squadron had an "A for Apple" etc and it was difficult to sort out which was which. As an interim measure, each squadron was allocated an identification number code for that station so that the aircraft were now marked "1-A", "2-A", "3-A" etc. There is evidence that No.53 used the number "2" on its Liberators whilst at St Eval. A list of identified individual codes for the squadron Liberators is given below.

A:	BZ754,	BZ781,	BZ819	
B:	BZ716,	BZ794,	BZ814	
C:	BZ804,	BZ818		
D:	BZ731,	BZ788,	BZ815	
E:	BZ745,	BZ871		
F:	BZ740,	BZ771,	BZ777,	BZ795
G:	BZ751,	BZ778,	BZ788,	BZ803
H:	BZ793,	BZ800		
J:	BZ774,	BZ796		
K:	BZ919			
L:	BZ817,	BZ944		
M:	BZ778			
N:	BZ720,	BZ769,	BZ781,	BZ816
O:	BZ730,	BZ945		
P:	BZ749,	BZ784		
Q:	BZ741,	BZ870		
R:	BZ750,	BZ793		

S:	BZ753,	BZ783,	BZ873
T:	BZ783,	BZ878	
U:	BZ820		
V:	BZ875		

In the summer of 1944, it was decided to go back to the old system, but to change the two-letter codes every three months. No.53 was allocated the letters "FH". As a result of the Normandy invasion and with the Germans retreating, it proved to be unnecessary to change the codes again. The letters "FH" were carried on the Liberators until 15 June 1946.

FH-A:	FK225			
FH-B:	KH279,	KH388		
FH-C:	EV877,	KH412		
FH-D:	EV879,	KH183,	TT343	
FH-E:	KH337			
FH-F:	EV953,	KH181		
FH-G:	EW302			
FH-H:	BZ985,	EV895,	KL622,	KH222
FH-J:	EV883,	KN748,	KH129	
FH-K:	EW300,	KH200,	KH132	
FH-L:	KH387			
FH-M:	EW293			
FH-N:	KH341			
FH-O:	EW297,	KL642		
FH-P:	KH178,	KH347		
FH-Q:	KH180			
FH-R:	KH143			
FH-S:	EW295			
FH-T:	EW289			
FH-U:	EW306,	KH413		
FH-V:	EW290,	KH198		
FH-W:	EV899,	KH346		
FH-X:	EW304			
FH-Y:	EW303,	KN743		
FH-Z:	EW291,	KH184		

No.53 was re-formed at Netheravon on 1 December 1946 by re-numbering No.187 and so inherited their code letters "PU". Known 53 Squadron Dakotas are as follows.

KK193/PU-F,	KN383/PU-V,	KN434/PU-U,
KN490/PU-B,	KN590/PU-H,	KN632/PU-W,
KN701/PU-N		

After the Berlin Airlift, the squadron Hastings carried the last three letters of their radio callsigns in large letters behind the roundel. For example, the callsign for TG604 was MOGAC.

TG529/GAB,	TG536/GAU,	TG564/JAZ,	TG574/GAJ,
TG604/GAC,	TG605/GAM,	WD488/JAM,	WD491/GAF,
	WJ329/JAY,	WJ332/GAY	

The 53 Squadron Beverleys carried a very large single identification letter on the side of the fuselage beneath the cockpit.

XB260/O,	XB263/K,	XB264/C,	XB265/A,
XB267/B,	XB268/D,	XB269/F,	XB283/G,
XB284/H,	XB285/J,	XB286/S,	XB287/T,
XB288/U,	XB289/V,	XB290/W,	XB291/X,
XH116/Y,	XH117/Z,	XH121/Z,	XL151/R,
	XM105/E,	XM105/P	

The Belfasts were named in 1969 after mythological giants and carried the name beneath the cockpit.

XR362 *Samson*   XR363 *Goliath*   XR364 *Pallas*
XR365 *Hector*   XR366 *Atlas*   XR367 *Heracles*
XR368 *Theseus*   XR369 *Spartacus*   XR370 *Ajax*
                  XR371 *Enceladus*

XR364 over Belfast prior to delivery to No.53 Squadron as 'Pallas'. (Short Bros & Harland)

Page 122: "No.53 Squadron at Bircham Newton" - Five missing
from Centre Row - Should read after "P/O Moira,
Unknown,....." -(ADD)- "S/L Aldridge, W/C Grant,
S/L Lilly, F/L Bunce, P/O Burne" then "P/O Fell,
P/O McLintock,.......".

Page 128: F/L Gillie Potier's crew - Delete the second Front
Row caption commencing "W/O W R Kinsman.....".

F/L J Ketcheson's crew - Back Row - Sgt "Hayr"
should be Sgt "Hayter".

Page 133: "F/O Ernie Gledhill...." and "Sgt Tony Wheeler..."
Photo credit should be "F/L E Gledhill".

Page 134: Top photograph: S/L "Moffet" should be "Maffet".

Page 135: These Hectors (K9714, K9704, K9700 plus one) were
allocated to 59 Sqn and not to 53 Sqn.

Page 136: "Blenheim L4852/TE-A...." - Photo credit should be
"G/C W S G Maydwell DSO DFC".

Page 138: "Martinet target tug JN680...." - "F/O Williamson"
should read "F/O Wilkinson".

Page 140: "L-1079" should be "L-1049".

Text:

Page 11: Paragraph commencing "Sgt H A Whatley (2056)...."
Delete last sentence "His brother, 2Lt W E Watt
was also serving on 53 Squadron at this time".
(this sentence belongs to the next paragraph).

Page 38: Last paragraph - Sentence "Later, the fuel tanks
of the Oxford exploded" should be "Seconds later,
the fuel tanks of the Oxford exploded".

"V6087" should be "V6087/O".

Page 41: "P/O S G Goatley" - "P/O S G Goatley (RCAF)".

Page 42: "AM521" should be "AM521/N".

Page 49: Paragraph commencing - "A submarine 'similar in
silhouette.......'" - the submarine concerned has
been identified as Spanish Navy submarine B 2.

Page 56: "LACW W Hutchinson and LACW M MacLean..." - "was"
should be "were".

Page 57: Last sentence - should read "....KN743/Y came back
from India on 9 June....".

Page 66: Chipmunk "WE660" should be "WB660".

Page 97: "TG529/GAB" should be "TG529/JAB".

Page 102: "27 May 1940" - "AC1 R H Trafford" should read
"AC1 R H Trafford (Can)".

Page 105: "17 Apr 1942" should read "16/17 Apr 1942".

Page 114: "G/C J B Wray CBE DFC" should read "the late G/C
J B Wray CBE DFC".

The entire extreme right-hand column is missing.
It should read:

"The 53 Squadron Association was formed at midnight
on 14 September 1976. Membership is free and is
available to all past members of the squadron and
their dependents. Reunions and other events are
organised from time to time and further details
can be obtained from either of the following:"

"UNITED IN EFFORT"

ERRATA

Photo Captions:

Page 7:   F.K.3 photograph - "in used" should be "in use".

Page 13:   Capt H L "Tracey" should be "Tracy".

Page 16:   "R.E.8 A4400 at Abeele......" - definitely not!
This is actually - "R.E.8 A3457 - ran into tree on
airfield boundary landing at Bailleul 16/7/17 -
2Lt H L Tracy and 2Lt W H Skinner unhurt".

"This crashed R.E.8......" - I have now identified
this as "B6464 - Engine choked on take-off from
Bailleul and crashed on edge of aerodrome 4/1/18.
2Lt L C Jarrett and Lt T B M Brown uninjured"

Page 24:   "Hectors with flares...." - Photo credit should be
"G/C W S G Maydwell DSO DFC".

Page 26:   "No.53's Blenheim IVs..." - Photo credit should be
"the late G/C Jack Butterworth".

Page 29:   "L4240" should be "L4840".

Page 32:   "Belgian schoolgirls" - "L4840" should be "L4860".

Page 39:   More likely to be "PZ-R flying from Limavady to
North Coates".

Page 42:   "Hudson AM540/C.." - "Langam" should be "Langham".

Page 57:   KN743/Y returned on "9/6/46".

Page 58:   Photo credits (and all subsequent references) -
"S/L" L T Bennett should be "M/S" (Master/Sig) - I
inadvertently gave Les a much deserved promotion!!

Lower photograph - "Utersen" should be "Ütersen".

Page 63:   "TG529/GAB..." should be "TG529/JAB".

Page 66:   Photo credit - "WJ333" should be "F/L E Gledhill".

Page 72:   "XE289/V" should be "XB289/V".

Page 119:   "C" Flight at Odiham - "KE" McIntyre should be
"KJ" McIntyre.

"At School of Army Co-operation...." - Centre Row
should commence P/O "R" Walton.

1

handwritten: XF 597 shown on front cover flown many times at Manby 1963/4

PROVOST PAIR

Britain now has a display team using the charismatic Percival Provost trainer. Ken Ellis reports on their restoration and future plans.

"I FLEW HER and fell in love with her." Alan House was offered a Percival Provost in 1983 and, after sampling the big trainer, bought it without a second thought. This love affair has turned out *not* to be monogamous – he now owns *three!*

Operating an historic aircraft is never an easy undertaking and there are always times when the determination of a team can be tested to the full. In July 1987, after five happy years and the acquisition of a second airframe for restoration to flying condition, Alan had to force-land *Romeo Yankee* through no fault of his own.

Lying there in a cornfield with the bottom of the fuselage and firewall badly damaged and the wing 'totalled', no consideration was given to stopping the restoration of No 2 and giving up the whole venture. The former Shuttleworth Collection Provost was carefully removed and put into store at Alan's workshop to await its turn.

Work on No 2 took on more vigour, the team being determined to get a Provost back into the air. This aircraft, *Fox Whiskey* flew again in the same year that No 1 went down, and the year in which the *Provost Pair* really should have made their debut. The pair were now to be completed by Provost No 3, a T.51 previously with the Irish Army Air Corps, which started its restoration after G-BKFW left the workshop.

Tracing its origins back to 1948, the Percival P.56 was a private venture from the Luton-based company based on their experiences (not all good) with the Prentice trainer designed to take over the helm from the Tiger Moth. At much the same time as Percival's

Heading: Putting the pair away – the team built the hangar as well! Above: G-AWRY being nursed back to health in the workshop. (Duncan Cubitt)

were working on the mock-up P.56 the Air Ministry had formulated Operational Requirement 257 for a very rugged and simple side-by-side trainer, fitted with the ubiquitous Armstrong Siddeley Cheetah, but with an eye to installing the Alvis Leonides.

This thinking crystallised into Specification T16/48 in December 1948. Percival's and Handley Page (Reading) – the salvaged elements of the Woodley-based Miles concern – won the first round and were asked to build prototypes in July 1949. While both looked much the same in terms of format, the P.56

was a superior beast, offering excellent aerobatic qualities over HP's HPR.2. Alvis's Leonides was quickly recognised as the best powerplant and 200 Provost T.1s for the RAF were ordered in 1951 with deliveries commencing in 1953.

Repeat orders and exports brought the production run of the Provost to over 400 and the last one, for Eire, was delivered in 1960. There were two basic export machines, the unarmed T.51 and the machine gun and hardpoint equipped T.53. (refurbished ex RAF airframes being designated T.52.) Provosts

FlyPast

Main picture: Peter Newbery at the helm of T.51 G-BKOS in full Irish Army Air Corps livery.

Right: Touch-down back at the Berkshire strip.

Middle: The team: Stan Lawrence, Alan House, Peter Newbery and Chris Wheeler.

Far right: The Pair in their element. (All Duncan Cubitt).

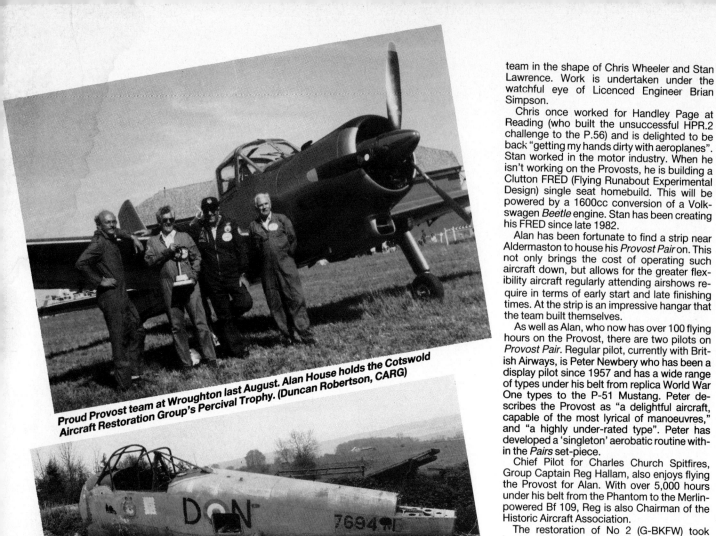

Proud Provost team at Wroughton last August. Alan House holds the Cotswold Aircraft Restoration Group's Percival Trophy. (Duncan Robertson, CARG)

Spares ship WV486 will be used in the rebuild of the fuselage of G-AWRY – providing datum for the jigs. (Duncan Cubitt)

team in the shape of Chris Wheeler and Stan Lawrence. Work is undertaken under the watchful eye of Licenced Engineer Brian Simpson.

Chris once worked for Handley Page at Reading (who built the unsuccessful HPR.2 challenge to the P.56) and is delighted to be back "getting my hands dirty with aeroplanes". Stan worked in the motor industry. When he isn't working on the Provosts, he is building a Clutton FRED (Flying Runabout Experimental Design) single seat homebuild. This will be powered by a 1600cc conversion of a Volkswagen *Beetle* engine. Stan has been creating his FRED since late 1982.

Alan has been fortunate to find a strip near Aldermaston to house his *Provost Pair* on. This not only brings the cost of operating such aircraft down, but allows for the greater flexibility aircraft regularly attending airshows require in terms of early start and late finishing times. At the strip is an impressive hangar that the team built themselves.

As well as Alan, who now has over 100 flying hours on the Provost, there are two pilots on *Provost Pair*. Regular pilot, currently with British Airways, is Peter Newbery who has been a display pilot since 1957 and has a wide range of types under his belt from replica World War One types to the P-51 Mustang. Peter describes the Provost as "a delightful aircraft, capable of the most lyrical of manoeuvres," and "a highly under-rated type". Peter has developed a 'singleton' aerobatic routine within the *Pairs* set-piece.

Chief Pilot for Charles Church Spitfires, Group Captain Reg Hallam, also enjoys flying the Provost for Alan. With over 5,000 hours under his belt from the Phantom to the Merlin-powered Bf 109, Reg is also Chairman of the Historic Aircraft Association.

The restoration of No 2 (G-BKFW) took longer than expected, following its pick-up from Oakington, where Alan had discovered it. (Pick-up being a most appropriate term, Alan has now moved Provosts several times using a

were exported to Burma, Eire, Iraq, Malaya, Oman, Rhodesia and the Sudan.

In RAF service the Provost was replaced by a dramatic revision of itself – the P.84 *Jet* Provost. The spindly-legged Armstrong Siddeley Viper powered prototype flew at Luton in June 1954 and looked every bit a P.56 with a faired-over nose, retractable undercarriage and jet in the rear fuselage.

From this prototype was to evolve the stalwart *JP* trainer for the RAF, ending up with the T.5s now being replaced by the Shorts Tucano (back to the prop four decades on...). Ultimate *JP* was the belligerent BAC.167 Strikemaster built at Warton with last customer deliveries taking place in 1988.!

So much for the Provost's credentials. Alan started flying in 1976 at Thruxton in a Cessna 150. He bought himself a Cessna 175 and then acquired Cessna Hawk XP II G-BHYD and ferried it over from Florida in late 1980 – and still operates this machine. He had long had his eyes on an historic type, but "hadn't really settled upon a real choice".

Shuttleworth's rationalised their collection in 1983 and several of their inmates were part of the Christie's auction at Duxford in April 1983. Provost G-AWRY did not find a buyer there, but soon afterwards Alan made that decisive flight and bought this lovely example.

Romeo Yankee broadened Alan's knowledge and skills and soon he had a support

XF597

Jan31, 1955	Awaiting collection at Percival's Luton, on Contract No 9850, as XF597.
Feb 10, 1955	Issued to 9 Maintenance Unit (MU) at Cosford.
Jan 9, 1956	Transferred to 12 MU at Kirkbride.
Jan 2, 1958	On charge with the RAF College, Cranwell.
Mar 31, 1960	Issued to the College of Air Warfare, Manby.
Apr 6, 1964	Retired to 27 MU Shawbury and declared a non-effective airframe Aug 4, 1965.
Nov 22, 1967	Sold to Flint Technical College, Connah's Quay, as an instructional airframe.
1982	Sold and moved to Oakington for restoration to flying condition. Registered as G-BKFW on Sept 21.
1987	Acquired by Alan House and flown again in Spring 1988 in Cranwell colours.

XF836

Jun 17, 1955	Awaiting collection at Percival's, Luton, on Contract No 9850 as XF836.
Jun 22, 1955	Issued to 12 MU, Kirkbride.
Apr 29, 1957	Brief issue to Manchester University Air Squadron for their Summer Camp.
Aug 30, 1957	Transferred to the RAF College, Cranwell. Coded 'J-G'.
Jul 11, 1960	To 49 MU Colerne for storage.
Jul 26, 1960	Issued to the Central Navigation and Control School, Shawbury. Coded 'R'.
Feb 11, 1963	Unit renamed Central Air Traffic Controller School.
Jan 6, 1969	Retired to 27 MU, also at Shawbury. Allocated instructional airframe number 8043M.
Apr 18, 1969	Acquired by the Shuttleworth Trust and flown to Old Warden.
1977	Repainted at RAF St Athan and returned to Cranwell colours.
Oct 29, 1981	Registered to the Shuttleworth Collection as G-AWRY.
Apr 14, 1983	Auctioned by Christie's at Duxford. Acquired by Alan House.
Jul 28, 1987	Force-landed following engine failure. Removed to workshops for rebuild following completion of 178.

Carcase of WV486 will be used in the recalibration of XF836's fuselage. WV486 was built in October 1953 and served with 6 Flying Training School (FTS) at Ternhill and 22 FTS at Syerston. It was used as an instructional airframe at Halton as 7694M from November 1960. In the mid 1970s it was acquired by Provost operator John Bradshaw as a source of spares for his G-AWPH before being acquired by Alan House.

178

May 27, 1954	Mk 51, delivered from Luton to the Irish Army Air Corps at Casement, near Dublin, as 178.
Feb 1980	Withdrawn from use at Casement by this date and offered for sale.
Dec 11, 1981	Acquired by Jim Cassidy and removed by road/ferry to Burtonwood for storage.
May 29, 1982	Moved by road to Woodvale for start of restoration to flying condition.
Feb 21, 1983	Registered as G-BKOS.
1986	Moved to Kingsclere, then acquired by Alan House and moved to his workshop in 1988.
Aug, 1989	First flown following restoration, painted as IAAC 178.

Stan Lawrence and Chris Wheeler with G-BKOS in the workshop prior to 'roll-out' in 1989. (Duncan Cubitt)

PROVOST PAIR

'skip' lorry. Without the 'skip' the swing-arms of such vehicles provide an easy way of moving a fuselage without recourse to a crane – a ploy worth remembering!) Previous 'restoration' work was found to be of a poor standard and accordingly the team went "all the way back" and started a ground-up rebirth.

With *Fox Whiskey* in the air, and *Romeo Yankee* down and out for a while, Alan then acquired No 3 so that the team could start again. This aircraft was a former Irish T.51 and acquired from fellow Provost collector Jim Cassidy.

Bedecked in the lovely spiralling Irish boss markings, G-BKOS flew last year and allowed Alan's frustrated *Provost Pair* to come to reality, albeit not with the airframes he at first envisaged. The pair have made several airshow appearances and there is hope for an expanded series of venues for 1990.

In terms of restorations Provost No 1 is now No 3. G-AWRY represents a very different proposition for the tightly-knit Provost rebuild team. As a damaged airframe "it will be a major challenge, even though we now know the type inside-out," said Chris Wheeler.

To assist in re-aligning the fuselage, a junked former instructional airframe Provost has been acquired. This will act as a 'jig' to calibrate the former Shuttleworth machine during the complex rebuild. More importantly, the team will need a new wing – with paperwork or known hours – to complete this project. Alan has a Leonides Major engine available for exchange and is keen to hear from anyone with leads on Provost wings.

Nobody will tie themselves down to a date when the alliterative *Provost Pair* become the *Provost Trio*, but Alan hopes to keep all three machines – this love affair runs deep. Alan is realistic about such an operation, "The third one can only be kept on if we get good airshow back-up..... no bookings and I must sell her."

Alan House is currently working towards his own engineering licences and the team are happy to consider work on other projects – with Provosts obviously being a speciality. Latest inmate in the workshop is a former RLS Saab Safir, which will be a welcome shape in UK skies, only one other currently flying here.

Work on *Romeo Yankee* is well underway at the workshop. Meanwhile, the *Provost Pair* looks forward to its first full airshow season. 1990 looks set to be the year the lovely Provost is taken much more seriously as a performer and a classic historic type.

(Contact Alan House on 0635 63433 or '66088 for details of booking the *Provost Pair*.)

A view of the workshop when G-BKOS was the height of attention – a Saab Safir now occupies this slot. (Duncan Cubitt)

G-AWRY at the Christie's Duxford sale in April 1983, Alan House bought her shortly after this. (Alan Curry)

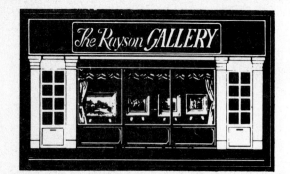

APPENDIX V

Roll of Honour

World War I

Date	Name	Role	Status	Aircraft
3 Dec 1916	Capt H N Steward	(P)	Killed	B.E.2 5837
	2Lt M Thornely	(O)	Killed	
6 Jan 1917	Lt D W L Young	(O)	Killed	B.E.2 7256
22 Jan 1917	Lt S E Goodwin	(P)	Wounded	B.E.2 6317
24 Jan 1917	Lt T F Preston	(P)	Killed	B.E.2 6308
	Lt C M Buck	(O)	Killed	
25 Jan 1917	2Lt J R Houghton	(O)	Wounded	B.E.2 6311
16 Feb 1917	Capt F W H Simpson	(P)	Killed	B.E 2 6313
	Sgt C J Edlington	(AG)	Killed	
26 Feb 1917	2Lt T H Butler	(P)	Injured	B.E.2 7250
	2Lt V G Southern	(O)	Injured	
4 Mar 1917	Lt R W Scoles	(P)	Injured	B.E.2 6311
	2Lt B A Morgan	(O)	Died of Injuries	
17 Mar 1917	Cpl T W Willis	(AG)	Injured	B.E.2 A2779
4 May 1917	Lt J R Geddes (Can)	(O)	Wounded	R.E.8 A4207
5 May 1917	2/AM C Day		Wounded	
	2/AM J J B Woods		Wounded	
12 May 1917	2Lt F Adams	(P)	Killed	R.E.8 A3243
	2Lt O R Kelly	(O)	Killed	
27 May 1917	1/AM J W Bridle		Wounded	
28 May 1917	2/AM J Briddon		Wounded	
1 Jun 1917	1/AM L E Tucker	(WOp)	Wounded	Gas attack
2 Jun 1917	2Lt R R Gyles	(O)	Wounded	R.E.8
	2/AM J S Baley	(WOp)	Wounded	Gas attack
7 Jun 1917	2Lt F P Brown	(P)	Wounded	R.E.8 A3240
	2Lt H E Wells	(O)	Wounded	
	Lt N J Wenger	(P)	Injured	R.E.8 A4308
	2Lt E B Hamel	(O)	Injured	
	Lt L S Bowman	(P)	Injured	R.E.8 A3464
	2/AM S T Jones	(WOp)	Wounded	Shell shock
8 Jun 1917	2Lt T C S MacGregor	(P)	Killed	R.E.8 A3684
	2Lt R W Spooner	(O)	Killed	
9 Jun 1917	2Lt J A Loutit	(P)	Wounded	R.E.8 A3463
	2Lt V J Holland	(O)	Wounded	
	2Lt C L Green	(P)	Died of injuries	R.E.8 A4292
	2Lt M D R Paton	(O)	Injured/Died 12 June	
12 Jun 1917	2Lt W Turnbull	(P)	Killed	R.E.8 A4207
	2Lt W B Protheroe	(O)	Killed	
18 Jun 1917	Lt M E Newton	(P)	Killed	R.E.8 A4617
	2Lt H M Jackson	(O)	Killed	
25 Jun 1917	Lt L S Bowman	(P)	Killed	R.E.8 A3847
	2Lt J E Power-Clutterbuck	(O)	Killed	
29 Jun 1917	2Lt W E Watt	(O)	Wounded	R.E.8 A4236
2 Jul 1917	Sgt H A Whatley	(P)	Killed	R.E.8 A3538
	2Lt F G B Pascoe	(O)	Killed	
	Capt W P Horsley MC	(P)	Killed	R.E.8 A3249
	2Lt A G Knight	(O)	Wounded	
12 Jul 1917	Sgt R Kay	(P)	Wounded	R.E.8 A4621
	Lt B W Binkley (Can)	(O)	Killed	
21 Jul 1917	2Lt L C Jarrett	(P)	Injured	R.E.8 A3858
	Pte W Metson	(AG)	Injured	

Date	Name	Role	Status	Aircraft
27 Jul 1917	2Lt P J Rodocanachi	(P)	Killed	R.E.8 A4303
	2Lt N L Watt	(O)	Died of Wounds	
31 Jul 1917	2Lt L W Collier	(O)	Wounded	R.E.8
10 Aug 1917	Lt G I L Murray(Aus)	(P)	Wounded	R.E.8 A3260
	Lt S H Short (Can)	(O)	Wounded	
	Lt A Binnie	(P)	Wounded	R.E.8
	2Lt J T Long	(O)	Wounded	
14 Aug 1917	2Lt J E Goodman	(P)	Killed	R.E.8 A3838
	2Lt F E Kebblewhite	(O)	Killed	
14 Sep 1917	2Lt H W Westaway	(P)	Wounded	R.E.8 A3238
	2Lt L Hodkinson	(O)	Killed	
18 Sep 1917	2/AM W H Hadcraft	(WOp)	Wounded	Gas attack
21 Sep 1917	Capt R N F Mills	(P)	Killed	R.E.8 A3617
	Lt W A Browne	(O)	Killed	
1 Oct 1917	Lt A V Dufton	(O)	Injured	R.E.8 A3771
2 Oct 1917	Lt H W Smith	(O)	Wounded	R.E.8 A4376
8 Oct 1917	2Lt H W Laird	(P)	Killed	R.E.8 A3261
	2Lt J T Long	(O)	Injured/Died 10 Oct	
29 Oct 1917	2/AM G Yates	(WOp)	Wounded	Shell fire
31 Oct 1917	Capt W A L Poundall MC	(P)	Killed	R.E.8 A4214
	2Lt E R Ripley	(O)	Killed	
	Lt J Barker	(P)	Wounded	R.E.8 A3865
8 Nov 1917	2Lt L W Middleton	(P)	Killed	R.E.8 A4664
	2Lt F J McCullough	(O)	Killed	
28 Dec 1917	Lt W R Bucknall	(P)	Injured	R.E.8 B6463
5 Feb 1918	2Lt F A Lewis	(P)	Killed	R.E.8 B6466
	Lt T McK Hughes	(O)	Killed	
22 Mar 1918	2Lt T E H Birley	(P)	Wounded/POW	R.E.8 A4400
	Lt E Dennis	(O)	Killed	
	2Lt B G Poole	(P)	Killed	R.E.8 A4438
	2Lt G F Moseley	(O)	Wounded	
	2Lt G B Knight	(P)	Injured/Died 7 Apr	R.E.8 B841
	1/AM A J Coleman	(IR)	Injured	
24 Mar 1918	Lt A A Miles	(P)	Wounded/POW	R.E.8 B6564
	2Lt C W Cook	(O)	Wounded/POW	
	Lt F J Pullen	(O)	Wounded	R.E.8 A3931
	Capt R H Martin (Can)	(P)	Killed	R.E.8 B5061
	2Lt G H Parker	(O)	Killed	
9 Apr 1918	2/AM M V Webb (99625)	Wounded	Gas attack	
11 Apr 1918	2Lt J Craig	(P)	Killed	R.E.8 B8890
	Lt K Hall	(O)	Wounded	
	2Lt R D Best	(P)	Wounded	R.E.8 B4021
	2Lt W R McCoo	(O)	Wounded	R.E.8 A4452
12 Apr 1918	2Lt F E Pashby	(O)	Wounded/Died 13 Apr	R.E.8 A3931
	2Lt F Green	(P)	Injured	R.E.8 A4376
	Lt A DeM Severne	(O)	Injured	
16 Apr 1918	2Lt C E Lovick	(O)	Wounded	R.E.8 ?5037
17 Apr 1918	2/AM W Cobban (99478)		Wounded	Accident
18 Apr 1918	1/AM D W C Newton (48792)		Wounded	
19 Apr 1918	2/AM R A Ryder (58063)		Died of Wounds	
21 Apr 1918	Lt E H N Stroud	(P)	Killed	R.E.8 C5037
	Capt C G White MC	(O)	Killed	
25 Apr 1918	Capt H M Gibbs	(P)	Wounded	R.E.8 B6615
	Lt A Lomax	(O)	Wounded	
	Lt G J Hutcheson	(P)	Wounded/Died 27 May	R.E.8 C2244
29 Apr 1918	2/AM A A MacLennan (50481)		Wounded/Died 30 Apr	
30 Apr 1918	Lt R A Carter	(O)	Wounded	R.E.8 D4690

Date	Name	Role	Status	Aircraft
3 May 1918	Lt H T Rushton	(P)	Wounded	R.E.8 C2311
	2Lt J B Sanders	(O)	Wounded	
7 May 1918	Lt G W T Glasson	(P)	Wounded	R.E.8
9 May 1918	Lt J W Foreman	(P)	Injured	R.E.8 C2259
4 Jun 1918	2Lt T E Read	(O)	Wounded	Accident
13 Jun 1918	Lt W H Williams	(P)	Injured	R.E.8 C2291
	2Lt L F Raby	(O)	Injured	
25 Jun 1918	2Lt K D Handel	(P)	Died of Injuries	R.E.8 D4966
	2Lt H Dyson	(O)	Injured	
29 Jun 1918	2Lt J N Gatecliff	(P)	Killed	R.E.8 D4834
	2Lt J Harrison	(O)	Killed	
1 Jul 1918	2Lt J W Perks	(O)	Injured	R.E.8 D4860
2 Jul 1918	Lt I B MacBean	(?)	Wounded R.E.8	
10 Jul 1918	2Lt H F Redmond	(P)	Injured/Died 11 Jul	R.E.8 B4090
	2Lt W Cowden	(O)	Injured	
17 Jul 1918	2Lt A F Stokes	(P)	Injured	R.E.8 C2503
	Lt H Walpole	(O)	Injured	
22 Jul 1918	2Lt J A Lewis	(O)	Wounded	R.E.8
31 Jul 1918	Lt K A Ranney	(P)	Killed	R.E.8 C2308
	2Lt H S Smith	(O)	Killed	
3 Aug 1918	2Lt C Whitehead	(O)	Wounded	R.E.8
11 Aug 1918	Lt G L Dobell	(P)	Killed	R.E.8 C2265
	2Lt A W Baker	(O)	Killed	
17 Aug 1918	1/AM A Hill	(?)	Killed	
1 Sep 1918	Lt S W Cowper-Coles	(P)	Wounded	R.E.8 C2244
	2Lt D C Burke	(O)	Wounded	R.E.8
3 Sep 1918	Lt B E Scott MC DFC (Can)	(O)	Wounded	R.E.8 C2377
22 Sep 1918	2Lt J P Sharp	(P)	Injured	R.E.8 C2506
	2Lt S A Bird	(O)	Injured	
2 Oct 1918	Lt J B Pierce	(P)	Killed	R.E.8 C2742
	2Lt M W Wakeman	(O)	Wounded/Died 19 Oct	
9 Oct 1918	Lt G C Brown	(P)	Wounded/Died 10 Oct	R.E.8 D6804
	2Lt L F Raby	(O)	Killed	
17 Oct 1918	Lt G W E Whitehead	(P)	Killed	R.E.8 D6799
	2Lt R H Griffiths	(O)	Killed	
30 Oct 1918	Lt P G Hutson	(O)	Wounded	R.E.8 C2558
3 Nov 1918	Lt A H Alban	(P)	Wounded	R.E.8

Post World War I

Date	Name	Role	Status	Aircraft
24 Nov 1918	2Lt W H Sissons	(P)	Injured	R.E.8 C2613
	2Lt J J V Barlow	(O)	Injured	

Pre-World War II

Blenheim

Date	Name	Role	Status	Aircraft
30 Jan 1939	P/O P F G Jameson	(P)	Killed	L4836

World War II

(NB: RP=Runnymede Memorial Panel No. OP=Ottawa Memorial.)

Date	Name	Role	Status	Aircraft
12 Feb 1940	AC1 T J Hotten	(WEM)	Killed	Accident
3 May 1940	P/O J L G Butterworth	(P)	Killed	L9329
	Sgt M G A Pearce	(O)	Killed	
	AC2 R A Wood	(AG)	Killed	

9 May 1940	Sgt D G B Falconer	(O)	Killed	R3634
10 May 1940	P/O J A A Read	(P)	Injured	Accident
	P/O J Butterworth	(P)	Injured	
11 May 1940	F/O A D Panton DFC	(P)	Wounded	L9459
	Sgt J Christie	(O)	Wounded	
	AC2 R W Bence	(AG)	Wounded/POW Stalag XII	
13 May 1940	AC2 W J Cavett	(AG)	Wounded	L9332
15 May 1940	P/O P K Bone	(P)	Killed	L9399
	Sgt W J Cronin DFM	(O)	Killed	
	LAC J Bromley	(AG)	Killed/RP 22	
16 May 1940	P/O M G L Lovell	(P)	Wounded	L4860
	Sgt D McLeod	(O)	Wounded	
	AC Kenneth	(AG)	Wounded	
	P/O R I C McPherson	(P)	POW/Stalag Luft III	L4843
	Sgt A T Morland	(O)	POW/Stalag 357	
	AC2 S Robinson	(AG)	POW/Stalag Luft I	
	F/L B B StG Daly	(P)	Injured	L4852
	Sgt W R B Currie	(O)	Injured	
	AC2 P J Blandford	(AG)	Injured	
18 May 1940	P/O L J Huggett	(P)	Killed	L4841
	Sgt A C Gothard	(O)	Killed	
	AC1 W A Christie	(AG)	Killed	
	P/O P G Royle	(P)	Wounded/POW Stalag Luft I	L4861
	Sgt E F Woods	(O)	Wounded/POW	
	AC2 A H Malkin	(AG)	Wounded/Escaped to UK	
23 May 1940	F/O S G L Pepys	(P)	POW/Stalag Luft III	R3691
	Sgt A J Haygreen	(O)	POW/Stalag 357	
	AC2 H Spear	(AG)	POW/Stalag 357	
26 May 1940	P/O G M Bailey (NZ)	(P)	Killed	L8863
	Sgt W J K Evans	(O)	Killed	
	AC1 A A Gillmore	(AG)	Killed	
27 May 1940	P/O P F C Villiers-Tuthill	(P)	Killed	R3735
	Sgt A H Payne	(O)	Killed	
	AC1 D B Mearns	(AG)	Killed	
	P/O K A Aldridge	(P)	Injured	R3703
	AC1 R H Trafford	(O)	Injured	
6 Jun 1940	Sgt H H Wilson	(WAG)	Wounded/Died 7 Aug	R3602
25 Jun 1940	LAC E E Wheeler(628716)		Missing in France/RP24	
14 Jul 1940	F/O A D Panton DFC	(P)	POW/Stalag Luft III	N3551
	Sgt A E Farrow	(O)	POW/Stalag Luft VI	
	Sgt L H Stride	(WAG)	Killed	
18 Jul 1940	F/O J E Mahony	(P)	Missing/RP 6	R3661
	Sgt D A Keetley	(O)	Missing/RP 16	
	Sgt G E Exton	(WAG)	Killed	
25 Jul 1940	P/O D B Starky (NZ)	(P)	Missing/RP 10	R3836
	Sgt H W Hunt (Can)	(O)	Killed	
	Sgt B Moriarty	(WAG)	Missing/RP 17	
4 Aug 1940	P/O H C Corbett	(P)	Killed	L9475
	Sgt S E Riddington	(O)	Killed	
	Sgt K W Crane	(WAG)	Missing/RP 13	
11 Aug 1940	P/O P J Coleson	(P)	POW	T1816
	Sgt I Inskip	(O)	Missing/RP 15	
	P/O G M Bardolph(Can)	(WAG)	Wounded/POW; Died 17 Aug	
13 Aug 1940	S/L D C Oliver	(Flt Cdr)	Killed	Air Raid
	F/O H M Aspen	(Sigs Off)	Killed	
	Sgt W H L Richards	(C/Rig)	Killed	
	Cpl W F Bateman	(Fit/1)	Killed	
	Cpl J I Price	(Fit/1)	Killed	

13 Aug 1940	LAC A F Dancaster	(Fit/2)	Killed	Air Raid
	LAC R O'Kelly	(Fit/2)	Killed	
	AC1 G Booth	(F/Rig)	Killed	
	AC2 J W S Smith	(W/Op)	Killed	
	Sgt D J Roberts	(WAG)	Wounded	
	Sgt K W Vowles	(WAG)	Wounded	
	LAC A H Roberts	(Elec/2)	Wounded	
	LAC R Park	(F/Mec)	Wounded	
	LAC G B Currie	(I/Rep)	Wounded	
	LAC J Jenkins	(Arm)	Wounded	
	LAC M R Powell	(ACH)	Wounded	
	AC2 R Foggin	(F/Mec)	Wounded	
	AC2 D H Lee	(F/Mec)	Wounded	
	AC2 A Topham	(F/Rig)	Wounded	
22 Aug 1940	F/L M G Stevenson	(P)	Wounded	T2132
24 Aug 1940	F/O S C Rochford	(P)	Killed	T2035
	Sgt W Briggs	(O)	Killed	
	Sgt D Brook	(WAG)	Killed	
28 Aug 1940	P/O W E Fitzpatrick	(P)	Missing/RP 8	T2046
	Sgt J Bann	(O)	Missing/RP 11	
	Sgt H Dunnington	(WAG)	Missing/RP 13	
30 Aug 1940	AC2 B Stone (639515)		Killed	Air Raid
	AC1 Jones (967859)		Wounded	
	AC2 Johnson (944766)		Wounded	
31 Aug 1940	W/C E C T Edwards	(CO)	Killed	T1940
	Sgt L L Benjamin	(O)	Killed	
	Sgt J T Beesley	(WAG)	Killed	
8 Sep 1940	P/O R G Hall (NZ)	(P)	Missing/RP 8	T2042
	Sgt J D Randall	(O)	Missing/RP 18	
	Sgt M B Conacher	(WAG)	Missing/RP 12	
	F/L I H Bartlett	(P)	Missing/RP 4	R3779
	Sgt R E Aldridge	(O)	Missing/RP 11	
	Sgt E D Sheldrick	(WAG)	Missing/RP 19	
19 Sep 1940	P/O C F Tibbitts (NZ)	(P)	Missing/RP 10	T2045
	Sgt R W Grace	(O)	Missing/RP 14	
	Sgt E Harrold	(WAG)	Missing/RP 15	
26 Sep 1940	Sgt R H Trafford (Can)	(O)	Injured	T2221
30 Sep 1940	P/O S R Bevan-John	(P)	Killed	T2044
	Sgt S Macquire	(O)	Killed	
	Sgt H A Shaw	(WAG)	Missing/RP 19	
5 Oct 1940	P/O K A Faulkner	(P)	Injured	R2771
	Sgt A R S Hall	(O)	Killed	
	Sgt G B Fielder	(WAG)	Injured	
8 Oct 1940	P/O J C Mallon (NZ)	(P)	Killed	T2036
	Sgt W P Whetton DFM	(O)	Killed	
	Sgt A T Shackleford	(WAG)	Killed	
21 Oct 1940	P/O H J W Meakin	(P)	Injured	R3699
27 Oct 1940	P/O R L Buckley	(P)	Missing/RP 7	L8789
	Sgt C Henderson	(O)	Missing/RP 15	
	Sgt P E J Neale	(WAG)	Missing/RP 17	
	P/O E Plumtree	(P)	Wounded	T2132
	Sgt Wood	(O)	Wounded	
	Sgt P M Kinsey	(WAG)	Wounded	
26 Nov 1940	P/O M M Barbour	(P)	Missing/RP 7	N3630
	Sgt A Cowling	(O)	Missing/RP 13	
	Sgt G A Hinton	(WAG)	Missing/RP 15	
	P/O R E Maurer	(P)	Missing/RP 9	V5371
	Sgt I S Macaulay	(O)	Killed	

Date	Name	Role	Status	Aircraft
26 Nov 1940	Sgt B L Bembridge	(WAG)	Killed	V5371
5 Dec 1940	P/O P E Gibbs	(P)	Injured	T2218
	Sgt Wood	(O)	Injured	
	Sgt Oram	(WAG)	Injured	
6 Dec 1940	P/O S R E Weatherley	(P)	Killed	V5420
	Sgt H S Parrott	(O)	Killed	
	Sgt S McAndrew	(WAG)	Injured	
7 Dec 1940	P/O A K Steel	(P)	Killed	T2395
	Sgt W R Hemsley	(O)	Killed	
	Sgt D Robson	(WAG)	Injured	
27 Dec 1940	Sgt J Hill	(WAG)	Wounded	V5399
28 Dec 1940	F/L J D Steuart-Richardson DFC	(P)	Killed	L9043
	Sgt J L Maguire	(O)	Killed	
	Sgt K W V Vowles	(WAG)	Killed	
4 Jan 1941	P/O P E Gibbs	(P)	Missing/RP 32	R2773
	Sgt H S Wall	(O)	Killed	
	Sgt H G W Martin	(WAG)	Killed	
	P/O G R H Newton	(P)	Injured	V5398
	Sgt K G Hughes	(WAG)	Wounded	
9 Jan 1941	Sgt H V Jackson	(WAG)	Missing/RP 46	V5370
4 Feb 1941	P/O G F Marriott	(P)	Injured	Z5765
	Sgt E L Strudwick	(O)	Died of Injuries	
	Sgt G T Hadnam	(WAG)	Died of Injuries	
	P/O C P Morris	(P)	Missing/RP 33	T2283
	Sgt G W F Ashwin	(O)	Missing/RP 38	
	Sgt I R W Clark	(WAG)	Missing/RP 41	
	F/L B B StG Daly	(P)	Missing/RP 28	T1992
	Sgt J L Jones	(O)	Missing/RP 46	
	Sgt R H Trafford (Can)	(WAG)	Missing/RP 53	
11 Mar 1941	P/O D K Plumb	(P)	Missing/RP 30	P4850
	Sgt R H S Maton	(O)	Missing/RP 48	
	Sgt C McL Calder	(WAG)	Missing/RP 40	
14 Mar 1941	P/O G R H Newton	(P)	Killed	V5399
	Sgt C Whitehill	(O)	Killed	
	Sgt J R Miller	(WAG)	Killed	
15 Mar 1941	P/O W H Leedam	(P)	Missing/RP 33	T2132
	Sgt F P H Oatley	(O)	Missing/RP 49	
	Sgt W E Williams DFM	(WAG)	Missing/RP 55	
27 Mar 1941	P/O R N Philpott	(P)	Killed	T2332
	Sgt C A C Goad	(O)	Killed	
	Sgt F G Manning	(WAG)	Missing/RP 48	
	P/O J M Fothergill MC	(P)	Missing/RP 32	V5865
	Sgt T P O'K K T Coady	(O)	Missing/RP 41	
	Sgt P R Parker	(WAG)	Missing/RP 50	
7 Apr 1941	P/O E L E Nicholson	(P)	Missing/RP 34	T2398
	P/O H A L Stone	(O)	Missing/RP 34	
	Sgt P M Kinsey DFM	(WAG)	Missing/RP 46	
9 Apr 1941	P/O I F Anderson	(P)	Killed	V5862
	Sgt H H Walker	(O)	Killed	
	Sgt E A J Fabian	(WAG)	Killed	
16 Apr 1941	P/O R C L Reade	(P)	Killed	V5518
	Sgt J D O'Connell	(O)	Killed	
	Sgt R H W A Camm	(WAG)	Injured	
17 Apr 1941	Sgt A F Brownlee	(WAG)	Killed	Accident
18 Apr 1941	P/O E W Thomas	(P)	Missing/RP 35	V6302
	Sgt S G Capel	(O)	Missing/RP 40	
	Sgt D H Trotman	(WAG)	Killed	
11 May 1941	AC1 D D Mackay (1358078)		Killed	Air Raid

11 Jun 1941	P/O N D MacLennan(Can)	(P)	Killed	V5933
	Sgt D C Taylor	(O)	Killed	
	Sgt W M Roberts	(WAG)	Killed	
23 Jun 1941	P/O D M Bolton	(P)	Missing/RP 31	V5647
	Sgt K E Corrie	(O)	Missing/RP 41	
	Sgt G K Kircher	(WAG)	Missing/RP 46	
	P/O E Hewson	(P)	POW/Stalag Luft III	V6125
	Sgt A R Dawson	(O)	POW/Stalag Luft VI	
	Sgt W G McCorkell	(WAG)	POW/Stalag Luft IV	
26 Jun 1941	P/O L J Francis	(P)	Missing/RP 32	V6309
	Sgt R A Whitley	(O)	Missing/RP 54	
	Sgt J StC Hopper	(WAG)	Killed	
	P/O D T Herrick GM (NZ)	(P)	Wounded/POW Died 30 Jun	V6087
	Sgt G F W Gahagan	(O)	Missing/RP 43	
	Sgt G L Wells	(WAG)	Missing/RP 54	
	P/O C E Greville-Heygate DFC	(P)	Missing/RP 32	V6122
	P/O G Troup	(O)	Missing/RP 35	
	Sgt C H Naylor	(WAG)	Missing/RP 49	

Hudson

10 Aug 1941	P/O A F Buck	(P)	Killed	AM672
	Sgt L H Wood	(O)	Killed	
	F/L I P Magrath	(WAG)	Killed	
	F/S T E Stepney	(WAG)	Missing/RP 37	
14 Sep 1941	P/O T M Gay	(P)	Escaped from France	AM777
	Sgt J M Powell	(O)	POW/Stalag 357	
	Sgt S Tyson	(WAG)	POW/Stalag 357	
	Sgt A H Graham	(WAG)	Escaped from France	
27 Oct 1941	F/L L J M Bunce	(P)	Injured	AM651
	F/S F D King DFM	(O)	Missing/RP 46	
	Sgt W C Cleaver	(WAG)	Injured	
	Sgt E Leverington	(WAG)	Missing/RP 47	
12 Dec 1941	P/O C Thomas	(P)	Missing/RP 39	AE656
	Sgt L Griffiths	(O)	Missing/RP 44	
	Sgt R Smith	(WAG)	Missing/RP 52	
	P/O F C Taylor	(WAG)	Missing/RP 35	
8 Feb 1942	F/S T S Aucott	(WAG)	Died/Hospital	
24 Feb 1942	P/O D A Ray (Aus)	(P)	Missing/RP110	AM563
	P/O R D Fairbairn(Can)	(O)	Missing/RP100	
	P/O K S Davies (Can)	(WAG)	Missing/RP100	
	P/O F S Knight	(WAG)	POW/Stalag Luft III	
9 Mar 1942	Sgt R Walbancke	(P)	Injured	AM877
	Sgt C S Milne (Can)	(O)	Killed	
25 Mar 1942	Sgt R Rayner	(WAG)	Wounded	AM584
8 Apr 1942	Sgt D C Thornhill	(P)	POW/Stalag VIIIB	AM549
	Sgt D O Moran (Can)	(O)	POW/Stalag VIIIB	
	Sgt M A May (Aus)	(WAG)	POW/Stalag VIIIB	
	F/S L A W Diamond	(WAG)	POW/Stalag VIIIB	
11 Apr 1942	F/O A N McLintock	(P)	Missing/RP 67	AM560
	F/S J Hanna	(O)	Missing/RP 74	
	Sgt J B Melvin	(WAG)	Missing/RP 75	
	Sgt D R I Morgan	(WAG)	Missing/RP 89	
17 Apr 1942	F/S D G S Corden	(P)	Missing/RP 73	AM803
Apr 1942	Sgt A R Clouston	(O)	Missing/RP 80	
	Sgt H Cliffe	(WAG)	Missing/RP 80	
	F/S G N Moore (Can)	(WAG)	Missing/RP105	

22 Apr 1942	P/O G G Shore	(P)	Missing/RP 71	AM542
	P/O S G Goatley (Can)	(O)	Missing/RP100	
	Sgt J M C Jenkinson	(WAG)	Missing/RP 87	
	F/S R H W A Camm	(WAG)	Missing/RP 73	
27 Apr 1942	Sgt R Rayner	(WAG)	Wounded	AM527
4 May 1942	F/S K M Nichols	(P)	Killed	AM530
	Sgt S E Smith	(O)	Killed	
	Sgt A W Newhouse	(WAG)	Killed	
	Sgt C Pottas	(WAG)	Killed	
	2Lt C L Summers	(USAAC)	Killed	
	P/O M G Gummer	(P)	POW/Stalag Luft III	AM565
	F/S J B Jones	(O)	Missing/RP 75	
	Sgt T McDamm	(WAG)	POW/Stalag VI	
	Sgt D E Round	(WAG)	Missing/RP 92	
8 May 1942	F/S C J Wyllie (BLAV)	(P)	Killed	AM683
	F/S A T Thompson	(P/O)	Killed	
	Sgt W J Rowe	(WAG)	Killed	
	Sgt W R McLeod	(WAG)	Killed	
	P/O J P Rickards	(P)	Wounded	AM540
	Sgt K Whitnall	(WAG)	Wounded	
	Sgt J Smith	(WAG)	Wounded	
15 Sep 1942	P/O G T Risbey (Aus)	(P)	Killed	AM727
	P/O J W P Walker(Aus)	(O)	Killed	
	Sgt A M Parkin	(WAG)	Killed	
	Sgt N F Brassington	(WAG)	Killed	
	AMM3C W M Boots Jr	(USN)	Killed	
28 Sep 1942	P/O A A Morris (Aus)	(P)	Killed	V9105
	AMM3C G M Nobes	(USN)	Killed	
	PFC J H Fischer	(USAAC)	Killed	
	PFC S L Shipes	(USAAC)	Killed	
	Pte Smith	(USAAC)	Killed	
10 Nov 1942	F/S R R Sillcock(Aus)	(P)	Missing/OP 2	V9253
	Sgt P G Nelson (NZ)	(O)	Missing/OP 2	
	Sgt R Millar	(WAG)	Missing/OP 1	
	Sgt W Skinner	(WAG)	Missing/OP 1	
	S1C H L Drew	(USNR)	Missing	

Whitley

26 Mar 1943	Sgt W G Kirby	(P)	Missing/RP156	EB331
	Sgt I D Bradley	(F/E)	Missing/RP142	
	Sgt C J H MacKenzie	(O)	Missing/RP158	
	Sgt V C Matthews	(WAG)	Killed	
	Sgt K Stainton	(AG)	Missing/RP165	
	Sgt S Westwood	(AG)	Missing/RP169	

Liberator

8 Jul 1943	F/O J Witts	(WAG)	Killed	BZ716
	F/S H A Pomeroy	(WAG)	Wounded	
18 Jul 1943	F/L J A Dewhirst	(P)	Missing/RP119	BZ731
	F/O K C Hollinson	(P)	Missing/RP125	
	F/O G R Rowland	(NAV)	Missing/RP129	
	F/O G W Snelling	(NAV)	Missing/RP129	
	Sgt J E Devine		Missing/RP147	
	F/S B G Kemp DFM		Missing/RP137	
	F/S T Chadwick		Missing/RP135	
24 Jul 1943	LAC H D Brown	(Fitt 2)	Killed	Accident

28 Jul 1943	F/L G F Davey	(P)	Killed	BZ740
	F/S J K G Freeland	(O)	Killed	
	P/O N A Gardiner(NZ)	(NAV)	Killed	
	F/S J Marshall	(WAG)	Killed	
	F/S N C Taylor	(WAG)	Killed	
	Sgt E A Phillips	(WAG)	Killed	
	F/S A V House	(F/E)	Killed	
30 Jul 1943	F/O W J Irving (Can)	(P)	Interned	BZ730
	F/O R E Dobson	(P)	Interned	
	F/O J N Haste	(NAV)	Interned	
	Sgt A J Pudifin(Can)	(WAG)	Interned	
	P/O R A Sharpe	(WAG)	Interned	
	Sgt J Wildon	(WAG)	Interned	
	Sgt J G Humphreys	(WAG)	Interned	
13 Aug 1943	F/O G F Wood DFC	(WAG)	Killed	P9228
21 Sep 1943	Sgt I R Heays (NZ)	(WAG)	Killed	BZ720
	Sgt I R W Thomson(NZ)	(WAG)	Wounded	
4 Oct 1943	F/L J Rintoul	(P)	Missing/RP120	BZ753
	F/O D B Stewart (Can)	(P)	Missing/RP175	
	F/S A Fieldhouse	(NAV)	Missing/RP136	
	F/O C W Foster	(WAG)	Missing/RP124	
	F/S D W McInnis (Can)	(WAG)	Missing/RP184	
	F/S F F Mercer (Can)	(WAG)	Missing/RP185	
	F/S W F Garrod	(WAG)	Missing/RP136	
	F/S W A Dearman		Missing/RP136	
	F/L E M C Guest DFC		Missing/RP119	
15 Nov 1943	F/O D R Cooper	(P)	Killed	BZ817
	F/S E F Barge	(P)	Killed	
	F/O D B Sinclair (Can)	(NAV)	Killed	
	F/O L H Lister	(WAG)	Killed	
	Sgt F Quinn	(WAG)	Killed	
	W/O G Young (Can)	(WAG)	Killed	
	F/S A J Pudifin (Can)	(WAG)	Killed	
	Sgt R J Clarke	(WAG)	Killed	
20 Nov 1943	S/L K A Aldridge DFC	(P)	Missing/RP118	BZ816
	F/O A J Trennery		Missing/RP129	
	F/L A G Warren	(SNAVO)	Missing/RP122	
	F/L J A Hoskin	(WAG)	Missing/RP119	
	W/O O H Hill	(WAG)	Missing/RP134	
	F/S A N Partington	(WAG)	Missing/RP138	
	F/S T L Anderson	(WAG)	Missing/RP134	
	F/S N Smith	(WAG)	Missing/RP139	
	W/O N R Bowman (Can)		Missing/RP179	
21 Nov 1943	F/O A Davis	(P)	Missing/RP124	BZ819
	F/L F Halliday (Can)		Missing/RP172	
	F/O B Hamilton	(WAG)	Missing/RP119	
	F/S W N Owen	(WAG)	Missing/RP138	
	F/S G E Shield	(WAG)	Missing/RP134	
	Sgt L E Terry		Missing/RP166	
	Sgt S C Johnson		Missing/RP155	
4 Feb 1944	F/O R S H Browning	(P)	Missing/RP204	BZ878
	P/O W L Englert (Can)		Missing/RP246	
	F/O F C Langridge		Missing/RP207	
	F/O A G Archibald (Aus)		Missing/RP257	
	P/O D A Rowat (Can)		Missing/RP248	
	F/S A Campbell	(WAG)	Missing/RP216	
	Sgt W F Reid (Can)		Missing/RP256	
	Sgt J M Thomlison (Can)		Missing/RP256	

Date	Name	Role	Status	Aircraft
4 Feb 1944	Sgt F W Gander		Missing/RP229	BZ878
	Sgt D F Taylor		Missing/RP238	
	F/L D A Bell	(P)	Missing/RP201	BZ795
	Sgt V T A Patey		Missing/RP235	
	F/S J O Lewis (Aus)	(NAV)	Missing/RP261	
	F/O N J Williams (Aus)	(NAV)	Missing/RP258	
	F/S S G Hill (Aus)	(WAG)	Missing/RP260	
	Sgt J W Churchman		Missing/RP227	
	F/S E J Fowler (Aus)	(WAG)	Missing/RP260	
	Sgt R D Howard		Missing/RP231	
	Sgt C Lidgitt		Missing/RP233	
17 Apr 1944	F/L F M Burton	(P)	Missing/RP201	BZ945
	P/O E J Hagen (Can)	(P)	Missing/RP246	
	P/O A E Buckley (Aus)	(NAV)	Missing/RP257	
	F/O K K Edwards	(NAV)	Missing/RP205	
	Sgt W A Hallett (Can)	(WAG)	Missing/RP254	
	Sgt T R McDennon (Can)	(WAG)	Missing/RP255	
	Sgt C R Newell (Can)	(WAG)	Missing/RP255	
	F/O L H Abbott	(WAG)	Missing/RP204	
	Sgt R L M Peirce	(WAG)	Missing/RP236	
	Sgt L G Reilly	(F/E)	Missing/RP236	
	F/O A D Critchlow	(P)	Missing/RP205	
	F/L G Roberts	(P)	Missing/RP203	BZ800
	F/O D J Moore	(P)	Missing/RP208	
	F/S M Box (Aus)	(NAV)	Missing/RP260	
	F/S J A Alexander(Aus)	(N)	Missing/RP259	
	F/S F H Nopper	(WAG)	Missing/RP221	
	F/S R J Lawrie (Can)	(WAG)	Missing/RP254	
	F/S J L Stubbs (Can)	(WAG)	Missing/RP254	
	Sgt R J Humbles	(WAG)	Missing/RP231	
	P/O H G P Reed	(F/E)	Missing/RP212	
16 May 1944	Sgt D L Coleman	(Fit/2)	Killed	Accident
21 May 1944	F/O G A Bowman	(P)	Missing/RP204	BZ873
	F/S J K Richards (Aus)	(P)	Missing/RP261	
	F/S R D Christie	(NAV)	Missing/RP216	
	F/S W W Moore (Aus)	(NAV)	Missing/RP261	
	W/O F W Atherton	(WAG)	Missing/RP213	
	F/O H W Watkins (Aus)	(WAG)	Missing/RP258	
	F/S G Harrison	(WAG)	Killed	
	F/S J T Kerr (Aus)	(WAG)	Missing/RP261	
	Sgt A F Johnson (Aus)	(WAG)	Missing/RP260	
	F/O W McTaggart DFM	(F/E)	Missing/RP207	
7 Jun 1944	S/L G Crawford DFC AFC	(P)	Missing/RP200	BZ778
	F/O D G Biggs (Can)	(P)	Missing/RP245	
	P/O R J Martin	(NAV)	Missing/RP212	
	F/O J G Smith	(NAV)	Missing/RP209	
	Sgt K V Jones	(WAG)	Missing/RP232	
	W/O H A Corns	(WAG)	Missing/RP213	
	F/S B G Barton (NZ)	(WAG)	Missing/RP263	
	F/S R A O'Kane (NZ)	(WAG)	Killed	
	Sgt R Stoten	(WAG)	Missing/RP238	
	P/O H Richardson DFM	(F/E)	Missing/RP208	
14 Jun 1944	S/L J W Carmichael DFC	(P)	Missing/RP200	BZ818
	F/S E E Stevens	(P)	Missing/RP222	
	F/S J T McKeown DFM	(NAV)	Missing/RP220	
	F/O A O Peters (Aus)	(NAV)	Missing/RP257	
	F/O V R White		Missing/RP209	
	F/S R H Curner (Aus)	(WAG)	Missing/RP260	

14 Jun 1944	F/S K J Campbell (Aus)	(WAG)	Missing/RP260	BZ818
	F/L J W Shaw		Missing/RP203	
	F/S I E Martin (Aus)	(AG)	Missing/RP261	
	Sgt V H Lusher	(F/E)	Missing/RP233	
31 Jul 1944	F/O J Osborne	(P)	Injured	EW306
	F/O J A D Caines	(P)	Missing/RP204	
	F/L J Morgan	(NAV)	Missing/RP203	
	F/S J Ingham	(WAG)	Missing/RP219	
	Sgt L Fairclough	(WAG)	Missing/RP217	
	Sgt P J W Burns (Can)	(WAG)	Injured	
	F/S F I B Ross (Aus)	(NAV)	Injured	
	W/O A L Walduck	(F/E)	Injured	
27 Aug 1944	F/L C McA Forbes DFC	(P)	Injured	EV899
	F/S H C Reay (NZ)	(P)	Missing/RP264	
	F/L T C Hood	(NAV)	Missing/RP202	
	F/S R J Mullins (Aus)	(NAV)	Missing/RP261	
	F/S W H J Barnes (NZ)	(WAG)	Missing/RP263	
	F/S C J Falconer (NZ)	(WAG)	Missing/RP263	
	Sgt W C Tatum		Missing/RP238	
	Sgt R Ashworth		Missing/RP224	
	Sgt E R Steer	(WAG)	Injured	
	Sgt B A Coombes	(WAG)	Injured	
18 Nov 1944	F/L W G Payne	(P)	Missing/RP203	EV895
	F/S L A Windress		Missing/RP223	
	F/O J C McIver (Can)		Missing/RP247	
	F/S A Palmer		Missing/RP221	
	W/O R A Scott		Missing/RP214	
	W/O J G Chamberlain (Can)		Missing/RP253	
	W/O H A Stephen (Can)		Missing/RP254	
	F/S K J Spackman		Missing/RP222	
	Sgt J Bassett		Missing/RP224	
	F/S G H Cockburn		Missing/RP216	
3 Mar 1945	F/O F W Snapes	(NAV)	Killed	EW293
	F/O J Yates	(NAV)	Injured/Died 6 Mar	
16 Apr 1945	F/O H Lewis	(P)	Missing/RP267	EW303
	F/O H Brown	(AG)	Missing/RP266	
	F/L T B Atkinson (Can)	(WAG)	Missing/RP278	
	F/O D J McL Robertson (Can)	(NAV)	Missing/RP279	
	W/O W Parry	(WAG)	Missing/RP269	
	F/S G L George (Can)	(AG)	Missing/RP281	
	From RAF Tain:			
	LACW W Hutchinson	(Clk/SD)	Killed	
	LACW M MacLean	(RTO)	Injured	
8 Jul 1945	F/L C Grayson	(P)	Killed	KH183
	F/L T H Topping	(P)	Killed	
	F/O W G L Mills	(F/E)	Killed	
	F/S P N Scott	(WAG)	Killed	

Post World War II

Liberator

22 Nov 1945	F/L L Mielecki (Pol)	(P)	Killed	KH126
	F/O G J Meyers	(P)	Killed	
	F/O S Kleybor (Pol)	(NAV)	Killed	
	F/O A Wize (Pol)	(WAG)	Killed	
	F/L J Brzezinski (Pol)	(F/E)	Killed	

Dakota

20 Dec 1947	F/O C Hore	(P)	Injured	KN439

Hastings

20 Dec 1950	F/L G Tunnadine	(P)	Killed	TG574
	F/L S L Bennett	(P)	Killed	
	F/S I A Johns	(NAV)	Killed	
	Sgt G J Bain	(SIG)	Injured/Died 24 Dec	
	Sgt P E Walker	(F/E)	Injured	
	Sgt W A Slaughter	(AQM)	Injured	
	From No.99 Squadron:			
	S/L W G James	(P)	Killed	
	From RAF Abingdon:			
	S/L T C L Brown	(MO)	Injured	
22 Jun 1953	F/L J Dodds	(P)	Killed	WJ335
	Sgt J W Mead	(P)	Killed	
	F/L E T Orringe	(NAV)	Killed	
	M/S H Mourant	(SIG)	Killed	
	Sgt L R Plummer	(F/E)	Killed	
	Sgt P J Buckley	(AQM)	Killed	
27 Jul 1953	F/L S E Judd	(P)	Injured	TG564

Beverley

5 Mar 1957	F/L N E H Gilbert	(P)	Killed	XH117
	F/L R G Wilcox	(NAV)	Killed	
	Sgt G M Woodhouse	(SIG)	Killed	
	Cpl J L A Spoel	(AQM)	Killed	
	F/L L A Andrew	(NAV)	Injured	
	F/O H J Ludlam	(P)	Injured	
	From No.47 Squadron:			
	F/S J Zarecky	(P)	Killed	
	Sgt W J Owen	(SIG)	Killed	
	Sgt D Robinson	(AQM)	Killed	
	F/L V J R Hurring DFC	(P)	Injured	
13 Apr 1963	F/S F Denby	(AQM)	Killed	XB268
	S/L M P Wells	(P)	Injured	
	F/O W C S Henderson	(P)	Injured	
	F/L C G Rogers	(NAV)	Injured	
	F/L D R May	(NAV)	Injured	
	F/S F A Brown	(SIG)	Injured	
	M/E A J Doyle	(F/E)	Injured	
	From RAF Abingdon:			
	SAC D E Marshall	(W/Mech)	Killed	

F/O John Wray on a Blenheim at Odiham early in 1939. He later became Gp Capt J.E. Wray CBE DFC

APPENDIX VI

Awards and Decorations

World War I

DSO

Major C S Wynne-Eyton (RFC)	1.1.18

Croix de Guerre (French)

Major G Henderson (38th Central India Horse)	21.9.18

MC

Lt H Blofeld (RFC)	26.7.17
Lt J E S P Bradford (West Riding Regiment)	26.7.17
2Lt R E J Fulljames (RFC)	18.10.17
Capt S G Hodges (Wiltshire Regiment)	26.9.17
Lt F H Holmes (Royal Engineers)	25.4.18
Capt J B Home-Hay (7th Argyll & Sutherlands)	26.7.17
Lt A Lomax (RFA)	30.4.18
Capt K R Napier (RFC/RAF)	17.5.18

Lt E L O'Leary (Canadian Field Artillery)	17.5.18
Lt J J Quinn (RFC/RAF)	30.4.18

DFC

Lt G Davis (RAF)	8.2.19
2Lt G L Pargeter (Royal Fusiliers)	3.12.18
Lt B E Scott (Canadian Field Artillery)	3.8.18

MSM

Sgt Major G Gillman (8398) (RFC/RAF)	3.6.18

Croix de Guerre

Cpl G Holmes (98931) (RFC/RAF)	15.4.18
Cpl W Metson (106809) (RFC/RAF)	15.4.18

World War II

DSO

Wg Cdr J R Leggate	22.5.43

OBE

Flt Sgt H G Christmas	11.7.40

DFC

Sqn Ldr K A Aldridge	28.7.42
W/O W Anderson (RNZAF)	2.6.44
Flt Lt A C Brown	23.7.40
Plt Off B S Bannister	17.5.41
W/O F E Bailey (RNZAF)	27.7.45
Flt Lt J W Carmichael	14.6.44
Sqn Ldr G Crawford	22.12.43
Fg Off D Destonis (RCAF)	22.8.44
Plt Off A P Dottridge	21.12.40
Fg Off K L Fogden	22.8.44
Flt Lt C Mc A Forbes	21.5.44
Wg Cdr R T F Gates AFC	18.8.44
Plt Off G E Greville-Heygate	17.5.41
Fg Off J F Handasyde	20.7.43
Sqn Ldr A E Hilditch	19.4.43
Fg Off W J Irving (RCAF)	22.8.44
Flt Lt E B A Le Maistre	27.7.45
Fg Off C K McPherson	10.10.44
Sqn Ldr T C P Maxwell	16.4.43
Sqn Ldr W S G Maydwell	23.11.40
Flt Lt R T Merrifield	8.7.43
Flt Lt R M Mottram	25.2.41
Sqn Ldr W B Murray	23.7.40
Fg Off A D Panton	8.3.40
Plt Off E Plumtree	29.10.40
Plt Off J P Rickards (RAAF)	19.10.42
Flt Lt G R D Sherwell	7.12.43
Plt Off J D Steuart-Richardson	29.1.41
W/O I R W Thomson (RNZAF)	22.8.44
Plt Off T DeR Waters	30.8.41
Flt Lt J S Wilkinson	9.9.44
Fg Off G F Wood	8.7.43

Bar to DFC

Flt Lt G G Potier DFC	7.9.44

DFM

Sgt B J Brooks	23.7.40
Sgt G H Cooper	23.7.40
Sgt W J Cronin	8.3.40
Flt Sgt D Diggles	31.10.41
AC1 H A Ferre	8.3.40
Sgt R W Gellard	25.2.41
Sgt F D King	21.12.40
Sgt P M Kinsey	29.10.40
Sgt R A Latham	23.7.40
Sgt J T McKeown	14.6.44
Sgt H J Mills (RNZAF)	7.7.44
Flt Sgt R Niven	8.7.43
Sgt H A Pomeroy	20.7.43
Sgt D J Roberts	23.11.40
Sgt W P Whetton	23.7.40
Sgt W E Williams	25.2.41

BEM

Flt Sgt W Springate	2.6.43
Sgt G M Jarratt	1.1.46

MID

Flt Lt I H Bartlett	1.1.41
Flt Lt H G Boreham	31 1.45
Cpl D Boulton	1.1.41
LAC C J Bubb	1.1.41
Plt Off J Butterworth	26.2.40
Cpl W M Chowns	1.1.41
Sgt A E Farrow	1.1.41
Plt Off J W Faulkner	14.3.41
Plt Off T M Gay	11.6.42
Flt Lt F Halliday (RCAF)	20.11.43
LAC D J Horsborough	1.1.41
Cpl K A Hides	14.6.43
W/O R G Marsh	14.6.43
Plt Off D P Massey	1.1.41
Sgt J P Rickards (RAAF)	8.5.42
Sgt E C Roe	1.1.41
LAC F Rogers	25.2.40
Sgt E D Sheldrick	1.1.41
Flt Sgt W H H Smith	1.1.41
Cpl W Springate	25.2.40
Plt Off J D Steuart-Richardson	1.1.41
Flt Lt S A Thompson	14.3.41
Flt Sgt G B Watson (RCAF)	14.6.43
Flt Sgt H Webb	14.6.43
W/O H C Westwood	25.2.40

APPENDIX VII

Abbreviations Used

AA	Anti-aircraft		LAC	Leading Aircraftman
AACU	Anti-aircraft Co-operation Unit		LACW	Leading Aircraftwoman
AASF	Advanced Air Striking Force		Lt	Lieutenant/Leutnant
AC	Army Co-operation		MC	Military Cross
ACAS	Assistant Chief of the Air Staff		MID	Mentioned in Despatches
ACM	Air Chief Marshal		MSM	Meritorious Service Medal
AC1	Aircraftman 1st Class		MU	Maintenance Unit
AC2	Aircraftman 2nd Class		NAS	Naval Air Station
AD	Aircraft Depot		NAV	Navigator
AFB	Air Force Base		NCO	Non-Commissioned Officer
AFC	Air Force Cross		NZ	New Zealand
AG	Aerial Gunner/Air Gunner		OBS	Observer
ALG	Advanced Landing Ground		OCU	Conversion Unit
AM	Air Marshal		Olt	Oberleutnant
ANGB	Air National Guard Base		OP	Ottawa Memorial Panel Number
AOA	Air Officer Administration		OTU	Operational Training Unit
AOC	Air Officer Commanding		P	Pilot
AQM	Air Quartermaster		PAR	Precision Approach Radar
ASC	Army Service Corps		PLE	Prudent Limit of Endurance
ASD	Aeroplane Supply Depot		P/O	Pilot Officer
ASV	Air-to-Surface Vessel		POL	Poland
Aus	Australia		POW	Prisoner of War
AVM	Air Vice Marshal		PRU	Photographic Reconnaissance Unit
BABS	Blind Approach Beacon System		PTS	Parachute Training School
BAFF	British Air Forces in France		P2	Pilot 2 (NCO Aircrew Rank)
BEM	British Empire Medal		RA	Royal Artillery
Can	Canada		RAAF	Royal Australian Air Force
CAP	Counter Attack Patrol		RAE	Royal Aircraft Establishment
Capt	Captain		RCAF	Royal Canadian Air Force
Cdr	Commander		RE	Royal Engineers
CinC	Commander-in-Chief		REME	Royal Electrical and Mechanical Engineers
CO	Commanding Officer		RFA	Royal Field Artillery
Cpl	Corporal		RFC	Royal Flying Corps
DC	Depth Charge		RGA	Royal Garrison Artillery
DCLI	Devon and Cornwall Light Infantry		RNZAF	Royal New Zealand Air Force
D/F	Direction Finding		RP	Runnymede Memorial Panel Number
DFC	Distinguished Flying Cross		Sgt	Sergeant
DFM	Distinguished Flying Medal		Sig	Air Signaller
DSO	Distinguished Service Order		S/L	Squadron Leader
DZ	Dropping Zone		SNCO	Senior NCO
EFTS	Elementary Flying Training School		SOC	Struck off Charge
F/E	Flight Engineer		SR	Special Reserve
FIDO	Fog Investigation Dispersal Operation		SU	Support Unit
Fkapt	Fregettenkapitän		S2	Signaller 2 (NCO Aircrew Rank)
F/L	Flight Lieutenant		TCEU	Transport Command Examining Unit
Flt	Flight		UAE	United Arab Emirates
F/O	Flying Officer		Uffz	Unteroffizier
F/S	Flight Sergeant		USAAC	US Army Air Corps
G/C	Group Captain		USAF	US Air Force
GCA	Ground Controlled Approach		USN	US Navy
GL	General List (RFC)		Vzfw	Vizefeldwebel
HLI	Highland Light Infantry		W/C	Wing Commander
HQ	Headquarters		W/O	Warrant Officer
KEH	King Edward's Horse		WOP	Wireless Operator
Kkapt	Korvettenkapitän		W/T	Wireless Telegraphy
Klt	Kapitänleutnant		1/AM	1st Class Air Mechanic
KRRC	King's Royal Rifle Corps		2/AM	2nd Class Air Mechanic
			2Lt	Second Lieutenant

ACKNOWLEDGEMENTS

I would like to offer my thanks to all of the following for their help and without whom I could not have written this history:

From 53 Squadron: W/O B L Abbott, S/L R N Alcock, F/L C A G Ashman, F/L A J Barnes, F/O R Baxter RAAF, S/L L T Bennett, W/C J G Brodie MBE AFC, Mrs E G Brookes, F/O A W G Brown, F/O F J Brown, F/O W G Brown, C S Carpenter, F/L D E Carter, the late F/L W C Cleaver, W/C P J Cundy DSO DFC AFC TD, F/L R E Dobson, the late Capt C Dowdall MC RFC, F/O L Esler RCAF, F/L R R Fabel DFC, F/L K FitzRoy, W/O C D Gethin, F/L E Gledhill, F/L P Gordon, Roy Groves, F/L S H Guy, F/O R M Hall, the late Lt Col A P C Hannay MC, W/O D A Harrington, F/S D E F Hayter, the late F/S G Holt, F/L R W Hurnall, F/O W R Kinsman RAAF, F/L R Kirkbride, G/C J R Leggate DSO, W/C L G W Lilly, P/O I F Little RAAF, F/L A MacLean, S/L D A G McLeod, S/L M May RAAF, G/C W S G Maydwell DSO DFC, W/C M J Middlemist, W/C E Miskiman RCAF, W/C R M Mottram DFC and Bar, Sgt R I Mowat, W/O A F Murray RAAF, W/C N A D Nugent, F/L F Nuttall, Air Commodore A D Panton DFC, F J Peebles, the late AVM E Plumtree CB OBE DFC, C/T J E Rhodes, S/L D J Roberts DFM, F/L C G Rowe, Sgt S Robinson, F/L E Skemp, S/L A Spooner DSO DFC, the late W/C B W Taylor DFC, the late F/L D Thomas, F/L D Turner, W/O V Udberg, F/L C Waldrop RCAF, S/L H Wallbank, S/L R Walton MC AFC, F/O L G Watt, F/L D Weir, Sid Williams, G/C J B Wray CBE DFC

Others who have helped: Gillian Anderson, Bob Andrew, Cornish Aviation Society, Chris Ashworth, Mrs N Berrill, Theo Boiten, F/L I Buckley RAAF, F/L E S Cheek AFC DFM, Mr A Day, S/L C H Goss, Wyb Jan Groendijk, C M Hobson, Philip Jarrett, Alwyn Jay RAAF, Lt Col A P De Jong RNAF, F/L R King, C/T A Lumsden, B McCann, J G Perkins, B T Richardson, Juan Carlos Salgado, John and Jean Shapland, Ken Smalley, Ray Sturtivant, Andy Thomas, Raymond Vann, Colin J Waugh, P G White,

Without wishing to single out any one person, I simply could not have completed this project without the help of my good friend Mr Richard Robinson who did an inordinate amount of "digging" on my behalf at the PRO, Kew and at the RAF Museum. Mr S H Clarke, Air Historical Branch (RAF), was of invaluable help in solving some of the more obscure mysteries and particular praise goes to Mr R M Coppock, Naval Historical Branch, who went to great lengths to make sure that I got the naval matters correct. Mr James J Halley MBE deserves a great deal of praise for his dedication in producing the Air-Britain RAF Aircraft series. These volumes have made the task of researching so much easier. Finally, my Dutch friend Hans de Haan provided me with the information needed to complete a list of 53 Squadron casualties and POW details for the whole of World War II, for which I shall be eternally grateful.

53 SQUADRON ASSOCIATION

The 53 Squadron Association was formed at midnight on 1 September 1976. Membership is free and is available to al past members of the squadron and their dependents. Reunion and other events are organised from time to time and furthe details can be obtained from either of the following:

Peter W Lewis
Secretary & Treasurer
53 Squadron Association
46 Bagley Wood Road
Kennington
Oxford   OX1 5LY

Jock Manson
Historian
53 Squadron Association
17 Barnside Avenue
Burgess Hill
West Sussex   RH15 0JU

LITERATURE CONSULTED

Aircraft versus Submarine	Alfred Price
A Penguin in the Eyrie	Hector Bolitho
Belfast	Molly O'Loughlin White
B.E.2 in Action	Peter Cooksley
Blackburn Beverley	Bill Overton
Flight From the Middle East	ACM Sir David Lee GBE CB
RAF Coastal Command	Chris Ashworth
R.A.F. R.E.8	J M Bruce
The Berlin Airlift	Robert Jackson
The Eye in the Air	Peter Mead
The Fighting Captain	Alan Burn
The Squadrons of the RAF	James J Halley MBE

Various Air-Britain publications
Various copies of Cross & Cockade

SCRAPBOOK

People and Planes and Places

Bailleul, 1917. Left to right: back row: Capt J.B. Home-Hay and two unknown. Seated: Capt J.O. Archer, Capt S.G. Hodges, Lt F.C. Elstob (Senior Observer). (The late Capt C.C.L. Dowdall MC)

Bailleul, 1917. Left to right: Major J.K. Kinnear (CO 42 Sqn), two unknown, Lt H.W. Smith (C Flt 53 Sqn). (The late Capt C.C.L. Dowdall MC)

2Lt F.G.B. Pascoe (7th Royal Irish Fusiliers. Shot down and killed on 2 July 1917 by Baron Manfred von Richthofen. (Hal Giblin)

2Lt S.W. Cowper Coles, Autumn 1918. Killed in action on 14 October 1918 in R.E.8 E33 of 7 Squadron, shortly after leaving 53 Squadron. (Colin Waugh)

Lt G.F. Wilson, Recording Officer, Bailleul, 1917. (The late Capt C.C.L. Dowdall MC)

2Lt S.F. Pickup, Capt C.G. White MC and Lt A.D.E.M. Severne

No. 53 Squadron at Clairmarais, 8 July 1918. (S St Martin collection)
Front row: Lt J.B. Sanders, Lt J.F. Vickerton, Lt W. Cowden, Lt G.L. Pargeter, Lt L.J. St Jean, Lt B. Pepper
Second row: Lt T.B.M. Brown, Capt Towler (IO), Capt W.S.C. Smith (OC 'A' Flt), Capt D.R. Hanlon (OC 'C' Flt), Major G. Henderson (CO), Capt A.W. Jones (RO), Capt K.R. Napier MC (OC 'B' Flt), Capt Duc, Lt D.W. Saunders
Third row: Lt K.A. Ranney, Lt J. Willson, Lt Harris, Lt G.L. Dobell, Lt. A.W. Baker, Lt T.G. Evans, Lt H. Walpole, Lt H.W. Auerbach, Lt G.C. Brown, Lt R.J. Aitken, Lt D.C. Dunlop, Lt C.C. Allinson, unknown
Back row: Lt Bowden USA, unknown, Lt T.J. Stannage, Lt. S.A. Bird, unknown, Lt B.E. Scott MC, Lt J.M. Calneck, Lt G. Davis, Lt Davies USA, Lt J.A. Lewis, Lt Hangfield (EO), Lt H.F. Redmond.
(S St Martin collection)

Below: Headquarters Flight at Sweveghem on Armistice Day, 11 November 1918

No.53 Squadron at Sweveghem on 11 November 1918. Top 'A' Flight, centre 'B' Flight and bottom 'C' Flight

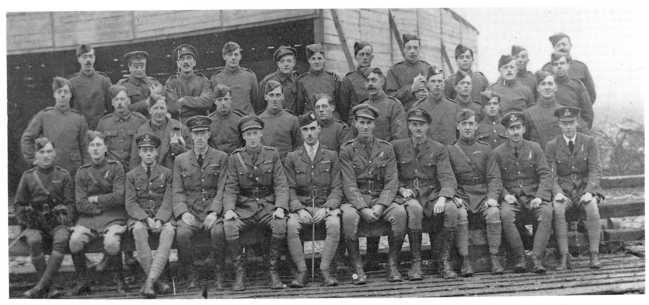

'C' Flight at Odiham in 1938. Front row; unknown, P/O P.F.G. Jameson, P/O D.P. Hughes, Capt K.E. McIntyre, P/O J.F. Hyde, two unknown. (C.S. Carpenter)

At School of Army Co-operation, Andover, with 59 Squadron personnel.
Back row: Sgt J. Culnane, two of 59, Sgt F. Haisell, one of 59;
Centre row: P/O F. Walton, P/O A. Fleming, one of 59, P/O R. Miles, P/O I.F. Anderson
Front row; Sgt E Allgood, three of 59. (S/L R. Walton MC AFC)

Refuelling Hectors at Evanton; left to right: P/O Peter Jameson, P/O Ian Jameson, F/O Jack Butterworth, P/O Jasper Read. (Gp Capt J.B. Wray CBE DFC)

At Kirkwall on 29 August 1938. Left to right: Capt Joyce, P/O Read, F/O Butterworth, P/O Wray, P/O Ian Jameson, Lt Maydwell, P/O Peter Jameson. (Gp Capt J.B. Wray)

AC 'Batt' Moriarty, an early Blenheim air gunner, shot down and killed attacking German convoy near Ameland on 25 July 1940 in Blenheim R3836. (B. McCann)

Sgt L.L. Benjamin at Detling. He was killed in Blenheim T1940/D flown by the CO, W/C E.C.T. Edwards, on 31 August 1940. (Ralph King)

F/O Jack Butterworth, Capt John McIntyre (Royal Tank
Corps), Capt M.D. Khalifa (Royal Egyptian Air Force)

RAF and Army officers at SAC Andover in 1938 Left to right:
P/O Ian Jameson, Lt 'Dizzie' Dayrell (Royal Artillery), P/O
Jasper Read, Lt Dick Maydwell (Somerset Light Infantry), Lt
Brian Daly (Lancashire Fusiliers) S/L Bill Murray, F/L Jack
Butterworth. (G/C J.B. Wray CBE DFC)

NCO aircrew at Bedruthan Steps Hotel, near St.Eval, Spring 1941. Some identified as follows:
Front row, left to right: Sgts Stevens, unknown, Fennel, unknown, Fabel, Hall.
Centre row: unknown, Sgts Archie Graham, Ian Graham, F/S Roberts DFM, four unknown, Sgt King DFM
Back row: unknown, Sgts Powell, Diggles, unknown, Allgood, Culnane, two unknown, McKechnie, unknown, Dennis, unknown
(S/L R. Walton MC, AFC)

No. 53 Squadron at Bircham Newton in July 1941

Back row: unknown, Sgt Jayne, Sgt McKechnie, Sgt Popplewell, Sgt Stead, Sgt Williams, Sgt A. Graham, unknown, F/S Cook, Sgt Wood, Sgt Templeton, Sgt Gotham, Sgt Smith, Sgt Powell, Sgt Perkins, Sgt Saunders, Sgt Varley, Sgt Carson, Sgt W.G. Brown, Sgt Carty, Sgt Melvin, Sgt Kyle, Sgt Mercer, Sgt Sewell, Sgt Poole, Sgt Owen, two unknown, Sgt King DFM, Sgt Boulton

Centre row: P/O Hayton, P/O Hilditch, unknown, P/O Grimsditch, P/O Thomas, P/O Abbott, unknown, P/O Waters DFC, unknown, P/O Buck, P/O Stevens, P/O Gay, P/O Moira, unknown, S/L Fell, P/O McLintock, P/O Dobson, F/L Hurnall, P/O Williams, P/O O'Brien, P/O Oldworth, P/O Coates, P/O Gibbs, unknown, F/O Wyles

Sitting: Sgt Anderson, Sgt Maslen, Sgt Fennell, Sgt Garcia-Scott, Sgt Lansdale, Sgt Brookes, unknown, Sgt Griffiths, Sgt Hall, F/S Roberts DFM, Sgt F.J. Brown, Sgt Diggles DFM, Sgt Jenkinson, Sgt Cleaver

No. 53 Squadron at Limavady in January 1942

Back row: Sgt Owen, Sgt Gardner, Sgt Kennard, Sgt Morgan, Sgt Frost, Sgt Weitzel, Sgt Wyllie, Sgt Moore, Sgt Morris, Sgt Corden, Sgt Poitevin, Sgt Jesty, Sgt Nevills, Sgt Thornhill, Sgt Moran, Sgt Rickards, Sgt Johnson, Sgt Guthrie, Sgt Clarke, Sgt May, Sgt Clouston, Sgt Diamond

Centre row: P/O Fairburn, P/O Gotham, P/O Goatley, P/O Davey, P/O Woodhall, P/O Jacob, F/O Guiver, F/L Dobson, S/L Aldridge, W/C Grant, F/L Hilditch, F/L Pemberton, F/O Stigner, F/O Wyles, F/O Hood, P/O Ray, P/O Davies, P/O Knight, P/O Middleton

Front tow: Sgt Foster, Sgt Smith, Sgt Hale, Sgt F.J. Brown, Sgt Rayner, Sgt Anderson, Sgt Garcia-Scott, F/S Roberts DFM, Sgt Udberg, Sgt Jenkinson, Sgt Newhouse, Sgt Cliffe, Sgt Abbott, Sgt Maher

P/O F/S Eddie Allgood, P/O Rae Walton, Sgt Jack Culnane, St. Eval, Spring 1941. (S/L R. Walton MC AFC)

P/O Alf Fleming and PO 'Wiggie' Wigmore at Thorney Island, January 1941 (S/L R. Walton MC AFC)

F/L I.P. Magrath; shot down by flak in Hudson AM672/P on 10 August 1941 off Friesians. He was washed ashore on Schiermonikoog on 16 October and buried with full military honours on 18 October. (Wyb van Groendijk)

P/O Peter Gibb, Bircham Newton, July 1941 (F/L W.C. Cleaver)

Sgt Thornhill's crew, North Coates, Spring 1942
Sgt Dickie Thornhill, Sgt Murray May (RAAF), F/S Jack Diamond, Sgt Dave Moran (RCAF)
This crew ditched with flak damaged near Sylt on 8 April 1942 in AM549/F and ended up in Stalag VIIIB, Lamsdorf
(S/L M.A. May)

Sgt Rickard's crew, North Coates, May 1942
Sgt G.R.G. Johnson (RAAF), Sgt John Rickards (RAAF), Sgt J. Smith, Sgt K. Whitnall
(F/L G.R.G. Johnson)

Sgt Arthur Newhouse (WOP/AG) North Coates, Spring 1942
Shot down by flak off IJmuiden in AM530/Q on 4 May 1942
(F/L F. Nuttall)

Sgt Bill Cleaver, North Coates, Spring 1942
(F/L W.C. Cleaver)

Crew members at Lachine, near Montreal, returning from Trinidad; Sgt 'Pom' Pomeroy, Sgt 'Squibs' Whorlow, F/S Jack Badger, P/O John Woodrow-Davies, Sgt Bill Cleaver, Sgt Dil Thomas. (F/L W.C. Cleaver)

F/O G.W. Winter's crew, Thorney Island, August 1943 F/S L. Hood, Sgt R. Pearson, P/O G.W. Winter (RCAF), Sgt L.G. Lewsey, Sgt H.S. Vince, Sgt E.J. Hawkins, P/O J. Gorman, P/O K.L. Fogden. (W/O H.S. Vince)

P/O Esler's crew, 20 February 1944
Back row: F/S A.W.G. Brown, F/S A.F. Murray (RAAF), P/O Len Esler (RCAF), Sgt T.H. Neilson, F/S R.J. Crompton (RAAF)
Front row: W/O W.R. Kinsman (RAAF), F/S F. Clegg (RNZAF), W/O R.C. Lauer (RCAF), Sgt D.M. Holden (S/L A.W.G. Brown)

F/L Davey's crew, July 1943
F/L G.F. Davey, F/S J.K.G. Freeland, P/O N.A. Gardiner (RNZAF), P/O J.P.P. Grignon (RCAF), F/S J. Marshall, W/O W.C. Cleaver, F/S D. Thomas
Four members of this crew were killed on 28 July 1943 in BZ740/F. (The late F/L D. Thomas)

F/O K.C.J. Boulter's crew, Thorney Island, Summer 1943

P/O Tony Buck and P/O Johnny Good at immediate readiness

Sgt 'Mac' McLeod (RCAF), North Coates, Spring 1942
(F/L Bill Cleaver)

F/O Frank Nuttall
(F/L F. Nuttall)

At readiness, North Coates, Spring 1942
P/O Guthrie, Sgt McLoughlin, F/S Wyllie, unknown, P/O Harman (standing), Sgt Cook, Sgt Nuttall, Sgt Osborne, W/O Marsh
(Sigs Officer), Sgt MacRoberts, Sgt Brookes. (F/L F. Nuttall)

F/S W. Anderson (RNZAF) sank U535 on 5 July 1943 in Liberator BZ751/G. (Gillian Anderson)

W/C R.T.F. Gates AFC at St.Eval, CO from November 1943 to August 1944. (IWM CH12369)

S/L Tony Spooner's crew, St.Eval, early 1944
Back row: W/O Ware, F/L Moore, S/L Spooner, F/O Wilkinson, F/L Wells; front row: F/S Mills (RNZAF), F/S Bailey (RNZAF), F/S Thompson (RNZAF), Sgt Hinchliffe, F/S Barnes. (S/L A. Spooner DSO, DFC)

S/L 'Flash' Henley's crew, St.Eval, summer 1944
Back row: F/O C.W. Dorey (RAAF), F/O G.V. Lorimer, S/L
E.P. Henley (Newfoundland), Sgt R. Browning, F/S I.F. Little
(RAAF)
Front row: F/O R.M. Hall, Sgt J.F. Dunglinson, F/O W.
James, F/O F.P. Brown. (F/O Ian Little)

F/L C. Waldrop's crew, Reykjavik, December 1944
Back row: F/S E.G. Mercer, Sgt J. Mitchell, Sgt C. Coffey,
F/S E.W. Puttrell, F/S N.F. Catt
Front row: W/O E. Arnold (RCAF), F/L A.H. Moore, F/L C.
Waldrop (RCAF), F/S H.R. Hook (RCAF), F/S J. McKay
(F/L C. Waldrop)

F/L 'Gillie' Potier's crew, St.Eval, 15 August 1944
Back row: W/O F.E. Bailey, F/O L. Cundy, F/L G.G. Potier
DFC, Sgt W. Strangward, F/O T.K. Archer (RAAF)
Front row: Sgt E. Butterfield, Sgt W. Bond, Sgt J.K.
Johnson, Sgt K.A. Kirkland (RAAF), Sgt K.S. Thue (RCAF)
Front row: W/O W.R. Kinsman (RAAF), F/S F. Clegg
(RNZAF), W/O R.C. Lauer (RCAF), Sgt D.M. Holden
(S/L A.W.G. Brown)

F/O 'Ed' Miskiman's crew, Reykjavik, 1945
Back row: Sgt S. Nunn, Sgt G. Holt, P/O Stokes, F/S A.
Owen, F/O A.G. Flippance, Sgt A.W. Vine
Front row: P/O A. Banwell, F/L W.H. Webb, F/O H.E.
Miskiman (RCAF), F/O R. Stansfield, F/S R.W. Rolph
(W/O G. Holt)

F/L Earnshaw's crew, Reykjavik, Spring 1945
Back row: F/S L.E. Avery, W/O S. Sheridan, F/S L.E.
Ashford, W/O A. Fishwick, Sgt R. Beacock
Front row: F/L R.J. Snedker, F/O R.W. Moran (RCAF), F/L
G.J. Earnshaw, F/O E.A. Rutland, P/O I.F. Little (RAAF)

F/L J. Ketcheson's crew, Reykjavik, March 1945
Back row: Sgt F.J. Davis, Sgt G. Baker, Sgt D. Hayr, F/S A.
Appleton, Sgt D. Benson, F/S R. Anderson
Front row: F/O W.Y. George, F/L J. Ketcheson (RCAF), F/O
B.L. Cawley, F/O A. Strickland (D.E.F. Hayter)

F/L J. Burton's crew, St.Eval, January 1944
Back row: Sgt E.A. Grover, F/S A.R. Baxter (RAAF), F/L J.
Burton, P/O M.B. Hurley (RAAF), F/S J.H. Hawkins (RAAF)
Front row: F/S M. Kohler (RAAF), F/S T.C. McGrath
(RAAF), F/S J.D. Hunter (RAAF), F/S J.A.V. Kelly (RAAF)
F/O A.R. Baxter)

F/L Stan Houghton's crew, St.Eval, August 1944
Back row: Sgt R.E. Brocksop, F/O L.G. Renn, F/L S.J.
Houghton, F/S A. Thompson, F/O R.A. Sharpe
Front row: W/O F. Clafton, F/S P.W. Johnson (RAAF), Sgt
C.D. Gethin, F/S J.A. Humphreys
(W/O C.D. Gethin)

F/L H. Nixon's crew, Reykjavik, April 1945
Back row: Sgt E.A. Mann, F/S D. McLintock, F/S J.
Bowman, Sgt T.W. Payne, F/S H. Wallbank
Front row: F/O J.A. Haw, F/L C. Gay, F/L H. Nixon, F/L J.
McAtamney
(S/L H. Wallbank)

F/L W.K.T. Brook's crew, Reykjavik, April 1945
Back row: W/O D.H. Smith, F/S J.B. Beirne (RNZAF), F/S
E.A. Duncan, Sgt C.A.G. Ashman, F/S K.S. Blakesley
Front row: F/S D.A. Harrington, P/O P. Hall, F/L W.K.T.
Brooks, F/S A.G. Middleton, W/O M.M. Stewart (RNZAF)
(F/L C.A.G. Ashman)

F/L F.M. Burton's crew, early 1944
Back row: F/O A.E. Buckley (RAAF), F/O K.K. Edwards,
F/L F.M. Burton, P/O E.J. Hagen (RCAF), F/O L.H. Abbott
Front row: Sgt R.L. Peirce, Sgt W.A. Hallett (RCAF), Sgt
C.R. Newell (RCAF), Sgt L.G. Reilly, F/S T.R. McDennon
(RCAF). (Ian Buckley)

F/O Harradence's crew, St.Eval, 7 July 1944
Left to right: F/S N.L. Tichenor, F/S V.E. Glasswell, F/S
R.J. Hall, W/O K.J. Brewer, F/O S. Coates, F/O C.W.
Harradence, P/O B.W. Hutchins, F/S R.D. Cochrane, Sgt W.
Martin, W/O L.G. Watt
(F/O Lloyd Watt)

129

Sgt R.J.C. Hall, port beam gunner, at St.Eval. (IWM)

W/C A.R. Holmes RCAF with HQ staff at Reykjavik

W/O A.P. McKinnon, RNZAF) with homing pigeons after a patrol over the Bay of Biscay in BZ818. (IWM CH12365)

F/O E.R. Skemp and F/L W.K.T. Brooks, Reykjavik, 21 March 1945. (F/L E.R. Skemp)

Unloading homing pigeons. Left to right: Sgt W.C. Tatum, Sgt J.S. Knapp RCAF, W/O A.P. McKinnon RNZAF. (IWM CH12364)

S/L George Crawford DFC, AFC. He and his crew were shot down on 7 June 1944 in BZ778/M. (IWM CH12368)

No.53 Squadron at Wunstorf in early 1950

Front row: S.2 J.P. McCarthy, P.3 J.M. Simpson, N.3 H.T.C. Farmer, N.3 P.M. Gibbons, E.4 A.N. Mitchell, S.2 M. Goacher, P.3 L.W. Marsh, N.2 J.I. Ludden, P.3 S.J. Adams

Second row: F/L W.T. Thornton, F/L S. Evans, F/L E.S. Davis, F/L D.J. Scott, S/L J.P. Trant, F/L F.W. Wincott, F/L D.F. Hanson AFC, F/L D.J. Doherty DFC, F/L R.R. Wheeler

Third row: P.1 D.W. Francis, Sgt E.J. Webb (Glider Pilot Regt), S.1 E.G. Green, F/L E. Goose, F/L J. Sinclair, F/L J.D. Beacham AFC, F/L M.P. Baillache, P/O O.H. Hoadley, P/O P.O. McCann, M/S R.D. Brown, S.1 J.K. Dands, N.2 T.A. Robinson

Back row: E.4 J. Vaughan, E.2 H. Barrows, P.2 R.F. McLaren, E.4 F. Bartle, N.2 W.H. Adamson, S.2 G.H. Taylor, E.4 T.H. Knight, S.1 N. Dodd, E.2 G.H. Taylor, E.4 R.B. Ives, E.2 S.F. Spencer, E.4 D.W. Thompson

No.53 Squadron detachment at Changi, July 1953
(F/L A. Maclean)

131

F/S Les Bennett, Netheravon, 1947. (S/L L.T. Bennett)

F/L Stan Guy (Engineer Leader) at Mauripur, Pakistan, 1953

No.53 Squadron at Abingdon, 1959

Front row: F/O A. Smedley, F/L F. Welch, F/L E.W. McDonnell, F/L K.C. FitzRoy, F/L C.J. Calvert, F/L H. Charnley, W/C B.W. Taylor DFC, F/L W. Thompson, F/L A. Scorey, F/L R. Kirkbride, F/L J.M. Bass, F/L F. Baker, F/L P.W. Lewis
Second row: F/L J. King, F/L A. Aked, M/N W. Todd, M/P J. James, F/O R. Statham, F/O G. Sutton, F/L R. Rowlands, F/L Jock McKay, F/L W. Deere, F/L R. Fisher, F/L J. Ludham, F/L M.H. Letton, M/P A. Obolewicz, F/L K.J. Parfitt, F/L D. Durling, F/L David, F/L J.H. Jones, F/L P. McComas (Adj)
Third row: F/L H. Crawley, F/L R. Sibley, two unknown, Sgt Trewatha, unknown, F/O R. Spiers, unknown, M/E F. Threadgold, M/E G. Hatt, three unknown
Back row: Four unknown, M/N C. Burgess, unknown, F/S G. Banks, two unknown, F/S M. Mercer, unknown, Sgt Nicholls

F/L Andy Wilson and crew, Fayid, December 1953; left to right: Unknown, F/O Gordon, F/L Wilson, Sgt Biddiscombe, Sgt Pemberton; kneeling: unknown. (F/L P. Gordon)

F/O Ernie Gledhill aboard Hastings WJ333 between Changi and Darwin, 10 May 1954

Sgt Tony Wheeler (Sig) aboard Hastings WJ333 between Changi and Darwin on 10 May 1954

F/L Dickie Dye on the steps of a Belfast, 1966

H.M. The Queen inspecting a squadron crew at Brize Norton, 12 March 1971
Left to right: F/S W.I. Hext, M/E P.E. Gregson, S/L K. Newman, F/L D.A. Ferguson, H.M. The Queen, F/L C.N. Murgatroyd

'Meester Selkirk's Last Flight'
Lajes - Brize Norton, 18 November
1974 in XR369 after more than 30
years service.
F/L Jock Manson, F/L Brian Prior,
MALM Roy Selkirk, Sgt Phil Lowe,
C/T Ginge Eves, S/L Tony Freeman,
S/L Sean Moffet, C/T Mo Morris,
ME Dave Frost

The Concorde Support Team,
June 1972
MALM Tony Thacker, F/L Eric
Taylor, S/L Tony Woodford,
Sgt Jim Duff, F/L George Embleton,
ME Ian Medlam

Presentation of the Berlin Gold Cup
to 53 Squadron, 6 December 1973
OC 24 Squadron with the 'Lord Trophy'
W/C M.J. Middlemist, OC 53 Squadron
with the 'Berlin Gold Cup'
OC 30 Squadron with the
'Air Despatch Trophy'

Planes

and

Places

An R.E.8 of 'A' Flight of No.53 Squadron detached to St.Omer returns in the evening, June 1918

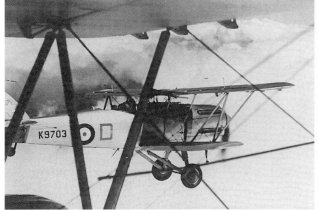

Hector K9703 seen through the struts and wires of another Hector. (G/C W.S.G. Maydwell DSO DFC)

Another view of K9703 shows the bomb racks under the wing and the flare brackets at the wingtips. (G/C Maydwell)

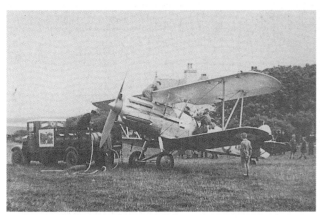

A Hector refuelling at Kirkwall from a civilian petrol tanker (G/C J.B. Wray CBE DFC)

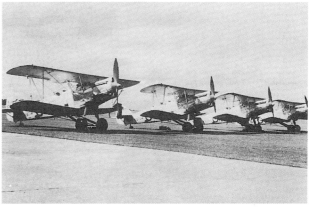

Hectors of No.53 Squadron lined up at Odiham (A. Thomas collection)

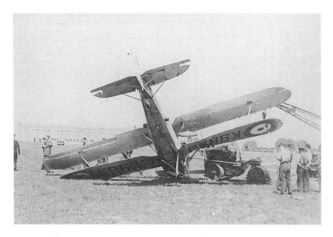

Hector K9688/K after collision with a road-roller that had been left on the airfield, Odiham, 16 June 1938. (G/C W.S.G. Maydwell DSO DFC)

Valentia K2344 during troop-carrying trials at Odiham in the summer of 1938. (Ken Smalley)

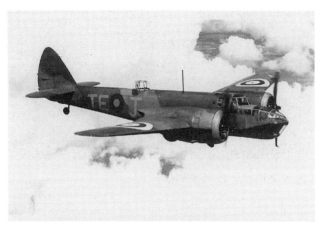

Blenheim IV L4843 TE-J. (RAF Museum P19542)

Blenheim L4852/TE-A in mid-1939

No.53 on parade at Poix, Spring 1940

The propeller of V9232 carved a gash in the fuselage when it overshot the runway at Guantanamo, Cuba

Loading depth charges on a Liberator at St.Eval in 1944. (IWM)

Photographed from EW291/Z is EW309/S of No.224 Squadron, 25 August 1944. (F/S L.C. Hatch)

Servicing a Liberator at St.Eval, 1944. (IWM)

Martinet target tug JN680 from No.4 Armament Practice Camp, Talbenny, formates with F/O Williamson's Liberator, 8 August 1944. (W/O E.F. Smith)

Dakota KN434/U at Rome/Ciampino airport in 1947 (S/L L.T. Bennett)

No.53's Dakotas taxying out for take-off, Abingdon, September 1947. (S/L L.T. Bennett)

Loading jeeps underneath a Hastings at Abingdon, September 1954. (F/L A. Maclean)

Hastings C.2 WJ332/GAY landing on a very wet runway. (MAP)

Beverley C.1 XB264/C. (MAP)

Beverley XB267/B framed by XB285/J at Nicosia

Belfast XR368 parked alongside Beverley XB284/H of No.47 Squadron at Nicosia in 1966. In the background can be seen three Hastings of No.70 Squadron, a United Nations Wessex, Lightnings and Javelins. At the civil airport behind are a L-1079 Super Constellation and two Viscounts

For a unique occasion, all ten Belfasts airborne in formation, 23 December 1971

Index

143

AIR-BRITAIN - THE INTERNATIONAL ASSOCIATION OF AVIATION HISTORIANS - FOUNDED 1948

For forty-nine years, Air-Britain has recorded aviation events as they have happened, because today's events are tomorrow's history. In addition, considerable research into the past has been undertaken to provide historians with the background to aviation history. Over 16,000 members have contributed to our aims and efforts in that time and many have become accepted authorities in their own fields.

Every month, *AIR-BRITAIN NEWS* covers the current civil and military scene.

Quarterly, each member receives *AIR-BRITAIN DIGEST* which is a fully-illustrated journal containing articles on various subjects, both past and present.

For those interested in military aviation history, there is the quarterly *AEROMILITARIA* which is designed to delve more deeply into the background of, mainly, British and Commonwealth military aviation than is possible in commercial publications and whose format permits it to be used as components of a filing system which suits the readers' requirements. Also published quarterly is *ARCHIVE*, produced in a similar format to *AEROMILITARIA* but covering civil aviation history in depth on a world-wide basis. Both magazines are well-illustrated by photographs and drawings.

In addition to these regular publications, there are monographs covering type histories, both military and civil, airline fleets, Royal Air Force registers, squadron histories and the civil registers of a large number of countries. Although our publications are available to non-members, prices are considerably lower for members who have priority over non-members when availability is limited. Normally, the accumulated price discounts for which members qualify when buying monographs far exceed the annual subscription rates.

A large team of aviation experts is available to answer members' queries on most aspects of aviation. If you have made a study of any particular subject, you may be able to expand your knowledge by joining those with similar interests. Also available to members are libraries of colour slides and photographs which supply slides and prints at prices considerably lower than those charged by commercial firms.

There are local branches of the Association in Blackpool, Bournemouth, Central Scotland, Exeter, Gwent, Heston, London, Luton, Manchester, Merseyside, North-East England, Rugby, Sheffield, Southampton, South-West Essex, Stansted, W. Cornwall and West Midlands. Overseas in France and the Netherlands.

If you would like to receive samples of Air-Britain magazines, please write to the following address enclosing 50p and stating your particular interests. If you would like only a brochure, please send a stamped self-addressed envelope to the same address (preferably 230 mm by 160 mm or over)

Air-Britain Membership Enquiries (Mil), 1 Rose Cottages, 179 Penn Road, Hazlemere, High Wycombe, Bucks., HP15 7NE

MILITARY AVIATION PUBLICATIONS

Royal Air Force Aircraft series: (prices are for members/non-members and are post-free)

J1-J9999	(£8.00/£12.00)	K1000-K9999	(see The K File below)	L1000-N9999	(£12.00/£18.00)
P1000-R9999	(£11.00/£14.00)	T1000-T9999	(£3.00/£4.50)*	V1000-W9999	(£4.00/£6.00)*
X1000-Z9999	(£4.00/£6.00)*	AA100-AZ999	(£6.00/£9.00)*	BA100-BZ999	(£6.00/£9.00)
DA100-DZ999	(£5.00/£7.50)	EA100-EZ999	(£5.00/£7.50)	FA100-FZ999	(£5.00/£7.50)
HA100-HZ999	(£6.00/£9.00)	JA100-JZ999	(£6.00/£9.00)	KA100-KZ999	(£6.00/£9.00)
LA100-LZ999	(£7.00/£10.50)	MA199-MZ999	(£8.00/£12.00)	NA100-NZ999	(£8.00/£12.00)
PA100-RZ999	(£10.00/£15.00)	SA100-VZ999	(£6.00/£9.00)	WA100-WZ999	(£5.00/£7.50)*

Type Histories

The Halifax File	(£6.00/£9.00)*	The Lancaster File	(£8.00/£12.00)*	The Washington File	(£2.00/£3.00)*
The Whitley File	(£4.50/£6.75)*	The Typhoon File	(£4.00/£6.00)*	The Stirling File	(£6.00/£9.00)*
The Anson File	(£15.00/£22.50)	The Harvard File	(£7.00/£10.50)	The Hampden File	(£11.00/£16.50)
The Hornet File	(£9.00/£13.50)	The Beaufort File	(£10.00/£15.00)	The Camel File	(£13.00/£19.00)
The Norman-Thompson File	(£13.50/£17.00)	The Defiant File	(£12.50/£16.00)	The S E 5 File	(£16.00/£20.00)

Hardbacks

The Squadrons of the Royal Air Force and Commonwealth (£15.00/£22.50)
The Squadrons of the Fleet Air Arm (£24.00/£36.00)
Fleet Air Arm Aircraft 1939 - 1945 (£24.00/£36.00)
Royal Navy Shipboard Aircraft Developments 1912 - 1931 (£15.00/£22.50)
Royal Navy Aircraft Serials and Units 1911 - 1919 (£15.00/£22.50)
Central American and Caribbean Air Forces (£12.50/£18.75)
The British Aircraft Specifications File (£20.00/£30.00)
The K File - The Royal Air Force of the 1930s (£23.00/£30.00)

Individual Squadron Histories

Strike True - The History of No.80 Squadron, Royal Air Force (£4.00/£6.00)*
With Courage and Faith - The History of No.18 Squadron, Royal Air Force (£5.00/£7.50)
Scorpions Sting - The History of No.84 Squadron, Royal Air Force (£11.00/£16.50)
Rise from the East - The History of No.247 Squadron, Royal Air Force (£13.00/£16.50)
* Currently out of print

The above are available from Air-Britain Sales Department, 5 Bradley Road, Upper Norwood, London SE19 3NT
Access, Visa, Mastercard accepted